# PROFITS FROM NATURAL RESOURCES

# WILEY TRADING ADVANTAGE

# PROFITS FROM NATURAL RESOURCES

## How to Make Big Money Investing in Metals, Food, and Energy

### Roland A. Jansen

**John Wiley & Sons, Inc.**

New York • Chichester • Weinheim • Brisbane • Singapore • Toronto

This book is printed on acid-free paper. ∞

Copyright © 1999 by Roland A. Jansen. All rights reserved.

Published by John Wiley & Sons, Inc.
Published simultaneously in Canada.

This publication is designed to provide accurate and authoritative information in regard to the subject matter covered. It is sold with the understanding that the publisher is not engaged in rendering professional services. If professional advice or other expert assistance is required, the services of a competent professional person should be sought.

*Library of Congress Cataloging-in-Publication Data:*

Jansen, Roland A., 1949–
   Profits from natural resources  :  how to make big money investing
in metals, food & energy  /  Roland A. Jansen.
      p.     cm.—(Wiley trading advantage)
   Includes index.
   ISBN 0-471-29523-X (cloth : alk. paper)
   1. Commodity futures.   2. Natural resources—Investments.
I. Title.  II. Series.
HG6046.J36   1998
332.63'28—dc21                                      98-16188

Printed in the United States of America.

10 9 8 7 6 5 4 3 2 1

# ACKNOWLEDGMENTS

I want to thank the following persons, who were instrumental in realizing this project:

Doris Booth of Authorlink, who offered me the possibility to publish a portion of my manuscript on the Internet; Authorlink (www.authorlink.com) is a Web site where publishers, literary agents, and writers can read manuscripts, exchange ideas, and give each other good advice. It is an excellent medium for writing talent to expose their works to the publishing world. Without Authorlink I would not have had access to the right people, and this book would probably not have been published.

My literary agent in the United States, Elisabet McHugh, who spotted my manuscript on Authorlink. She liked it and took me on as a customer. She introduced the manuscript to John Wiley & Sons.

Pamela van Giessen, editor at John Wiley & Sons, who has guided me in presenting a proper manuscript.

Marc Häberlin, my dear friend for life, my partner in crime, former Swiss rowing champion, second in the BMW World Golf Amateur championships, and one of the best Feng Shui Masters in Europe. He opened my eyes to ancient Chinese cultures and never stopped giving me good advice in pursuing my goals. He kept me focused on this book, presented me with new ideas, and taught me to concentrate on the important things in life. We are going to write our second book together.

Franz Maurer, president of the Floorball Club Schaan (Liechtenstein) and computer wizard, for helping me to manage the database.

My beloved Anna, who keeps believing in me and supports me through thick and thin. Anna is a very successful business woman herself, and her intelligence, wisdom, advice, and criticism have been a big contribution to this book. She made a lot of compromises and stayed beside me in her free time supplying me with endless delicacies out of the kitchen. She made it easy for me to focus on writing this book. She also made me work hard because initially I wrote the manuscript in German, and in the middle of the process she convinced me to rewrite the book in English.

My dear mother of 85, who is still very alert and interested in financial and ecological matters. She lives in Belgium and she mailed me an endless supply of newspaper clippings on natural resource matters.

Hans-Willem Baron van Tuyll van Serooskerken, director of Cargill Investor Services, Inc., who gave me interesting information about Cargill.

Kurt Kissling, vice president Near and Middle East, Central Asia, and Africa of the Hilti Corporation in Liechtenstein, for giving me a firsthand description of the oil-exploration business in such remote places as Azerbaijan and Kasakhstan.

Maaike Jansen, my niece who works for the United Nations in New York, for updating me with the latest UN articles on ecological matters.

I wrote this book in the Principality of Liechtenstein, tucked away in the heart of Europe between Switzerland and Austria.

ROLAND A. JANSEN

# CONTENTS

# Part One

## WHY YOU SHOULD BUY NATURAL RESOURCES

# 1

## THE FACTS SPEAK FOR THEMSELVES

### INTRODUCTION

The world we live in is characterized by megatrends: quickly developing technologies and telecommunications, turbulent stock markets, megamergers, the fall of communism, new democratic societies, life sciences, pharmaceuticals, exponential population growth, increased energy use, a quickly deteriorating ecology, and new epidemics. Our society is increasingly built on material values, egocentric short-term thinking, gigantism, merger mania, quarterly company reports, conveniences, instant gratification, and advertising based on hype and dreams. World society, and especially the United States, is becoming more and more a consumer society that thrives on the service sector, creates global brands, and outsources the actual production to cheap-labor countries.

This book deals with the biggest issue of the twenty-first century: it is about the state of Mother Earth and investing in one of the biggest "themes" in the coming years—the availability of natural resources like water, grains, energy, and metals. This topic, natural resources, will become just as important as the technical revolution and the Internet. We will be forced to focus more and more on our deteriorating ecology. So far, Homo sapiens does not think enough about the long-term consequences of irresponsible short-term behavior.

Because a scarcity in several natural resources can very well develop and *alternative* natural resources will become the *main* resources in the twenty-first century, a part of your assets should be invested in these "hard assets" *now*. You should invest *before* prices rise substantially, and over time you will realize *unnatural profits* in this field.

Reading this book is like doing your homework. The book has two main parts: Part One explains what the main forces in natural resources are. It gives you the necessary fundamental background information on *why* you should invest in natural resources stocks, certificates, physical commodities, limited partnerships, or funds. It describes the main causes that can lead to even a small squeeze in some natural resources, which would result in catapulting prices.

Part One takes a close look at the fundamental *supply* situation of raw materials, then switches to the *demand* side for natural resources and explains for which purposes and to what extent natural resources are needed. An entire chapter is devoted to China, a country whose demand for natural resources is increasing quickly. China is the so-called "swing factor." The final chapter of Part One highlights ecological aspects.

Part Two guides you through the maze of investing in natural resources. It describes how you can derive rewarding profits from your investments and avoid pitfalls.

## KEY FACTORS IN NATURAL RESOURCES

1. Humanity multiplies itself exponentially and soon will consume annually more food than Mother Earth can produce.

The population boom does not take place in Europe and North America, but in Asia and Africa. All in all, 90 million to 95 million people are added to the global population every year.

In the past 45 years, world population has doubled. Today about 5.7 billion people live on the earth. According to many experts, the global population will grow to 8 billion people by the year 2020. *And all of the growth will take place in developing countries in Asia and Africa.*

2. Due to consumption increases, humanity has consumed substantial parts of the already low world-commodity stocks.

3. Devastating pollution influences the global climate very strongly. It causes an acceleration of global warming. It reinforces hurricane activity, long dry spells in one area with floods in other areas, earthquakes, and water scarcity. It strongly diminishes the chances of abundant crops in the future. It has already been the main cause for small crops in countries close to the equator, like Indonesia and Malaysia.

4. More and more densely populated countries cannot produce enough food to feed their own people, thus becoming dependent on expensive imports.

5. Standards of living are improving rapidly in developing nations, and the competition among the nations to import commodities will increase substantially. Also, in times of an economic crisis like that in Asia, the Mercedes Benzes, the Gucci bags, and the Louis Vuitton luggage may go, but people still need to nourish themselves. This leads to rising prices for energy, base metals, and staple commodities such as grains, cotton, sugar, cocoa, and coffee.

China alone has experienced an increase in its gross national product of 57 percent in the past five years. And other emerging markets in central and eastern Europe and South America show a strong economic growth as well. Several hundred million people enjoy a higher income, improve their standard of living, and, last but not least, improve their eating habits. In China people do not want any more green tea and rice but a chicken and a beer.

6. The most precious commodity on Earth is water. Our bodies consist mainly of water, and without water we cannot live. If we don't preserve water, a water scarcity in the twenty-first century could lead to water wars among competing countries.

7. Not only for water, but also for other natural resources like energy, fish, corn, wheat, rice, silver, palladium, and paper, demand is soaring.

8. More and more countries are forced to import rice and other grains. On world markets, these commodities are priced in U.S. dollars. The U.S. economy enjoys healthy growth rates, and therefore the dollar is strong and makes food expensive for countries with devalued currencies.

9. When prices of basic nourishment are escalating, millions of people who are barely surviving cannot afford a daily meal any more. This situation can lead to famine— like in China in 1962—and can escalate into social unrest, riots, and crime. In the days of the Roman Empire, Nero recognized explosive situations: he kept his people sedated with *"Panem et Circenses"* (bread and plays). In today's and tomorrow's world, the *play* is abundant, but the *bread* will be missing.

Very often people ask me why the described dangers become so apparent now. The real reason lies in the fact that all the elements that can lead to a squeeze in natural resources, rising prices, and a food catastrophe have been *accelerating* greatly during the past few years. Imagine Mother Earth as an ecosystem that annually produces grains, oil, water, trees, plants, and animals like fish. *Total human consumption exceeds the earth's supply more and more, and therefore the substance of the earth is eaten away.* In real terms this means you can read regularly in newspapers like the *Wall Street Journal* and the *London Financial Times* that existing global reserves of oil, grains, and nonferrous metals are getting smaller and smaller. Sometimes they go down to record-low levels. Less and less fertile land, crops, and intact nature are being left unspoiled until in some parts of the world they are all gone and the system collapses. Remember the oil crisis in 1973? Oil prices tripled, and long lines of cars were found at the gas stations. But people tend to forget very quickly. If nothing changes, the coming grain squeeze will dwarf the oil crisis. Humanity can survive without oil—it can and must be replaced with other energy sources—but it cannot survive without food and water.

**The most important themes on earth in the future will not be political events or industrial mega-mergers, but the competition for water, food, and energy among importing countries and the escalation of prices for raw materials in general.**

When food prices escalate further, living conditions for humanity will deteriorate, and the portion of income spent on food will increase substantially.

## THE SHIFT IN WORLD DEMAND

In 1997 an economic crisis erupted in Asia. Currencies were tumbling, and at the same time man-made fires developed into an ecological disaster and threatened the lives of people in Indonesia, Malaysia, and Thailand. In September 1997, a plane crashed in Borneo in the haze due to bad visibility caused by smoke, killing 200 people.

Economic problems in Japan and the above-mentioned countries were dramatic but fairly regional. China was not affected.

Therefore the composition of global natural-resources demand shifted to other regions: positive economic news continued to come out of the United States and Europe and in particular out of central and eastern Europe and South America. This demand-shift is a continuation of a slowing growth in Asia and an accelerating demand in central and eastern Europe and South America. *The net result of total global demand is a fairly small change: the overall trend is and remains firmly up.*

The Asian economic crisis has the following impact on natural resources:

1. Governments, corporations, and private households of Indonesia, South Korea, Malaysia, Hong Kong, and the Philippines have been riding a booming economy. But simultaneously, governments and legislations did not keep up with modern times. Some countries like South Korea had accumulated huge debts and had spent too much money. The reality check came when the air escaped out of the Asian economic balloon and people woke up and were confronted with a *different* reality. Confidence in governments and outdated legislations was gone, currencies were halved, stock markets collapsed, interest rates soared, and people panicked. The *Asian demand for goods, services, and natural resources shrank dramatically,* creating a *temporary* negative impact on worldwide commodity prices, natural resource stocks, and natural resource stock funds. (This book on how to invest in natural resources is printed in the middle of this crisis.)

If you look back a few years from now, I think your timing for investing in low-priced natural-resource investment products *now* could not have been better.

2. There is another far worse phenomenon of the Asian crisis: people are losing their jobs and *cannot afford to buy food anymore with their currencies worth 50 percent less than in mid-1997.* In the streets in Indonesia, people were crowding the trucks that unloaded grain and sugar, literally fighting for those

commodities to stay alive. Who thought six months ago that this drama in Asia would unfold?

Asia is the most densely populated continent in the world. Taking current problems into account I think that poverty, outbreaks of epidemic diseases, hunger, and even starvation will increase.

3. The Asian economic crisis has not affected China so far, and the future of natural resources depends very much on China. Read Chapter 4: "Swing Factor China."

**My Opinion: In general, Asians are extremely tough and resilient, and therefore I think the Asian recovery will take place faster than many analysts in the Western world are thinking. New governments and legislations will restore confidence, and demand for goods and services will pick up again and drive natural resource prices to new highs— especially when the China factor kicks in.**

## GLOBAL WARMING

The influence of global warming on global crops will continue to increase. In autumn of 1997 the influence of El Niño causing a 5 percent temperature increase in the Pacific Ocean became visible everywhere. It was the reason why the long-awaited monsoon rains in Indonesia and Malaysia were delayed and failed to extinguish the forest fires there. Rice crops were small, and thousands of people were suffering from respiratory problems. It is estimated that 15,000 people in Malaysia had to be treated in hospitals. Asthma cases increased by 61 percent.

I do not think the global warming problem will be solved in the short term because politicians keep on bickering over who should do what. Emerging markets like China and India do not want to reduce carbon emissions because they fear a downturn in national production and thus an overall economic downturn. They like to see an easing of the burden for poorer nations. Like most emerging markets, they blame North America and Europe for all the existing pollution. So, they argue, those two continents must take the blame, bear the consequences, and reduce emissions the most. The majority of the nations do not start with themselves but prescribe what other countries should change. As long as these attitudes prevail, pollution will only get worse.

The United States with only 4 percent of the global population is the biggest polluter on earth and is responsible for 22 percent of total pollution. The U.S. government will not take all the blame for pollution and insists on including developing nations in the reduction of emissions. Strong leadership in the United States is now needed to reduce carbon emissions, for instance, by putting an extra dollar of tax on gasoline to reduce sales and usage. But the American gas-guzzling car and cheap prices for gas are two sacred cows, and a stiff tax on gasoline would tarnish Bill Clinton's popularity.

The European Union insists on reducing emissions by 15 percent by 2010. Japan wants an easy way out by a reduction of only 2.5 percent by 2010.

It all relates to the "resonance principle." In private and in political life, adult human beings cannot change the behavior of other human beings. But people can *change habits themselves* and act in a responsible way so that others might change their own habits for the better. If other countries saw that the biggest polluting country on earth—the United States—showed leadership and set the right example by reducing pollution substantially, they would do the same thing. Unfortunately this did not happen in the climate conference in Kyoto in December 1997. As long as everybody keeps on polluting and telling everybody else what should be changed, emissions will get worse, living conditions on earth will deteriorate, crops will be reduced, and *prices will rise.*

# 2

# THE SUPPLY OF
# NATURAL RESOURCES

## GRAINS

### Global Food Deficit

Millions and millions of people go to bed every night with a
hungry feeling in their stomachs. Explosive growth in world
population, especially in Asia, disastrous global pollution, and a
lethargic attitude of governments put this planet on a course
where Mother Earth cannot produce enough food anymore for
an increasing number of hungry mouths. Either the grain or
rice is not available, or the bulk commodity is already too expensive to be bought or is not distributed to the end-users.
According to the latest figures of the United Nations Food and
Agricultural Organization, close to 800 million people are hungry. Every year, another 90 million people are born on this
planet. In 20 years, the earth will need to produce twice as much
food as today to feed everyone.

**The main problem governments will have to deal with in the coming years is how to restore the balance between the exploding world population and the shrinking supply of natural resources.**

Global agricultural production has barely kept pace with an explosive global population. Yet today close to a billion people in developing countries suffer from chronic malnutrition, and almost 200 million children under the age of five suffer from protein deficiencies. Presently there are 88 "low-income food-deficit countries" (LIFDCs): 42 in sub-Saharan Africa, 19 in Asia and the Pacific, 9 in Latin America and the Caribbean, 6 in the Near East/North Africa, and 12 in Europe/Commonwealth of Independent States. Simultaneously the aid of industrialized nations to developing countries has declined dramatically from U.S. $10 billion in 1982 to U.S. $7.2 billion in 1992.

Twenty percent of the total population of the developing countries consists of hungry people. Will they be able to buy food in a bidding war or grow the grain they need in the future?

On one hand the world population is growing exponentially, and on the other hand the availability of arable land is not increasing but decreasing. World crops cannot meet future demand, and therefore world leaders at the highest political level must assess immediately the state of global food security. During many environmental and food conferences, political leaders have expressed their so-called "deep concern." For instance, at the twenty-seventh session of the Food and Agriculture Organization (FAO) Conference in November 1993, member nations stressed that "the world's major problems in food, nutrition, and sustainability require immediate action at national and international levels in order to attack the root causes of persistent food insecurity, notably the inadequate overall development and, particularly, agricultural and rural development."[1] These are good intentions. It sounds all fine and dandy, but unfortunately the actions of the world political leaders have been confined to "deep concern" only. Global nutrition has not improved, Western aid to underdeveloped countries has diminished, and the dismal situation is worsening.

## Global Grain Production Analysis

If you wanted to enlarge your grain crop a hundred years ago, you simply had to cultivate more land and plant more seeds. Times have changed. From 1950 until 1990, grain production expanded from 600 million tons to 1.78 billion tons. The global grain production *tripled* in this period with the help of new production methods, machines, irrigation, disease-resistant seeds, and fertilizers.

*But today the global grain production is approaching the capacity limits of Mother Earth.* In the period from 1990 to 1995, global grain crops did not expand greatly, and simultaneously reserves went down significantly. The 1996 and 1997 harvests in the United States, Argentina, Brazil, and Australia have improved greatly. Russia had a poor crop in 1996 and a big one in 1997. China expanded its crops in these two years but faces major crop problems for 1998. Reserves remain very low, and with the slightest crop problems, grain prices can rise significantly.

**What is more important is that grain demand is at a record high, and low reserves guarantee great price volatility in the foreseeable future.**

A major factor in crop enlargement is gentechnology. A new generation of "generic grains" will come to the market and, on paper, crops will be abundant. These newest types of grain require great amounts of water and fertilizers and often need to be "fogged in" by pesticides that are applied by aerial spray. The questions have not been answered yet if these crops bear health risks and if the consumer will accept these new bioengineered products.

Growth of the global grain crop is being reduced by the following long-term factors:

- The absolute quantity of cropland has been shrinking since 1981.

- Fertilizer use is scaled down because of the limited absorption capacity of the earth.

- Water for irrigation purposes is not as readily available as it was 10 years ago.

- Global warming and droughts will have a negative impact on crops in the southern hemisphere.

**As Figure 2.1 shows clearly, the global grain crop has expanded only marginally (5 percent) in the last seven years. In the same period, world population increased by 10 percent.**

But now the warm gulf stream off the coast of Peru—El Niño—can have a negative effect on the next global soft commodities

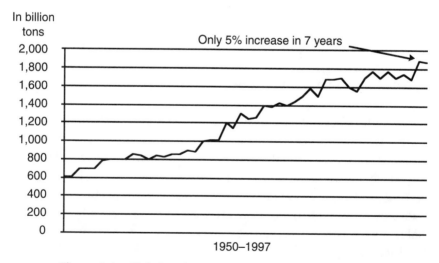

**Figure 2-1**  Global grain crop, 1950–1997. (*Source:* USDA.)

and grain crop. Crops close to the equator can be especially reduced by droughts.

The biggest unknown factor in forecasting the size of grain crops is the impact of global warming on world agriculture. The accumulation of carbon dioxide and other gases in the atmosphere is causing the heating up of Mother Earth, but it is impossible to quantify exactly what the damage to future crops will be.

An important reason for the present stagnation of global grain production is the shrinking land availability. Less and less land is available for agricultural purposes. In 1981, 732 million hectares (1,808 million acres) of land were available for grain production, but in 1995 the total surface had shrunk to 669 million hectares (1,652 million acres). The main causes were erosion, urbanization, industrialization, and transformation of cropland into pastures to breed herds of cows, sheep, and so on.[2]

For 30 years, the global grain production was growing faster than the increase of the global population. These times are over now, and we are confronted with the reverse situation whereby a slow but sure squeeze is developing: the global population grows by 90 million people every year. Simultaneously Asia— China and India in particular—improves its living standards and requires better quality food. Grain production will not increase in the same proportion. So the gap between supply (the crops) and demand (hungry mouths) will widen.

Lester Brown of the World Watch Institute in Washington estimates that an annual grain crop expansion of 28 million tons (78,000 tons a day) is needed for a world-population growth of 90 million people annually. If the rising standards of living are taken into account, this production increase must be even bigger.[3]

## Grain Stocks in Consumption Days

The human being needs a shock every now and then to change its habits. There will be a time when the northern part of the globe—the wealthy part—will also start to worry seriously about basic and safe nutrition. Today the balance between supply and demand is so delicate that it only needs a spark, an ignition, and food prices will skyrocket. Such a spark could be floods, a drought, or unexpectedly large Chinese imports.

As a squirrel can nibble on his winter stocks of nuts, humanity is happily eating away its grain stocks and taking a "mortgage" on the future. The United States Department of Agriculture (USDA) publishes figures on the number of days it would take humanity to consume total grain stocks without taking the annual crop consumption into account. In 1986 grain stocks would have been depleted after a comfortable 100 days of consumption. From 1987 to 1996, grain stocks became practically depleted to dangerously low levels. Luckily 1996 and 1997 were good crop years, and stocks have been rebuilt somewhat. But they are still close to a record low, and grain stocks hover around the lowest levels since World War II. The slightest crop disappointment or the slightest increase in export demand will provoke price spikes.

Goldman Sachs issued the following forecast on the number of days it would take humanity to empty its grain bins during the 1997–1998 crop.[4]

Wheat:      78 days

Corn:        44 days

Soybeans:  50 days

These numbers represent grain supplies that are shown as percentages of annual global consumption in Figure 2-2.

If we put all the grains together and weigh them according to world production, we empty our bins in only 61 days[5] (see Figure 2-3), or, expressed differently, global grain stocks represent only 16.6 percent of total global consumption. This is dangerously low.

Even with a record soybean crop for 1998, stocks will only be

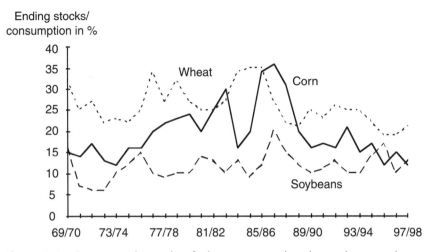

**Figure 2-2** Reserve grain stocks of wheat, corn, and soybeans (expressed as a percentage of annual global consumption). (*Source:* Goldman, Sachs & Co., © 1997. Reprinted with permission.)

rebuilt to their level of the previous year. Corn stocks for 1998 as a percentage of annual consumption are projected to be around 10 percent, and this is the lowest on record. This "drawdown" of commodity reserve stocks occurs when demand exceeds supply,

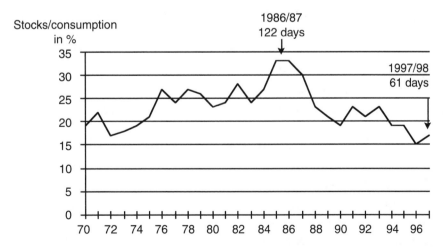

**Figure 2-3** Global ending stocks of all grains (expressed as a percentage of annual global consumption). (*Source:* Goldman, Sachs & Co., © 1997. Reprinted with permission.)

and that is the prerequisite for commodity investment returns to start becoming very interesting.

If the Chinese were to buy massive amounts of grains in the Western world, global grain stocks would become very critical, and the United States would have to declare an embargo on its exports. This *force majeure* could very well become reality in the coming five years. If the United States is sold out, importing countries will have to seek their grain in such countries as Canada, Argentina, Australia, and Brazil, and prices will sky-rocket. Already in the autumn of 1997 analysts of Goldman Sachs forecast a 20 percent lower grain crop for China in 1998 due to El Niño.[6]

## Global Area Harvested

An important factor from a supply point of view is the land suitable for crops: How much cropland is available on earth? Is it expanding or shrinking? How intensively is it used? And what is the relation of cropland to the exploding global population?

In 1981 the total cropland of the earth was a record 732 million hectares or 1,809 million acres (this number is used as the base, 100 percent, in Figure 2-4). From 1981 to 1995 crop–land had shrunk to 669 million hectares (1,652 million acres).[7] The actual usage of the land today is slightly more intensive than in the top year, 1991. If we take the global acreage har-vested as a percentage of the maximum area harvested in the preceding 25 years, we can conclude in Figure 2-4 that the global area harvested for the 1996/1997 and the 1997/1998 crops is forecast to be only 3 percent above the record 1981 levels.[8] And with all the pollution and construction going on (especially in Asia), I think the total surface and usage of cropland will shrink and not expand in the future.

"During the early [nineteen] nineties 3,000 industrial parks gobbled up 1,215,000 hectares of farm land," said Lester Brown,

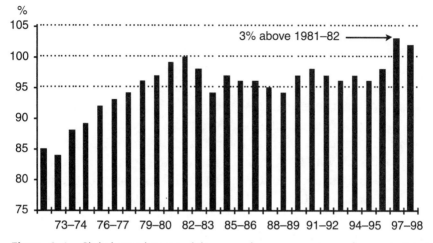

**Figure 2-4** Global area harvested (expressed as a percentage of annual global consumption). (*Source:* Goldman, Sachs & Co., © 1997. Reprinted with permission.)

president of the World Watch Institute in Washington (1,215,000 hectares = 3,001,050 acres). Mr. Brown sees higher agricultural prices in the future because "we are now in a transition from half a century dominated by food surpluses to a future dominated by food scarcity."[9]

If the shrinking surface of arable land in Asia continues at the same pace, Asia will run out of cropland around the year 2020. The main reasons are industrialization, urbanization, and erosion.

The United States suffers from heat waves, topsoil erosion, the depletion of aquifers (which hampers irrigation), and climate change. For instance, dry and mild areas like California and Florida experienced record rainfalls in December 1997 with plenty of flooding. I happened to be right in the middle of it.

But the most important reason for the whole worrisome development is the careless human attitude toward ecological issues. The man-made smog that hung over southeast Asia in September 1997 is a prime example. The woods set on fire on the islands of Sumatra and Borneo caused an ecological disaster.

The most important thing for the average Asian is to make money. He does not care about his environment. He neither appreciates nor has respect for nature. All his waste, including chemical waste, is just thrown on streets or dumped in rivers and seas. And local authorities do not seem to care very much either. When the smoke covered Sumatra, Borneo, and Malaysia, the local newspaper in Serawak's capital, Kuching, the *Serawak Tribune*, wrote: "Everything under control." In that city, visibility was less than 10 meters (32 feet), and everybody was covering their mouths with facial tissues so they could breathe at least a little in the smoke. Many thousands of people were treated in hospitals for respiratory problems. Despite these disasters the Asian mentality does not seem to change.

In the United States the attitude of the general public and more importantly of American industry toward the environment must improve. One example of unenvironmentalism is that of food packaging. In many American households, all the adults work, leaving little time for cooking meals. More and more Americans take their daily nourishment outside their own homes, and fewer families sit down at the dinner table and eat together. The fast-food industry meets the increasing demand for cheap and fast food, eaten either in the restaurant or at home, and it has transformed American eating habits. Many fast-food chains offer coffee, soft drinks, and hamburgers in nondegradable styrofoam cups and packages. Free supermarket bags, often made of plastic, are another example. You do not see this in Europe. There, cups are often made of degradable glass or cardboard, and supermarket bags are made of paper—and you pay for them. Imagine a one-day collection of all American nondegradable cups, knives, forks, and so on used in connection with food. It would be phenomenal. You could fill a few *Titanics* with them. In 1966 environmentalists organized an interesting experiment in Germany. They visualized how much pollution a single baby in the Western world was causing. They piled on a village square the total number of nondegradable diapers an average baby used in his first couple of years. It looked like a 30-

foot-high white haystack. And all these polluting products find their origins in fossel-fuel energy: oil. The ecological awareness of the average American adult and child is far behind Europe. When will an American Green Party catch a major part of the votes? As long as the big industries have a strong lobby in Washington, it is probably an illusion.

Especially in Europe ecological issues are much more important and become a political force. In Germany the Liberal Party has shrunk to an insignificant group and has given way to the upcoming Green Party.

In Asia ecology is not an issue, and people prefer to chop trees for a new car or a new television rather than leaving the rain forests intact.

## Available Cropland per Person

An interesting picture gives us the availability of cropland per consumer. In the past 30 years, production increases were not so much achieved with more plantings on a larger crop surface as with better production methods, more fertilizers, and so on. The output increase has now reached its limits, and more and more agricultural land is being transformed from cropland into plots suitable for industry and urbanization. Cropland is again becoming a precious commodity and a good investment. As Figure 2-5 shows, total available cropland has decreased dramatically.[10]

Cropland per capita of global population has shrunk in the past 45 years by 50 percent. In 1950, 0.25 hectares (0.62 acres) of land per capita was available; today it is no more than 0.12 hectares (0.29 acres).

In the past the increased yields per acre were outweighing the loss of cropland. But the improvements of the yield per acre in the past 10 years were so minimal that in absolute terms the loss of cropland was bigger. Meanwhile the demand for grain grows continuously. Annual global consumption is starting to

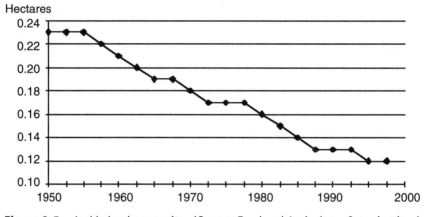

**Figure 2-5**   Arable land per capita. (*Source:* Food and Agriculture Organization.)

exceed Mother Earth's annual production, which means that each year part of the existing grain reserves will be consumed.

Given the increasing demand for food, our world cannot afford to lose more cropland through erosion, urbanization, and industrialization. This world cannot feed a population that increases by 400 million people in five years without stopping the further reduction of cropland.

**The gap between a slowly increasing supply and a fast rising demand continues to widen, and grain prices will climb in the coming years.**

### The Bottom Line

Here are key influences in today's grain market:

1. Crop forecasts are quite positive for the United States, Europe, and Eastern Europe. But demand is very high, too.

2. El Niño causes extraordinary heating of sea temperatures off the coast of South America and diminishes crops in

Australia, Indonesia, Africa, and China. Forecasts call for long dry spells, a lack of rain, and, thus, smaller crops. What is important in autumn 1997 is that the markets have not yet fully discounted the impact of these developments. In other words, it is not too late to invest in grains.

3. Grain prices are gradually on the rise again. The Goldman Sachs Commodity Index (GSCI) Agricultural Total Return Index posted gains of 9 percent between July and the end of September 1997. The bullish fundamentals are solid, and we can expect substantial price advances in the coming years. The Asian crisis has a bigger influence on declining sales of Gucci bags and Mercedes Benzes than on grain sales. Nourishment is and remains a basic need of humanity, and world population continues to explode as never before.

4. Grain stocks are still close to record lows.

## Conclusion

Grain markets in the United States are more focused on record grain crops than on El Niño and crop reductions in China. Importing countries are waiting for lower grain prices before they buy and jump on the bandwagon. With present record low grain reserves, it will only take a spark (bad weather, disappointing crop results, and so on) to make grain prices catapult again. Watch what happens to grain prices when a lower crop forecast for China hits the market or when it becomes public knowledge that China has made substantial purchases in the West. You should be in grains before this happens. Read about GSCI Total Return Index Certificates and GSCI Agricultural Total Return Index Certificates in Chapter 12. The global economic expansion continues, and that is the reason why the market can absorb the record crops of 1996 and 1997 easily.

Grain stocks are low, demand is high, and demand will outpace supply.

## Enlarging the Grain Crops: Genetic Engineering

If you are seriously contemplating investing in natural resources, the *food complex* must be a part of your investments. An integral part of food and agriculture is "'life science." This is a euphemism for genetic engineering. Developments in this field influence the enlargement and quality of world crops more and more. Can genetic engineering catch up with an exploding population and with global climate changes? The importance of genetic engineering in food production will undoubtedly grow exponentially in the coming 10 years. Genetic engineering is already a billion-dollar business, and it will probably provide the best answers for enlarging global crops, providing humanity with more food, and fighting hunger. The largest companies in bioengineering are Monsanto in St. Louis, Missouri (United States), and Novartis in Basel (Switzerland). Novartis is the new name for the merger of Ciba Geigy with Sandoz. Monsanto, an old-line chemical company, has sold its chemical industries and now concentrates fully on "life sciences."

Genetic engineering involves the manipulation of genetic material to alter genes and hence the characteristics of an organism. It might in the future create crops that are disease resistant, carry high yields, or need less water. Crops that are destroyed by bacteria, viruses, and flies are as old as Methuselah. Until recently, chemicals (fertilizers and pesticides) were the only answer to these threats. But now genetic engineering opens new possibilities for saving crops with a reduced use of pesticides. Plants are equipped with new genes in order to protect themselves against diseases and infecting flies.

### What Is at Stake?

1.  By changing genes of grains, disease-resistant grains are created, and on paper, world grain crops can be enlarged substantially in the future. Especially in regions close to the equator, arable land often lacks water and crops are invaded by insects. The soil contains too much salt, and despite intensive labor, the size of the crops is disappointing. Genetic engineering could adapt plants to local conditions and make them resistant to certain insects. This would certainly increase the yields per acre, and more desert land could be converted into arable land.

2.  It is not known yet which alterations (if any) the modified genes might have on human beings and animals as well. Continuous research is in progress. Genetically engineered grains should be seeded only when it is shown that the newly implemented genes cause no damage to humanity and wildlife and no disturbing side effects.

## The Corn Borer

On the silver screen, Arnold Schwarzenegger is the "Terminator" or the "Eraser." The Terminator for corn is the *corn borer fly*. It eats its way through the corn stem and destroys the arteries that transport the juices. Due to the interrupted nutrition flow, single parts of the plant die, such as the cob. The corn plant thus becomes useless for consumption. It is difficult to battle the corn borer with chemicals because the fly sits well protected against pesticides in the middle of the plant.

Genetic engineering can help to solve the problem: genetically produced corn now has a protein that is poisonous for the corn borer only. Thus the corn can protect itself against destruction. The same protective protein has been used in vegetables for 40 years. Gen Suisse (the Swiss Genetic Engineering Association) states that long-term experience has demonstrated that this protein is not damaging to the health of human beings and animals.[11]

### Buying Market Share

The big agrochemical companies in this world are investing billions of American dollars and Swiss francs in genetic engineering. They merge; they buy small- and medium-size biotechnology companies with specialized know-how in genetic engineering. The purpose is to accelerate their own transformation into life-science companies. In many cases ground-breaking technology is not developed by the chemical giants but by small-sized biotech companies. When the chemical giants buy these companies, they buy know-how, which from that moment on is no longer accessible to the competition. So in fact they are buying market share. Three examples:

1. Monsanto bought Calgene.

2. DuPont invested $1.7 billion in Pioneer Hi-Bred International.

3. Agrevo invested $550 million in Plant Genetic Systems. Agrevo is the joint venture formed in 1994 between Hoechst and Schering. Plant Genetic Systems is a small Benelux genetic-research concern with sales of just $5 million.

### A Short Excursion to Rice

Not only in Formula One racing are new prototypes being tested, but also in the high-tech world of rice. And Switzerland plays a very prominent role in food research. At the University of Zurich (Eidgenössische Technische Hochschule), Professor Ingo Potrykus is revolutionizing the most basic food of humanity: rice. He is a very important researcher in new rice prototypes.

Rice feeds 3 billion people, and in 30 years 2 billion additional people will depend on rice for their daily nutrition. Why is rice so important?

- The majority of humanity eats rice as their basic food.

- Twenty-one percent of the global nutritional energy is derived from rice.

- Traditionally Asians are not carnivorous. They eat rice daily, and rice production has a dominant place in Asian society. In 50 years, twice as many people will need to be fed.

In Asia, possibilities to enlarge agricultural land are very, very limited. Between 1980 and 1993, the total surface of rice fields increased by only 2.4 percent. But even the existing fields are threatened with partial disappearance in the future: Klaus Lampe, the former director of the International Rice Research Institute (IRRI) in Manila, estimates that in the coming 50 years, 20 to 25 percent of the total arable land in the world will be lost through erosion, salinization, steppe formation, exhaustion of the soil, or urbanization. So the challenge to feed Homo sapiens is colossal.

Every year 40 to 46 percent of the total rice crop is lost due to insects, diseases, or weeds. This amounts to a total of 240 million tons.[12] If rice farmers stopped using protective methods completely, up to 83 percent of the potential yield would be lost.

### The Shotgun Marriage

One of the worst rice destroyers is the *yellow stem borer*. Professor Ingo Potrykus has developed a new rice prototype that is resistant against the yellow stem borer. For 40 years, scientists have been trying with traditional methods to develop insect-resistant rice. But rice does not contain genes that can protect the plant against the insect, and experiments failed.

The Swiss story goes like this: Professor Potrykus developed a new rice plant that carried the bacteria "bacilus thuringiensis," which produces resistant protein. This protein kills the borer-fly. But experiments failed, and the flies kept on happily eating their way through the rice stems. A breakthrough came when the chemical giant Ciba Geigy, at no cost, provided Professor Potrykus with a synthetic gene. Ciba had successfully used this gene to produce corn resistant to the "corn borer." The new corn gene was literally shot on little gold pellets into the rice cells, like a shotgun marriage, and experiments in Zurich were very successful. The new rice prototype develops with the new gene the necessary protein that makes it resistant to the insect. Today the resistant rice prototype is being successfully tested in the greenhouses of the IRRI in Manila.

The new resistant rice types could prevent large crop losses in the future. The rice yield per acre can be increased by 20 to 25 percent as soon as this rice prototype becomes used commercially around the year 2000. An extra 85 million tons of rice can be produced, which would be enough to feed the increase in the Asian population for three years.[13] Professor Potrykus is the first biologist in the world who succeeded in equipping rice with a defense mechanism against the yellow stem borer. I think he should get a Nobel Prize for his work.

But how long will it be before Nature strikes back and the yellow stem borer will have pierced the resistance of the rice? Probably a few years, and therefore Professor Potrykus is busy developing the transfer of a second, a third, and a fourth gene into rice prototypes, making them more resistant.

Instead of commercializing his invention on a grand scale by utilizing a big company like Ciba or Monsanto, he gave the rice prototype to the IRRI in Manila for free testing. And when the institute completes the tests successfully, the new rice will be made available to all rice growers in the world. Local farmers have to pay for the seeds only once. They can then cross the seeds themselves with their own local rice types, multiplying the new rice into as much seed as they need.

Testing is rigorous in Switzerland and Manila alike. Professor Potrykus stated that the testing is more intensive than with the most dangerous viruses on earth. "So we are absolutely sure," he said, "that we can offer, health-care wise, an impeccable product."

Europeans are very skeptical of genetically altered products and fear that they can cause allergies. Professor Potrykus states: "Not a single one of the innumerable allergies is caused by genetic manipulation." Genetically altered plants have a built-in resistance to insects. Therefore the year-long use of pesticides and fertilizers can be reduced. And this is a very positive development that will stimulate a sustainable use of arable land.

For Professor Potrykus the rice plant resistant to insects, fungus, and viruses is only a first step. Rice does not contain vitamin A, and a monotone rice diet can lead to vision problems. Potrykus stated: "We are now successfully developing a rice prototype that is genetically altered in such a way that it contains high doses of vitamin A and iron. In Third World countries, over 1 billion women and children suffer from a lack of iron, and 150 million children lack vitamin A. Due to this deficiency, 5 million children turn blind."[14]

### Hybrid Rice Plants Increase Yields

The biggest and safest potential lies in hybrid rice plants. By crossing two inbreeding lines, A and B, a new high-yield rice plant can be cultivated. This is the area in which large yield increases of 20 percent can be realized without damaging ecosystems. It should be understood that hybrid rice plants are not genetically engineered; they are the result of a normal cultivation process. The peculiar side of the process is the fact that only two inbreeding lines are crossed, not two healthy rice types carrying different positive characteristics. The new plant has a 20 percent higher yield, but the second generation does not carry the high-yielding characteristics. So the farmer is forced to buy new seed every year. The University of Zurich is researching ways to reinforce the second generation of hybrid rice genetically and arm it with the same high-yielding feature.

The Chinese have been experimenting since 1976 with hybrid rice, and already 20 percent of the rice crop is realized with hybrid rice. The negative side is that these new hybrid rice types (Turbo-Rice) consume three times as much water as regular rice, and water supply is already a big problem of global nourishment.

### Thermal Underwear—Genetically Altered

In the United States, a team of plant molecular biologists are testing genetically altered cotton plants. The cotton produces fibers that can retain warmth much better and that can therefore be used for thermal underwear. Two extra genes are endowed in the plant, and each fiber is a mixture of normal cotton and small amounts of polyhydroxyburate. At harvest time the researchers studied the raw fibers and spun yarn out of them. Clothes were knitted, and they felt like real cotton. The material can hold 12 percent more heat than traditional cotton. Charles J. Arntzen, president of the Boyce Thomson Institute for Plant Research in Ithaca, New York, adds: "This use of a bacterial gene is something that could never have been accomplished with standard plant breeding. This is only one example of what might be done to improve cotton fibers with foreign genes. Dye-binding properties and greater stability of the fabric are going to appear in the next generation."[15]

Moral of the story: The long johns are genetically altered, but the content of the underwear remains genetically intact.

## Farming by Satellite

Do you remember the CNN pictures on your television screen of military targets in Iran during the Gulf War? As a spectator you had the same view as a U.S. pilot. You could see how a missile was launched off a fighter plane, and you saw the rocket flying toward the target. The next second, you witnessed with your own eyes the precision bombing raids. The same technique is now used in high-tech American agriculture. It is now possible for a tractor during planting time to have a real-time link with a satellite. In this high-tech farming the satellite measures every square foot of the farmer's land and checks the salinity of the soil. A computer calculates how much pesticides the soil needs and disperses automatically the exact necessary quantity. Irrigation systems can also be adapted to avoid saturating areas. This precision agriculture allows farmers to improve crop yields dramatically and thus enhance the net profit of farming.

The spatial information helps the farmer to minimize the excesses and avoid contamination. This stands in sharp contrast to traditional farming in which an acre of arable land is regarded as a single tract and fertilizers and pesticides are uniformly dispersed across the entire area. Now, new-generation tractors create an electromagnetic field in the soil where they are riding, and the satellites measure the electricity in those fields. The amount of electricity indicates the exact degree of salinity. So some areas might need more chemicals, while other areas can stay chemical-free. The net result is that this fascinating technique is enabling farmers to reduce the use of agrochemicals greatly and to farm in a more ecologically friendly way.

Using satellite data, farming can be improved in the following areas:

### Tilling

Satellite data allow farmers to map the land exactly before tilling starts. Global positioning systems inform the farmer where to start each row of a field, where to turn the tractor, and how large the distances between the rows should be. In the end it saves the farmer hours of extra work.

### Fertilizer and Pesticide Spraying

Sensors measure the speed of the tractor and adjust the amounts of fertilizers and pesticides dispersed on the field. Supplies are used as economically as possible, and the soil is not being inundated with chemicals in spots where spraying is superfluous.

### Planting

Again, sensors measure the speed of the tractor and constantly adjust the seeding. Optimal spacing of the seeds avoids clogging of the plants in a later stage.

### Harvesting

Sensors calculate in real time what the yield per acre is. The farmer can make faster decisions on how much grain he should store, hedge in the futures market, or sell immediately. He no longer has to wait until all the grain is in the bins.

### Weather Forecasting

The farmer's computer can be linked to weather forecasting services to get a precise weather forecast for his fields. The farmer benefits from data in such areas as rain forecasts, moisture content, wind, and temperature. Therefore he can plan the operational use of his slow-moving tractors better.

## OIL

### The United States Dependency on Oil

Today the United States is more dependent on oil imports than it was 20 years ago, and no one in the States seems to realize or to care about the fact. The more the United States depends on oil imports, the more vulnerable America is. But Americans do not worry about oil supplies, and 1973, the year of the oil embargo with long lines at the gas pumps, seems long forgotten. Way back then, America imported 35 percent of its energy needs; that figure dropped to 28 percent by 1982. But with today's booming economy, imports are way up to an unprecedented level of 46.3 percent of total needs, and imports have surged to 8.3 million barrels daily.[16]

Americans are again driving gas-guzzling cars and big family vans as never before. Therefore the shock will be big when a new oil crisis occurs. The United States has a huge appetite for fossil-fuel energy and burns more oil than any other country in the world. Its output of greenhouse gases has continued to rise instead of slowing down, as was generally agreed at several climate conferences. Stringent measures that are necessary to reduce emissions are politically explosive and costly as well.

During the environmental conference in Rio de Janeiro under the Bush administration, nonbinding goals were set to limit greenhouse gases by the year 2000 to the levels prevailing in 1990. The United States and most other countries did not meet that goal. Americans fear an economic disruption if indeed they reduce carbon emissions by 20 percent. The American government has relied in the past purely on voluntary approaches to reduce carbon emissions without binding targets.

## Forecast World Oil Demand

In 1995 oil prices started their new upward trend, a development that is still in the preliminary stages. The situation is as follows: Japan, Thailand, Malaysia, The Philippines, and Malaysia suffer a temporary economic setback with a slackening oil demand. The weakness in Asia is more than offset by rising demand in central and eastern Europe plus South America. This will push the market into a significant deficit in 1998–1999. Over time the devalued Asian currencies will strengthen the Asian export position. The Asian countries will be extra competitive again, which will strengthen their oil demand in the future.

In the past decade oil production and oil demand were down in the communist countries. But because these former centrally planned economies have positive economic-growth figures, the need for oil in these countries will be added to the rapidly growing demand for oil in the industrialized countries in the West and the developing countries in Asia. Presently one-fourth of the total oil demand is coming from Asia, and that number is growing. In the year 2000 Asian demand (including China) will be bigger than American demand. Forty-five percent of the total global population lives in China, India, and Indonesia, and their economic development adds a huge quantity of oil consumption.

**My Opinion: All in all, by the year 2010 demand for oil may rise by an additional 20 to 23 million barrels per day (mbd), totaling 91 mbd. Therefore, you have to invest in oil or in the oil industry today.**

This consumption forecast is based on growth rates of 2.5 percent in the developed market economies, 3.5 percent in the transition economies, and 5 percent in the developing economies. When a higher growth rate of 3 percent in industrialized countries is assumed, the demand rises to 94 mbd. The increasing energy use is a result of continuous urbanization and rising living standards. The greater use of motor vehicles accounts for much of the increase.

Three-quarters of the growth in demand will come from the developing countries, which will increase their demand share from 31 percent to 41 percent by 2010.

Will there be adequate supplies in the future? Production in the North Sea and Canada is expected to increase, while production in the United States is expected to decline. Russia has vast untapped supplies and will remain a big net exporter. Countries like Saudi Arabia, Iraq, and Iran also have vast supplies and will regulate the oil faucet. Yes, the world has enough oil, but because of steady increases in demand, suppliers will be able to let the price gradually rise (and let consumers pollute their environment even more).

What do we consume per annum? (See Table 2-1.)

Please note the big difference in oil consumption: the average American consumed 24 barrels in 1994, and the average Chinese consumed only 0.9 barrels. Far more significant is the fact that the per capita consumption in China from 1970 to 1994 increased by 350 percent and in the United States by only 11.1

TABLE 2-1   Per Capita Oil Consumption in Selected Countries[17] (Barrels per Person per Year)

|                   | 1970 | 1980 | 1990 | 1994 |
|-------------------|------|------|------|------|
| India             | 0.2  | 0.3  | 0.5  | 0.6  |
| China             | 0.2  | 0.6  | 0.7  | 0.9  |
| Republic of Korea | 2.0  | 4.4  | 8.7  | 14.4 |
| Japan             | 11.2 | 11.7 | 15.7 | 16.5 |
| United States     | 21.6 | 21.6 | 23.9 | 24.0 |
| World             | 3.9  | 4.1  | 4.4  | 4.5  |

Source: United Nations, "World Economic and Social Survey," 1995, 170.

percent. *And this Chinese acceleration is continuing.* China has not been affected by the Asian crisis. What will happen to oil prices when Chinese consumption rises further by 1 barrel per person per year? With a population of 1.2 billion people, where will those 1.2 billion extra barrels come from?

Physical demand for fossil-fuel energy, both for heating oil and for gasoline, is very high. American refiners became advocates of just-in-time inventories. This means that companies keep stocks low and let raw materials be delivered only just before they are needed for the manufacturing process, thus saving storage costs.

As you can see in Figure 2-6 (weekly crude oil stocks) and Figure 2-7 (weekly gasoline stocks), stock levels in 1998 are above those of 1997, due to the Asian crisis. But after the first quarter of 1998, Asian demand is picking up again, and the probability is high that stocks will come down in the second half of 1998.

Rising prices cause blockbuster earnings for the major oil companies. The International Energy Agency predicted that the consumption growth rate for 1997 would be just as "healthy"

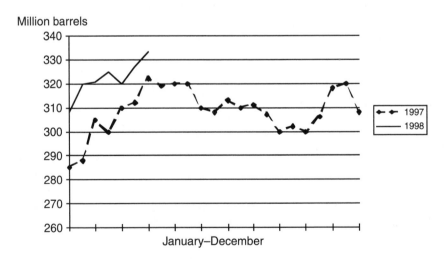

**Figure 2-6**  U.S. weekly crude oil stocks. (*Source:* Goldman, Sachs & Co., © 1997. Reprinted with permission.)

Million barrels

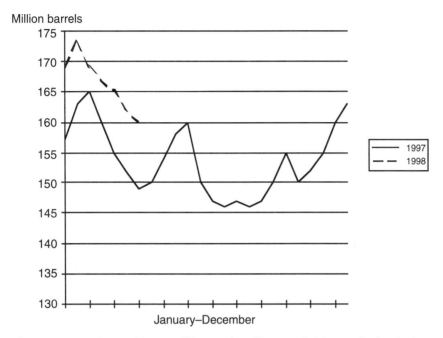

**Figure 2-7** U.S. weekly gasoline stocks. (*Source:* Goldman, Sachs & Co., © 1997. Reprinted with permission.)

as in 1996, mainly driven by economic expansion of developing nations. The Paris-based agency forecast that global growth in oil demand would increase by 1.8 million barrels a day in 1998 or by 2.5 percent to 73.6 million barrels a day. Other analysts estimate that this rise in demand is low and that demand will even swell further by another 100,000 barrels a day.[18]

In 1993, there were 5,000 active oil rigs and fewer than 1,000 mutual funds in the United States. Today, there are over 5,000 mutual funds in the United States and fewer than 1,000 oil rigs.

In 1960, there were 100 million cars on the road compared with 500 million today. All cars still consume oil, and world demand for oil is at an all-time record high level and expanding at a rapid rate.

The oil story is still about demand growth. It is about the billions of people in Asia, central and eastern Europe, and South

America who are improving their lifestyle. Everybody wants to own a car, a refrigerator, and an air-conditioning system. Consumption increase is far bigger than the oil industry has anticipated.

## China's Oil Consumption on the Rise

China is a net importer of oil since 1993 and is widely expected to consume about 8 mbd by 2010, which is nearly three times its consumption level at the end of 1997. Some economists compare China's development with the development of South Korea. They project China's consumption to Korea's consumption level of 1994—well before the 1997 Asian crisis. They assume China will reach Korea's 1994 consumption level a few years from now. This exercise leads to staggering results in the oil market. China's per capita consumption in 1994 was only 0.9 barrels. In the United States it was 24 barrels, and in South Korea it was 14 barrels. If China had reached Korea's level in 1994 (and it will in a few years), China would have consumed 45 million barrels per day, or two-thirds of world consumption. This is how the near future will look. In Part Two you can read how you can make unnatural profits in oil and how other people have done it already.

## Sacred Cow #1: The Car

What will your age be in 30 years? If you think of your life expectancy, do you have a fair chance to be alive on this planet in 30 years? If the probability is yes, you must imagine that you are now living in the year 2028. On the highways, *1.5 billion cars* try to move forward. They are clogging the roads and causing permanent traffic jams. And all those cars need a parking space as well. In Asia today, some cities have already taken rigorous legal measures to curb traffic, and I expect similar laws to be introduced in western Europe and the United States in the future. A few examples:

1.  Already today in a city like Tokyo, you can buy a car only when you can prove you have a parking place.

2.  In Singapore, taxes on cars are unbelievably high, as are the purchase prices: a new Honda costs $60,000 and a second-hand BMW $100,000. You can buy, own, and drive a car only with a special permit. The advantage is that there are not too many cars, so traffic flows very well.

It is estimated that car owners in Bangkok, Thailand, spend an average of 44 days a year in traffic jams.

The small country of Holland has 15 million inhabitants, and on some days there are traffic jams with a total length of 280 miles or more.

The spiraling costs of owning a car will gradually spread all over the world and will affect your life and mine.

The United States is technologically the most advanced country in the world but, unlike France or Japan, it does not have a good public rapid-transit system. Or to make the comparison, where are the ultrafast trains (traveling 150 miles an hour) between New York and Chicago? They don't exist, so Americans do need cars to go from point A to point B, and the car will remain the most important transport vehicle in the foreseeable future. As long as hydrogen has not replaced gasoline as the prime energy source, cars running on gasoline will remain one of the big polluters and a big factor in energy demand.

In the coming five to ten years, rapid-transit trains will run all over Europe, replacing more and more short plane flights. Already today, taking the Eurotrain from London to Paris is a very viable alternative to flying.

As shown in Figure 2-8, in the United States today, there are about 580 cars per 1,000 inhabitants. In China where economic development goes forward with lightning speed, there are only

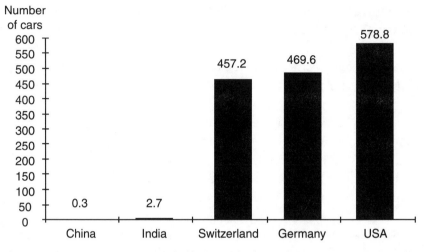

**Figure 2-8**   Cars per 1,000 inhabitants in 1997. (*Source:* CASH, Die Wirtschaftszeitung der Schweiz.)

0.3 cars per 1,000 inhabitants. China plans to build up to 3 million cars by the end of the century and a total of 22 million new cars by 2010. It is also interesting to note that cars built in China are *added* to the world fleet. Cars built in the United States are *replacements of old cars.*

Because of the huge Chinese population of 1.2 billion people, any slight improvement of the social status is immediately translated into a big increase in the number of cars and a big increase in oil demand. When the Chinese have the same living standards as the Americans—and they might accomplish this in 20 years—the ecology of the earth will be changed completely. If this situation were reality today, we all would have to stay home because we could not breathe the air outside due to the half-billion extra cars running in China.

We all know we should avoid this. But the possession of a car is a very emotional thing, and when emotions run high, rational thinking is left way behind.

Energy use keeps on rising, and *carbon dioxide ($CO_2$) output will increase dramatically as well.*

The number of cars is growing at a near exponential rate,

just like the world's population (see Figure 2-9). In 20 years, the parking lots on this globe will more than double in area. This is a megatrend and one more reason why you must invest in a natural resource called oil. Car companies like Mercedes Benz and Toyota are investing billions of dollars to produce clean-energy cars. But it will take at least 20 years before *all* cars run on clean hydrogen instead of gas.

## Reduction of Global Oil Stocks

In Europe governments are scrambling to raise income, sell off assets and cut budgets in order to meet the criteria for the new Euro currency in 1999. And the newest game in town to raise cash and manicure budget deficits is selling off strategic oil reserves.

Figure 2-10 shows that the United States and Germany hold

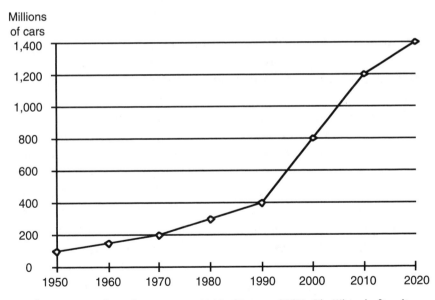

**Figure 2-9**  Number of cars, 1950–2020. (*Source:* CASH, Die Wirtschaftszeitung der Schweiz.)

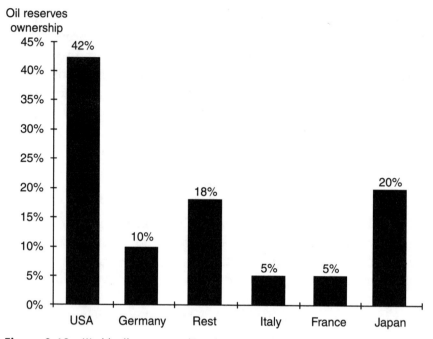

**Figure 2-10** World oil reserves. (Reprinted by permission of *The Wall Street Journal* © 1997 Dow Jones & Company, Inc. All rights reserved worldwide.)

more than half of the West's strategic oil reserves (52 percent). At the same time, both countries are heavily dependent on imports: 97 percent of the total German oil consumption is imported.

Remember the Arab oil embargo and the Iranian Revolution? They drove inflation in Western countries to double-digit levels. That is the reason why strategic oil stocks were built by such countries as the United States and Germany. The leaders of the West created the Paris-based International Energy Agency to stock petroleum and to administer a plan for oil distribution in an emergency. This stockpile is a kind of insurance policy against price shocks. All the Western countries plus Japan are members.

And although global oil demand is surging now, the United States and Germany are quietly selling off parts of their oil reserves, betting that an oil crisis will not occur again. In 1997, Germany sold 15 million barrels of the country's emergency oil stocks of 55 million barrels to raise approximately 400 million marks just to reduce the country's budget deficit. Germany needs to reduce its budget deficit to qualify for entering the European Monetary Union's single currency. The German government intends to continue to sell more oil in the future.

Roughly the same story is true for the United States. The United States makes a huge effort to reduce budget deficits and has already quietly sold 30 million barrels of oil in the past one and a half years. It intends to sell a further 10 million to 12 million barrels from its current strategic reserves of roughly 564 million barrels. The White House has further proposed selling $1.1 billion worth of oil in the year 2002.[19]

Many oil experts think countries should add to their oil reserves, not draw them down. Central Bank selling of gold is one thing because the practical use of gold is extremely limited. But selling energy is a far riskier business. Because of soaring demand (see Figure 2-11), the world's unused production capacity—its safety cushion—is only 3 million barrels a day. And this is the lowest level in more than 15 years. What is worse is that two-thirds of this unused capacity is in just one country: Saudi Arabia. One natural disaster or one Middle

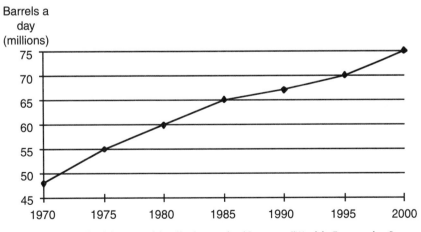

**Figure 2-11** Gushing world oil demand. (*Source:* "World Economic Survey 1995." The United Nations is the author of the original material.)

East war, and the vulnerable consuming nations will see the price of energy soar. The biggest oil consumer is the United States, where two-thirds of the oil used is consumed by the transportation sector: gas guzzlers are on the road again as never before. In total, U.S. dependence on oil imports is close to 50 percent.

## ALTERNATIVE ENERGY SOURCES

### Introduction

An energy revolution has started. The twenty-first century will be the century of energy sources we still call "alternative." It will mean *clean energy* and the *decentralization of energy generation*: no more oil-refining plants and Three Gorges Dams, but local windmills and local solar panels. When these alternative energy sources can be produced for mass markets on a grand scale, their costs will fall like the cost of a television set has fallen over the past 20 years.

Solar power generators or wind turbos in one region can be connected into a super system, which can then monitor and steer the energy flow. The major oil companies have perceived that the oil and coal market grows by 1 to 2 percent a year, but wind and solar energy markets grow much faster (see figures in the next section, Tailwind for Wind Energy). The strategy of several big oil firms now is to invest big money in alternative energies and to develop solar and wind energy products for the near future. These renewable energy sources differ from oil in two important ways:

1. They are not endangered by limited supply constraints. An oil well will run dry, but the sunlight and the wind do not.

2. They are both clean sources of energy and do not pollute our environment.

## Tailwind for Wind Energy

Wind energy is growing at an extraordinary rate. It is already the fastest growing source of energy around the world. And the future is very promising. Wind power is now a $2 billion-a-year business and has an annual growth rate of 25 percent.

The potential growth of wind energy is much greater than the growth of energy derived from hydropower, which provides a fifth of the world's electricity. There is so much wind in Europe that it could easily provide the energy needs for the total electricity consumption. Windmill energy is booming in Europe because of falling costs and improved technology. The European Union (EU) made a commitment that energy in Europe from renewable sources like wind energy and solar energy should be 8 percent by 2005. Under the EU plan, wind energy will supply 2 percent of electricity by 2005.[20] Rampant wind-energy development is also taking place in the United States.

Countries like Holland, Denmark, and northern Germany are very much in favor of wind energy. These countries are already surpassing EU targets: in the German state of Schleswig Holstein, for instance, wind supplies 4 percent of electricity needs, and Denmark plans to derive 10 percent of its energy needs from windmills by 2000.[21] Denmark will build 500 windmills standing on their own poles in the sea. This is an excellent idea because modern windmills do not embellish the landscape—they are not the pretty sight of Dutch windmills in Old Master paintings.

Wind energy produces today about seven times more electricity than solar energy. The use of wind energy more than doubled in the past 6 years. In 1994 alone, wind energy increased by 30 percent. Europe now is the biggest user of wind power, with 2420 megawatts of installed capacity in 1995 against 1700 megawatts installed capacity in the United States.[22]

Because of declining costs, wind power is a very desirable alternative source of energy and should be exploited much more. Turbine capacity has risen from 75 kilowatts to 600 kilowatts in

10 years, and since 1989, costs have been reduced by 30 to 50 percent. (See Figure 2-12.)

In terms of cost reduction and competitiveness to oil and gas, wind energy comes closer than other alternative energies. This is the story: In the 1980s, wind turbines were costing $3,000 per kilowatt, producing electricity at a price of more than 20 cents a kilowatt-hour.[23] Subsequently wind turbines became larger and more efficient, and by the late 1980s costs for the turbines had come down to $1,000 to $1,200 per kilowatt. So in the early 1990s the energy produced cost 7 cents per kilowatt-hour. Right now, developers of wind turbines using the newest technologies have signed contracts to sell wind energy at less than 5 cents per kilowatt-hour.[24] This compares vary favorably with the price of 4 to 6 cents that power plants fueled by natural gas and oil are charging.

Very ambitious goals have been set by the Spanish province of Navarra. By the year 2010 Navara plans to be self-sufficient in electricity. It wants to generate the energy from hydroelectric plants and windmills. As a country Spain is growing very

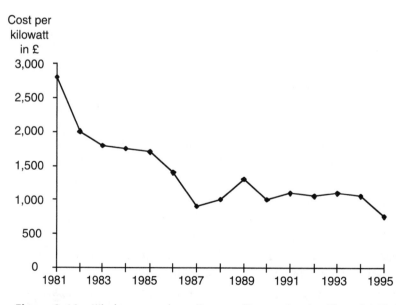

**Figure 2-12**  Wind power price—Europe. *(Source: London Financial Times.)*

quickly in wind power use and added 300 megawatts of installed capacity in 1997.[25] And the potential is just enormous. In the summer of 1997 I spent a day in the windsurfer's paradise of Tarifa. This Spanish beach village is situated in the south, close to Gibraltar. On the rocks above the beaches, you overlook the Strait of Gibraltar, and you have a splendid view of the African coastline. You also see hundreds and hundreds of windmills generating cheap, clean, continuous energy. Not the United States but Spain shows leadership in pollution reduction: Spain wants to generate 10 percent of its energy needs with windmills by the end of 1998. Imagine the United States supplying up to 10 percent of its electricity with wind energy. It would be a prime example for other nations to follow and it would be a giant step forward in the reduction of pollution worldwide.

Another country with great wind energy potential is Great Britain. As an island it is the country in Europe where wind is the largest untapped source of energy.

All in all, wind energy can greatly reduce pollution in Europe: if wind power generates 2 percent of Europe's energy needs, seven 1,000-megawatt coal-fired plants can be closed, and carbon dioxide emissions can be reduced by 30,000 tons a year.

Global warming can only be reduced when alternative sources of energy, not coal and crude oil, become the main sources of energy. We are only at the beginning of the development of alternative energy sources today: wind energy produces only 0.1 percent of the global energy needs, but as you can see in Figure 2-13, the energy produced by wind turbines has double-digit growth figures during any typical year.[26]

## The Solar Century

The twentieth century is the fossil-fuel century, and the twenty-first century will become the solar century. The sunlight that reaches the earth daily contains 6,000 times more energy than is used by all countries combined today.[27]

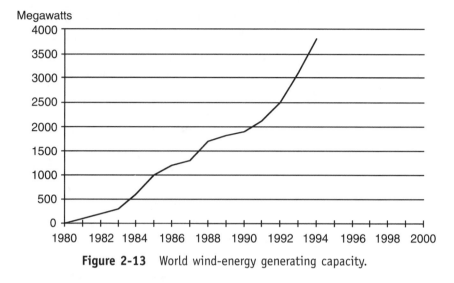

**Figure 2-13**   World wind-energy generating capacity.

To achieve a sustainable economy, we have to phase out gradually the use of fossil fuels, which are the largest contributor of carbon dioxide ($CO_2$) to the greenhouse effect. To slow global warming, the use of oil and coal as energy has to be reduced. Demand for electricity in developing countries is doubling every eight years, and solar power looks very promising as one of the alternative energy resources to replace fossil fuels. Photovoltaic cells (PVs) can convert sunlight into electricity. The sales of photovoltaic chips produced in California's Silicon Valley jumped by more than 50 percent between 1990 and 1994.[28] In 1996 PV producers sold solar systems totaling 90 MWp (megawatts at peak) with a total value of $1 billion. A total sales increase of 30 percent, to 120 MWp, was recorded for 1997. It is expected that by 2010, PV shipments will reach or exceed 800 MWp. The World Bank together with its lending arm the International Finance Corporation is setting up a Solar Development Corporation and a PV Market Transformation Initiative. This is to help poor people install a so-called solar home system (SHS). The SHS could generate 20 to 100 watts for a house, enough to generate electricity for four light bulbs and a small black-

and-white television set. In Kenya, 20,000 SHSs have already been installed by eight domestic companies. When these SHSs really take off, the use of solar power can reach 4,000 MWp a year.[29]

A very hopeful trend is the decrease in production costs of PVs. In the past, production costs were so high that solar energy was commercially too expensive as compared to traditional polluting energy sources. Despite falling prices the average wholesale price of PVs in 1993 was still between \$3.50 and \$4.75 a watt, or roughly 25 to 40 cents a kilowatt-hour. It is expected that the cost of solar energy will be brought down to 10 cents a kilowatt-hour by the year 2000 or perhaps to 4 cents by 2020.[30] If the downward trend in production costs continues, PV production can become an industry comparable in size to the computer hardware or software industries, and the twenty-first century will be the solar century.

Solar power is especially useful in remote areas, which do not benefit from hydroelectric power plants. It is already the cheapest form of energy for remote homes that are not connected with a regional electric grid.

## High Hopes for Fuel Cell Electric Cars and the Airline Industry

Big progress is being made with electric cars that derive their energy from hydrogen ($H_2$). The first prototypes of cars with fuel cells had the problem of huge hydrogen tanks on the roof. The tanks had to be big because it takes 140 cubic feet of hydrogen to produce the same energy as 1 gallon of gasoline. The second generation of these fuel cell electric cars will carry much smaller tanks. The big difference between traditional cars and the fuel cell car comes out of the muffler: instead of carbon gases, it is nonpolluting hydrogen.

The essence of the technology is a simple chemical reaction: two parts of hydrogen are fused with one part of oxygen ($O_2$), and the net result is energy and water. The energy then is transformed into electricity. Daimler Benz is experimenting with its second-generation Necar II (New Electric Car II). The car has a maximum speed of 68 miles per hour and its travel radius is 155 miles. According to Daimler Benz it will take another 10 to 12 years to commercialize these cars. If all cars in the world ran on oxygen and hydrogen, the biggest polluter would be a thing of the past. Hydrogen does not contain $CO^2$, and it is much lighter than kerosene. It could be used for planes, and Tupolev in Russia is experimenting with it.

**My Opinion:  If you want to invest in companies that are going to be the major players in solar energy, you can buy shares of Royal Dutch and British Petroleum (see Natural Resources Stocks in Chapter 13).**

**If you want to invest in car companies with the know-how and commitment to develop clean-energy cars, invest in Toyota, Mercedes Benz, and Ford Motor Company.**

## Electricity Generation

Oxera (Oxford Economic Research Associates), estimates that global energy demand can double by 2020. This will require an investment of $3 trillion in new electricity generation alone.[31] The United States and China would remain the biggest energy users in the world. In 20 years India can hold the number three spot. In the past 10 years Asian-Pacific energy demand grew by 60 percent, while American energy demand grew by only 20 percent. So Asia is catching up very fast. And what is important for you as an investor? Governments will not be able to provide their countries with the necessary energy infrastructure: it will have to come from the private sector, and you must be invested in it.

# METALS

## Introduction

The following pages explain the status of the metal markets around December 1997. I want to stress the following points about metals:

1. The Asian crisis that erupted in autumn of 1997 had a substantial dampening effect on industrial metal prices. Nobody knows how long the slump in Asia will last and, consequently, how long metal prices will be influenced by the slackening Asian demand.

2. Metal prices are very volatile and react to short-term market factors. If you are not a professional speculator, you should not invest in metal futures directly but invest instead in metal mining companies, metal funds, and metal accounts. These investment possibilities are clearly described in Part Two of this guide.

3. The following pages give you the long-term picture, which should be your focus when you make investment decisions. Predicting short-term impacts on prices is very difficult. If you concentrate on the big picture, your investment course will not be distorted by short-term diversions.

4. As you will see, not all metals were negatively influenced by the Asian crisis. Metals like palladium, silver, titanium, and lithium keep rising in price.

Nonferrous metals are copper, aluminum, lead, tin, zinc, and nickel. Precious metals are gold, platinum, palladium, and silver. Before the eruption of the 1997 Asian crisis, squeezes had developed in several metal markets, such as zinc, lead, and aluminum. A *squeeze* means that prices are rising due to tight physical nearby supplies. Everybody wants to have the physical material, and everybody is prepared to pay more for an immediate delivery. In this case, cash prices rise over prices for future delivery. This situation is called a *backwardation*. When supply and demand are orderly, cash prices are *lower* than future prices, and we speak of a *contango*.

The coming years will see cycles with sustained price advances on the London Metal Exchange (LME). There will be several bull markets, low stocks, high demand, and price backwardations. This will be especially true for nickel, zinc, and tin.

The buzz word in business is *"just-in-time" production* with good logistics. Money tied up in inventories is very expensive. So industry keeps inventories low, and today we have low global commodity stocks in grains, oil, and several metals.

Many analysts underestimate the demand for metals, which is driven by infrastructure development in central and eastern Europe, China, and South America. Combine this demand with low stocks, and you have the main ingredients for substantial price advances. Generally low stocks in commodities can be the catalyst for higher prices.

## Nonferrous Metals

### Lead

The lead market is heading for a period of supply tightness, low stocks, and recovering global demand. Lead stocks on the LME fell dramatically in 1995 and 1996 (see Figure 2-14), and further supply reductions are highly likely, resulting in higher lead prices.

The lead stocks are being drawn down to meet surging demand. From the second half of 1994 until the first half of 1996, lead stocks declined from 360,000 tons to 90,000 tons. Eastern Europe is a traditional lead exporter, but this situation is revers-

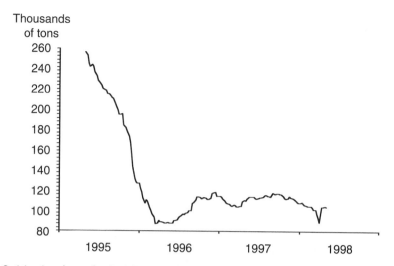

**Figure 2-14** Lead stocks in LME warehouse (May 1995–May 1998). (*Source:* Datastream.)

ing. Because it is producing 15 to 25 percent less lead, eastern Europe is now exporting 30 percent less, and in the future it might have to import the metal to meet demand.

Due to a temporary slackening demand from Asian countries like Japan, Malaysia, and Indonesia, lead cash prices came down (see Figure 2-15) and are now at very attractive levels to buy.

### Zinc

The zinc market is characterized by consumption at record levels, which is outpacing refined production for the second successive year. According to the International Lead & Zinc Study Group, there was a total world supply deficit in 1996 of 218,000 tons and in 1995 of 198,000 tons.[32] In the previous years zinc supply *surpassed* zinc consumption. Zinc is experiencing the most sustained price rally since 1992. Zinc stocks are being drawn down quickly. Half of the zinc production is used to make anticorrosive galvanized steel used for automobile parts such as

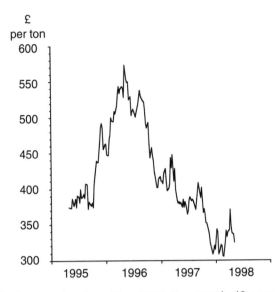

**Figure 2-15**  Lead cash prices (May 1995–May 1998). (*Source:* Datastream.)

hoods and panels. But galvanized steel is also used in the construction sector: it is used for many construction applications such as roofing and building support. Many analysts estimate the growth rate in zinc will become 3 percent annually. Galvanizing capacity in the United States is enlarged by 4 million tons, and this of course requires a lot of zinc. And zinc stocks are very low (see Figure 2-16).

In 1999 and 2000, new zinc mines and added melting capacity will increase the supply.

### Nickel

The nickel supply depends to a great extent on the Russian firm Norilsk. Strikes, supply problems, and increased demand cause a deficit between mining production, stocks, and demand. In nickel the question is always: Are the Russians exporting or not? Exports in 1995 and the first half of 1996 were greatly reduced. After mid-1996, exports were resumed, and nickel stocks rose

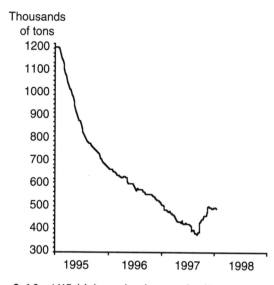

**Figure 2-16** LME high-grade zinc stocks (January 1995–May 1998). (*Source:* Datastream.)

from 40,000 to 60,000 tons from mid-1996 (see Figure 2-17) until January 1998.

## Aluminum

There is a fair chance that aluminum prices can double in the years from 1998 to 2003. The aluminum industry simply does not have enough smelting capacity to satisfy demand. Aluminum producers are showing more interest in expanding their smelting capacity, but the process is very slow. "New capacity does not come quickly enough onstream to avert a threatening shortage," according to Tony Bird, author of a thorough aluminum analysis.[33] According to his analysis, prices are not driven by "evil" speculators but by a persistent underlying industry demand (see Figure 2-18). Bird sees demand outpacing supply in markets outside the former Soviet Union by 333,000 tons in 1997, by 27,000 tons in 1998, by 345,000 tons in 1999, and by 540,000 tons in 2000.

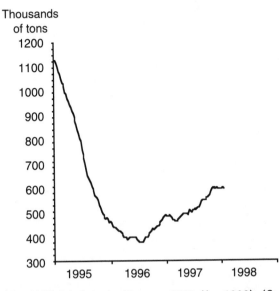

**Figure 2-17**    LME nickel stocks (January 1995–May 1998). (*Source:* Datastream.)

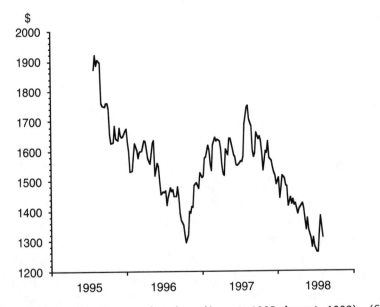

**Figure 2-18**    Aluminum cash prices (August 1995–August 1998). (*Source:* Datastream.)

The Economist Intelligence Unit suggested the same in a report of November 1997. The deficit between committed capacity and required production to satisfy demand will widen considerably. This will induce aluminum prices to go up.

Also aluminum stocks are being drawn down due to strong demand (see Figure 2-19).

### Copper

Copper is one of the oldest metals known to humanity, but it plays a prominent role in sophisticated technologies and modern conveniences. You use it every day when you switch on a light and the current is carried over copper wires or when you turn the tap and water flows through copper pipes. It is used in plumbing and telecommunications and in a huge quantity of

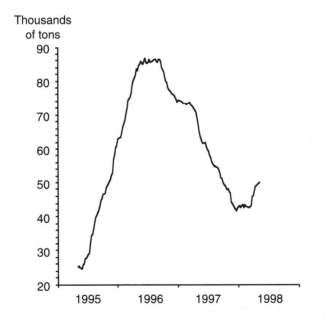

**Figure 2-19** Weekly LME aluminum stocks (May 1995–May 1998). (*Source:* Datastream.)

TABLE 2-2    Aluminum Supply-and-Demand Balance[34]

| World Primary Figures, tons per year | 1996 | 2000 | 2005 | 2010 | 2015 |
|---|---|---|---|---|---|
| Required production | 20,810 | 23,424 | 25,720 | 28,610 | 32,874 |
| Required capacity | 21,905 | 24,657 | 27,074 | 30,116 | 34,509 |
| Committed capacity | 23,543 | 24,744 | 24,744 | 24,744 | 24,744 |
| Surplus/Deficit | 1,638 | 87 | −2,330 | −5,372 | −9,765 |

Source: Kenneth Gooding, "Warning on Aluminum Growth," *London Financial Times*, November 16, 1997.

consumer goods and cars. Wherever electricity is used in your car (windshield wipers, lights, etc.), it is running through copper wires. In top-of-the-line cars, you can find over a hundred electrical motors all equipped with copper wires. The average family car requires 0.62 miles of cable which contains about 33 pounds of copper.[35] And the more that global warming causes higher temperatures, the greater will be the demand for air conditioners and thus for huge tonnages of copper.

Three big factors will influence copper prices in the coming years:

1. New production capacity comes on stream in Latin and Central America—particularly in Chile—and the market is forecast to have production surpluses. Global production surpluses are forecast to rise to 400,000 tons in 1999.

2. Asian copper demand is roughly a third of global copper consumption, and since the Asian economic crisis erupted in autumn 1997, demand has been slackening but picking up in the second half of 1998.

3. The big unknown demand factor in the copper market is China. Generally the bigger the demand for electricity is, the bigger the demand for copper. Take this example: according to Chinese officials, China is facing an annual shortage of at least

100 million tons of iron ore and will need to import vast quantities of copper by 2000.[36] China's largest copper producer, Jiangxi Copper, recently forecast a yearly shortage of 200,000 to 300,000 tons per year over the next few years. As soon as the Chinese Three Gorges Dam is completed, the Chinese company CPG (China Power Grid) will start to install 5,642 miles of power lines all over the country. This requires an investment of $7.2 billion and an awful lot of copper.

Richard Osborne, the chairman of Asarco, is of the opinion that many analysts underestimate China's appetite for copper. He believes that Chinese copper consumption will increase by more than 10 percent a year through 2000, based on official Chinese estimates of an 8 percent annual gross domestic product (GDP) growth. Actual GDP growth rates have been substantially in excess of that in recent years.

In December 1997 cash copper prices were depressed because of the slackening Asian demand and swelling global production. Currently copper is in a cycle in which inventories are rising against a backdrop of receding Asian consumption. When currencies in Asia are halved in value and interest rates rise, demand for expensive dollar-priced industrial metals slows down. However, I think the Asian recovery will come faster than the majority of market analysts think and prices will go up again in the years ahead. All in all, as a private investor, you should not speculate in metal futures yourself but should invest in good metal funds and first-class mining companies, and open metal bank accounts before prices start to rise.

### Lithium

A fascinating metal is lithium. It is already widely used in battery cells to power consumer products such as camcorders, laptop computers, cellular phones, watches, and electric cars. The Argonne National Laboratory in the United States is devel-

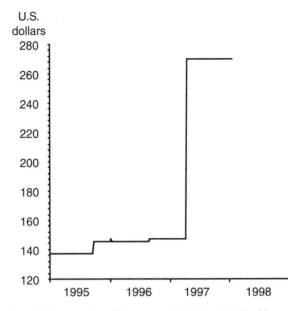

**Figure 2-20** Lithium prices (January 1995–May 1998). (*Source:* Datastream.)

oping a rechargeable bipolar lithium-metal sulfide battery that can enhance the power and energy densities of long-life batteries for electric and hybrid vehicles. The batteries last up to 100,000 miles and run 250 miles before they must be recharged. Fuel-cell technology can make electric cars a common sight on our roads in the twenty-first century. The next step will be the commercial use of fuel cells that produce electricity and that *do not need to be recharged*. The demand for lithium is increasing, and the price for lithium nearly doubled between mid-1996 and mid-1997 (see Figure 2-20).

## Precious Metals

### Gold

In December 1997 gold lost its luster. This is because gold is not a prime industrial metal and because gold has been a security against inflation. The inflation threat is not acute, and central banks have been big sellers. They have sold large quantities of gold to raise cash and to diminish government deficits. According to government statistics we live more in a time of deflation than inflation, so the role of gold as a hedge against inflation is a minor one.

Gold is a beautiful metal for jewelry, but I would not recommend it as an investment today. Other precious metals are much more attractive. The tide might turn for gold when inflation signs loom on the horizon.

## Palladium

Palladium is a precious metal, and it is used for some components of portable electronic equipment such as mobile telephones and laptop computers. It also can be found in catalytic converters that remove pollutants from car exhaust. Traditionally palladium came out of Russia. Russia produces 70 percent of the world's palladium consumption, but now demand is bigger than the supply. In 1997 Russia stopped exporting palladium for six months, which drove prices up to the highest level in 18 years to $296 an ounce (see Figure 2-21). According to Johnson Matthey, who is the world's biggest marketer of platinum and palladium, we will face a serious shortage of palladium after the year 2000. When Russian stocks are exhausted, supplies will greatly depend on the production of the Russian company Norilsk Nickel.[37]

**My Opinion: Many investors argue that the general price level of natural resources is very low. This is certainly true for oil. But looking more closely at other commodities, we can see that prices of several commodities, such as tea, lithium, and palladium, are already skyrocketing. If you look at Figure 2-21, you will see what is likely to happen to**

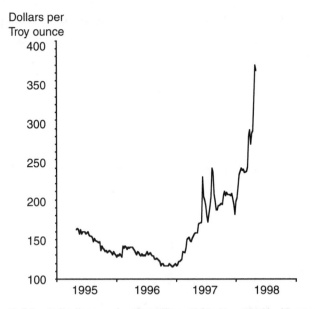

**Figure 2-21**   Palladium cash prices (May 1995–May 1998). (*Source:* Datastream.)

**other commodities in the first 10 years of the new millennium.**

### Platinum

The story for platinum is virtually the same as for palladium. Demand is rising and supplies are limited. The biggest producer of the metal is not Russia but South Africa, which is producing at close to full capacity. Higher shipments from South Africa are a dream. The tightness boosted platinum prices in 1997 from $350 to a peak of $495 an ounce in June 1997 (see Figure 2-22). Johnson Matthey forecasts a shortage because Russia—the second largest producer—failed to export platinum due to virtually depleted stocks. Platinum demand is especially rising in China. The Chinese love to

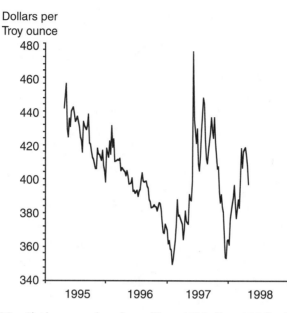

**Figure 2-22** Platinum cash prices (May 1995–May 1998). (*Source:* Data-stream.)

wear platinum jewelry, and because population numbers are huge in China, any slight increase in demand can catapult prices further. Platinum demand in China increased by 50 percent, and China has overtaken Japan as the biggest platinum user.[38]

> **My Opinion:** As you can see, platinum prices are extremely volatile, and I do not recommend a private speculator to buy the metal highly leveraged on the Comex Futures market in New York. Buying cash platinum or even better buying platinum in U.S. dollars in a metal account in a Swiss or Liechtenstein bank and leaving it for several years is a very viable alternative and does not cause sleepless nights. Prices are very cheap at these levels.

### Silver

Silver is a very interesting case. Silver has been the subject of huge squeezes and speculations since the Hunt days 26 years ago when the Hunt family of Texas drove up prices from $5 per Troy ounce to over $50 per Troy ounce. Interestingly the smart money is moving into silver again. In 1997 the smartest investor in the United States, Warren Buffett, baffled Wall Street once more as he bought a fifth of the world's silver supply—130 million ounces. Analysts estimate that he invested around $700 million and the holdings were around $1 billion by April 1998. Ironically Mr. Buffett called his purchase a nonevent. He started to buy the metal around $4.40 in mid-1997 (see Figure 2-23). Mr. Buffet perceived that bullion inventories had fallen substantially because of an excess user demand over mine production and reclamation. He interpreted this as a clear *buy* signal. Traditionally Buffett is a long-term investor. The silver investment, though, represents only 2 percent of the Berkshire

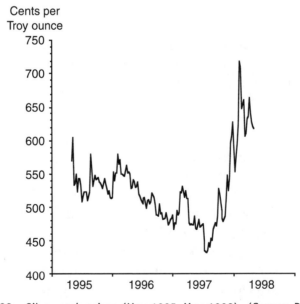

**Figure 2-23**   Silver cash prices (May 1995–May 1998). (*Source:* Datastream.)

Hathaway holdings, and it is rumored in the market that Buffett is already taking some profits.

This is a perfect example of how Buffett outsmarts the average investor who neglects commodities because of low price levels. Commodities are cheap, and that is the best moment to buy before the herd does likewise.

**My Opinion: The advice for platinum also holds for silver for the private investor: buy the metal in a silver account in U.S. dollars in a Swiss or Liechtenstein bank.**

### Titanium

Maybe you wonder why your titanium golf clubs are so expensive. Titanium consumption is rising fast, and part of the answer is the boom in golf and the use of titanium golf clubs. America has 22 million golfers. America is graying, and so are the golfers, who are also wealthier. Every golfer wants to hit the ball straighter and further. If you are on a golf course anywhere in the world, you see many people walking around with $400 titanium drivers. The price for this pleasure rose by 57 percent from 1995 to January 1998.

## WATER

### Water Wars

Water to a great extent is the natural resource of which you and I are made. It is the most precious commodity on earth. For most Americans it goes without saying that water is available in unlimited quantities at low prices, and the first thing you get in many American restaurants, without asking, is a glass of water.

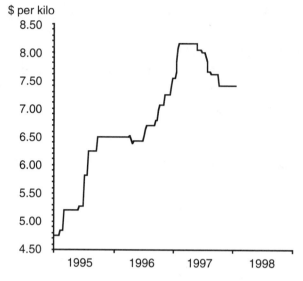

**Figure 2-24** Titanium cash prices (January 1995–May 1998). (*Source: Datastream.*)

In many other parts of the world, the situation is totally different: often there is not enough water, and when it is available it is wasted and polluted on a grand scale.

*Water, our most valuable and vital resource, can in the future cause wars among nations.* Defense and attacks on water wells can become the heart of armed conflicts. The supply of clean fresh water is limited, and many nations stand under huge pressures to provide their citizens with this commodity, which is getting more and more precious every day. Global population expands exponentially, and so does the demand for clean water.

The United Nations and the Stockholm Environment Institute issued a report and predicted that by 2025 two-thirds of the global population will be affected by water shortages. The gap between supply and demand is widening very rapidly. The former British ambassador to the United Nations expressed the problem like this: "World demand for water doubles every 21 years, but the volume available is the same as it was in Roman times."[39] Water consumption tripled in the past 40 years. The average American family consumes about 528 gallons a day. In some developing countries, families survive on about 40 gallons a day, and often they have to walk far and pump deep to get it.

In developing countries water often carries bacilli of killing diseases like diarrhea and even chemicals that can cause cancer. Contaminated water also has a negative effect on the endocrine system of human beings and animals. In general, human fertility around the globe is reduced continuously, and scientists fear that water carries the hormone killers which influence reproduction negatively.

## The Importance of Water

Let's go back to the basics: to grow a crop you need land, fertilizers, and water in large quantities—and water is irreplaceable.

**About 1,000 tons of water is needed to produce 1 ton of grain.**

Because the temperature of Mother Earth is rising, the subject of "irrigation" becomes more and more of a touchy one. As water cannot be replaced, water scarcity becomes visible instantly. As water becomes more and more scarce, the price for water rises constantly.

Two-thirds of water from rivers, lakes, and groundwater is used for agriculture. The problems are that:

- Groundwater levels are retracing more and more.

- Rivers are more and more polluted.

- Water reservoirs become clogged with mud due to erosion and deforestation.

- Industry and urbanization claim more and more water from agriculture.

- As ground water levels sink, salinization of the water increases.

- Floods become more and more frequent.

An essential part of food production is achieved with ecologically damaging use of water. This means that when more water is being pumped from lakes, rivers, and groundwater than what is being added annually, water deficiency becomes evident. When a farmer pumps more water than the quantity that is being added annually in the form of rain, the level of groundwater sinks. Pumping becomes more expensive, and on lower levels in the earth the salt content of the water increases.

Water or a lack of water is the determining factor for abundant or poor crops. Irrigated crop land is only 16 percent of the total global arable surface. *But this 16 percent prime cropland produces 40 percent of the world's grain crops.*[40]

## Water Deficiency

There are 26 countries containing a total of 230 million inhabitants in which water deficiency prevails and hinders food production, economic development, drainage systems, and environmental protection. Ten countries in this group consume more water than they annually produce. They just pump too much groundwater. More and more countries will fall into this water-deficient category. Some astonishing facts:

- The World Bank has published figures that 1 billion people lack access to clean drinking water and 1.7 billion people do not have clean sanitary facilities. Dirty water is the reason why 2 billion people in the Third World catch a disease.

Ten million children die yearly due to dirty water. When in the year 2025 over 8 billion people will be living on this planet, water demand will rise by 625 percent according to the World Bank.[41]

- Countries like America, India, Pakistan, Libya, Iran, and Saudi Arabia pump enormous quantities of groundwater. They satisfy short-term needs and take a mortgage on their future.

- It is estimated that on 10 percent of China's arable land more groundwater is being pumped than is being replaced by rain.

- In the Great Plains in the United States, the bread basket of America, more water is pumped than is replaced. Thousands of acres of frugal arable land in Texas are being lost annually because of a lack of groundwater. Statistically it has been proven that in agricultural areas the population grows or shrinks with groundwater levels: when the level falls, agriculture collapses, and the younger generation and also regional industries move away to areas with a sufficient infrastructure.

- If you look at a map of the United States, the Colorado River is a blue line ending in the Gulf of California. In fact this is wrong: the location where water was once gushing into the ocean is now no more than a trickle in a desert. On the maps "the mighty river of the West" should be nothing more than a brown stripe. In the beginning of this century, this was a green delta, and now it is a desert landscape. But the same story is true for the Nile, the Ganges, the Yellow River, and the Jordan. The rivers are pumped empty before they even reach the seas. The Colorado River irrigates 1.97 million acres of agricultural land. Twenty-one million people have drinking water, and Las Vegas is lit in neon lights at night.

• The Sacramento and San Joaquin rivers are also being emptied before they reach the ocean. In California most of the rain falls in the northern part of the state, but agricultural land lies in the south. From the Colorado River aqueduct, water is being transported to Los Angeles—250 miles south of the river. In California people say: "Water flows uphill to the money." There is no law in California that restricts farmers from pumping unlimited water out of the underground aquifers. So they pump much more than what is flowing back to the earth in the form of rain. There is not a place on earth where per capita water consumption is higher than in California. Grain meant for animal feed grows on irrigated land. Therefore *2,400 gallons of water are needed to produce 1 pound of California cattle hamburger meat.*[42] No, this is not a misprint, and it illustrates perfectly how unecological the consumption of hamburgers is.

In fact water means power. Those who have power can buy water. Countries without sufficient water are usually the poor countries. And drought combined with a lack of irrigation means poverty and causes the need to import grain at high prices in expensive dollars.

The competition for water among agriculture, urbanization, and industrialization, especially in Asia, is very intense. Asia is the most artificially irrigated area in the whole world. If water-usage patterns in Malaysia, India, and Indonesia continue, the supply of water will be 30 percent less than the demand.

## Global Water Consumption

Sandra Postel, who is one of the most prominent water experts today, gave an excellent analysis of water needs and consumption in the book, *State of the World 1996,* issued by the World Watch Institute. She divided up water consumption from rivers,

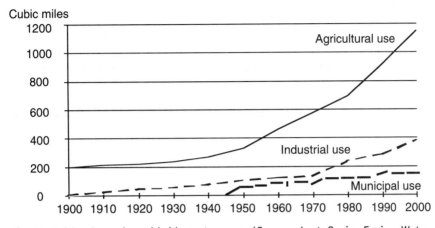

**Figure 2-25** Annual worldwide water use. (*Source: Last Oasis: Facing Water Scarcity* by Sandra Postel, © World Watch Institute. Reprinted with permission.)

aquifers, rainfall, and so on, as follows: worldwide agriculture, 65 percent; industries, 25 percent; and private households, 10 percent.[43] Figure 2-25 illustrates the differences in water use among the three sectors. Agricultural use has a higher rate of increase than industrial or municipal water use.

The significant fact is that 65 percent of water consumption is used for grain reserved for animal feed. This means that animals who are fed on animal feed like corn account for 65 percent of water consumption, and the human race (industry and private consumption) gets only 35 percent (see Figure 2-25). The cows come first, even if you are plainly forbidden to water your garden in the summer. And because most of the water consumed is used for agricultural purposes, agriculture is the area where an acute water shortage will be felt first.

Groundwater levels in the United States sink according to region between 6 inches and 6 feet per year. Consequently irrigation becomes more expensive every year because pumping takes place in deeper and deeper levels.

The main reasons for the declining irrigation of arable land include:

1. More pumping of groundwater than is being replaced.
2. Rivers that run dry due to heat and excessive pumping.
3. Freshwater stocks turning salty due to deforestation and erosion.
4. Industry claiming water that was reserved for agricultural purposes earlier.

As mentioned before, climate changes have a major influence on water levels. Scientists do not yet agree on what impact a continuous warming of Mother Earth will have on our environment. On one hand, global warming causes more heat in one area but maybe far more evaporation, which causes tropical storms, in other areas. In some hot regions at latitudes close to the equator, evaporation is more significant, and in other regions intensive rainfall is prevalent. Generally countries in higher latitudes suffer less evaporation than do countries situated at lower latitudes.

## FISH

### Ocean Catch

Two-thirds of the globe is covered with water, and from outer space the earth looks like "The Blue Planet." But oceans are not unlimited sources of nutrition. Big parts of oceans are infertile grounds where fish do not reproduce themselves. Compared to land, these parts of oceans are like deserts. In order to be fertile grounds for fish, the habitat must meet two conditions:

1. It must be in the upper layers of the ocean where sunlight can penetrate.
2. Ocean currents must transport nutritional elements like plankton from the deep layers to the upper layers.

Good examples of fertile grounds are for instance the Skagerrak or the North Sea. Wide open oceans like the Atlantic Ocean do not meet both conditions. Because of the dominating westerly winds in this world, these fertile grounds are mainly located on west coasts like Peru, California, and European shorelines, including Norway.

The FAO concludes that the global annual catch is around 100 million tons of fish and that oceans are reaching their limits of output-capacity to produce these quantities yearly.[44] The FAO also concludes in its study that the demand for salt- and freshwater fish is increasing sharply due to exploding population growth. Because of the limited supplies, fish prices will continue to rise, and especially in emerging markets fish will become unaffordable. Because of overfishing, more and more sorts of fish are slowly diminishing in population. This is true especially for salmon, trout, and sturgeon, which have died out in the North Sea. The fish catch in the North Sea is one of the most abundant catches in the whole world and amounts to 2.5 million tons yearly. This means an average catch of 7.29 tons per square mile. Oceans produce in general 20 times less fish than the North Sea catch.[45] In the Caspian Sea the supply of caviar is becoming more and more rare. Fishermen say there won't be any caviar left in two years if overfishing continues. A little glass pot of caviar in Russia already costs $50. Fish and chicken have one thing in common: if you breed them, they have roughly the same conversion ratio, that is, it takes 2 pounds of animal feed to produce 1 pound of fish or chicken. The fish catch in the oceans has reached its limits. So the growth in animal protein supplies can only come from animals living on land. We will see that the breeding of cattle, most of all, is a very uneconomical and unecological way to produce protein. The human diet—especially in Asia—likes to take protein from animals. The relatively advantageous fish conversion ratio is very economical compared to cattle breeding—one head of cattle eats 9 pounds of grain to produce 1 pound of meat. If humanity continues to consume ever-increasing amounts of meat, the pressure on grain supplies will intensify to satisfy the human diet, and grain prices will rise further.

The FAO states now that 11 of the world's 15 main fishing grounds are seriously depleted. There are too many fishing boats, and the expansion of the fleet continues. Fishing-rights conflicts erupt all the time, and they will intensify in the future. The United Nations states that over a hundred nations are engaged in fishing-rights disputes.[46]

## Fish Farming

World production of aquaculture is expanding and has a great economic value of $25 billion. One of the most important institutes in the world on food research is the Consultative Group on International Agricultural Research (CGIAR), with research laboratories around the world. They are developing new fish varieties that can double the returns of small aquaculture farmers in a few years. The farm fish has flavor equal to the best free-running freshwater and marine fish.

## SACRED COW #2: MEAT

### De Gustibus Non Disputandum Est

This Latin expression means: "You cannot argue about taste." And it is meaningless to discuss the taste of a hamburger. But in this investment guide, a brief excursion to cows and pigs is necessary for the simple reason that cows and pigs consume a huge quantity of natural resources: water and grain.

**American cows consume 10 times more grain than that consumed by American citizens directly.**

Most people do not realize that the cattle herd in this world has a disastrous effect on our ecology and on our civilization. A fifth of humanity is privileged to eat meat from cattle that has been bred on grain as animal feed. Another fifth of humanity cannot buy grain and feed itself directly with the minimum of calories and protein because the grain is too expensive. This is one of the most serious problems of our civilization. At the same time we have the absurd situation that millions of people die in the Western world from eating too much meat.

Meat plays an important role in analyzing the cause of death due to heart attacks and cancer. According to the National Research Council in America, beef is the second largest source of nutrition that causes cancer because of its pesticide content. The largest source of nutrition that causes cancer is tomatoes.

*Cattle eat over 70 percent of the grain produced in the United States.* Worldwide this figure is much lower: cattle eat about a third of the global grain crop. Simultaneously a billion people, or 20 percent of the global population, suffer from permanent famine.

I don't want to argue about taste. I am not a strict vegetarian, and every now and then I also like a little steak. The human being eats meat for a variety of reasons. It tastes good, it contains protein, and especially in Asia it is a symbol of a high standard of living. In Europe, meat consumption is in decline, but in Asia it is increasing strongly. Apart from the health aspects, eating meat is totally uneconomical and unecological as well.

**The grain consumed annually by cows is sufficient to feed a few hundred million people. All in all, the demand for grain as animal feed regulates to a big extent the price of grain. As long as humanity multiplies itself exponentially and as long as humanity loves to eat meat, the price of the commodity needed to produce the meat will go up.**

## A Final Little Story about Cows

There are several ways to make Europeans eat succulent beef. And there are many ways to make money in the food business. One of the most unusual aspects of the food trade is the American bull semen worth $90 million annually exported to Europe in liquid-nitrogen-cooled tanks.[47] Upon arrival, the bull semen is injected into European cows. New calves are born, bred, slaughtered, and served on plates. Don't tell the French that their chateaubriand or filet has American origins.

# 3

# THE DEMAND FOR
# NATURAL RESOURCES

## THE PAST, THE PRESENT, AND THE FUTURE

### The Big Grain Robbery—Part 1

I know that people have short memories, but even so let's look back briefly at what happened in 1972. Russia was suffering from a long spell of dry heat that resulted in catastrophic grain crops. And the communist central planning system in Moscow did not give incentives to farmers in Russia's bread basket—the Ukraine—to grow larger crops. The farmers always received more or less the same amount of rubles for their grain, and they were not motivated to get maximum production out of their cropland. They did what was dictated by Moscow and did not plant a grain seed more.

But the communist government had to feed its population, and suddenly the central Russian purchase agency, Exportklep, discreetly chartered freighters on the Baltic Exchange in London. Freight rates started to climb, and grain prices in Chicago mysteriously started to rise as well. Shortly afterward, Exportklep bought over 20 million tons of grain from the big grain-trading companies like Cargill, Bunge, Continental Grain, and Louis Dreyfus.

This was all done very discreetly, and one grain company did not know what the other grain company had contracted. The net result was catapulting grain prices on the Chicago Board of Trade. The Americans had abundant grain crops—mostly in the hands of Cargill—so they happily provided the commodities to Russia with huge profits. U.S. Secretary of State Henry Kissinger concluded that agriculture is too important to be left to farmers alone, and he called a world food conference to prevent a similar shock in the future. More market openness and emergency aid commitments now regulate the supplies to Russia.

The global grain trade is in the hands of a few family-type giant trading companies and Cargill is the biggest of them all. They thrive on the global demand for food, and today they control 25 percent of America's grain exports. They have a finger literally in many pies, and when you drink a Coke or a Pepsi or when you eat a hamburger from McDonald's, corn flakes from Kellogg's, or orange juice from Tropicana or Granini, you are eating or drinking a product that contains commodities supplied by Cargill. Together with Mars, it belongs to the largest family-owned company in the United States. Cargill and Mars are not public but privately held companies, and unfortunately you cannot buy their stock on a stock exchange. I worked seven years for Cargill Investor Services trading commodity and financial futures on behalf of Swiss financial institutions and high-net-worth individuals. Cargill is a great company, and I have very fond memories of that period of my life.

## The Big Grain Robbery—Part 2

The French have a saying: *C'est l'histoire, qui se répète* (history repeats itself). I think we will see "The Big Grain Robbery—Part 2" in the near future. The players in this drama will be partly the same, partly different. The cast of sellers will be largely the same, plus some additional players from Australia, Argentina, Canada, and Brazil. The main role among the buyers will not be played by the Russians but by the *Chinese*. And the dimensions of the grain purchases will be far bigger.

In the commodity markets China is the so-called "swing factor." If you involve China in any business deal, the numbers are automatically staggering. Nothing is small in China, and deals are done on a grand scale. So if China buys grain, it is *big* business and the quantities are huge. World grain prices will be dictated by the China factor. China used to be a grain *exporter*. But this country became in 1995 the second largest grain *importer* in the world after Japan. In 1994 it imported 6 million tons of grain, and in 1995, 16 million tons. These imports can mount to 50 million tons annually in the coming years. Chinese imports seen against a backdrop of unprecedented environmental constraints can, over time, push grain prices up much higher. *There will come a time when China's import requirements are too large to handle by any one country.*

Chinese demand can be the catalyst for higher food prices all over the world. You and I will notice that we have to lay out substantially more money for our daily basic needs. In supermarkets prices for meat, bread, milk, eggs, poultry, and all products made from grain (salad oils, potato chips, etc.) will rise sharply. There have already been demonstrations in American streets of housewives who protested against rising meat prices in 1972. When this phenomenon is repeated, billions of people who live on the borderline of poverty will no longer be able to afford basic nourishment. *Therefore you must invest now in the food and agricultural industry, not after the fact.*

## Skyrocketing Grain Demand

Grain plants like wheat, corn, and rice are the most important sources of nutrition for humanity. They provide the human species with 50 percent of its energy needs. The other 50 percent is also mainly derived from grains, but it functions first as animal feed and comes back in the form of meat, eggs, and milk. Taking the global grain production of 1.8 billion tons, one-fifth of humanity has an ample supply of food and three-fifths is just scraping by. The last fifth—close to 1 billion people—suffers from chronic malnutrition. Between 18 million and 22 million people die annually because of hunger. To feed the 1 billion people who will be added to the global population at the end of this century, the grain production must be enlarged substantially. It remains an undeniable fact that in the past 50 years the evolution of agriculture has been phenomenal. In the past 20 years alone, food production increased by 50 percent, and the global population grew by 40 percent. But now *global population grows exponentially* and food production has practically stalled. Next to faltering distribution, destruction of traditional agriculture through erosion, industrialization, and pollution is one of the major reasons for existing famine. According to UN Food and Agriculture Ogranization (FAO) Director-General Jacques Diouf, food production must increase by 75 percent over the next three decades to keep up with an expected population of some 9 billion people.[1] Mr. Diouf is optimistic that this world can feed all those hungry mouths through biotechnology, expanding water control, pest control, and plant nutrition.

A very positive development is that 100 years ago, 30 percent of the population had to work as farmers to feed the nation. Today only 1 percent are farmers. And this 1 percent not only produce top-quality nutrition but also relatively cheap food. Prices in real terms for the main food types have halved in the past 20 years.

But this *earth will have to feed over 10 billion people by the year 2050*, and our children will be confronted with a different reality. This means that with today's standards and statistics, twice as much grain must be produced, which is a near-impossible task. To feed the second category of people who are "just scraping by" with just enough food for everybody, *three* times more grain is needed. To feed the whole earth with the same high food standards as the people living in the northern part of the globe, *five* times more grain is needed. Optimists—mainly chemical engineers and economists—think humanity can fulfill this gigantic task through genetically modified foods. Pessimists—mainly ecologists—think this is not possible without doing harm to our environment. Personally I believe that genetic engineering will enlarge crops greatly but that the new techniques will not be sufficient to feed everybody and simultaneously control all future health risks.

The following factors influence supply and demand in the global food business:

1. An exponentially growing population—and this is a long-lasting trend that gets stronger every day.

2. A population that improves its living standards and eating habits.

3. A global population that pollutes its own environment.

4. Grain production that will be enlarged through genetic engineering.

5. A distribution system that does not allow the abundant crops from the north to reach countries in the southern hemisphere at a cheap price. The crops do not reach the millions of hungry people. This distribution problem is not going away with the new bioengineered soybeans, corn, wheat, and tomatoes. The crops in the north will be large, but people in poor countries will not be able to afford to buy the high-priced grain in U.S. dollars. There will not be enough food for everybody in the first quarter of the third millennium.

For the 800 million jobless and homeless people in the Third World, escalating food prices are way too high. Between July 1995 and June 1996, the price of U.S. No. 2 hard winter wheat, ordinary protein, rose by 70 percent. The price of U.S. No. 2 corn escalated in the same period by 80 percent. Today over 80 countries are forced to buy grain on world markets to complement their own crops. The imported grain has an inflationary effect on the overall price level of the country in question. Governments try to stabilize price levels and regulate imports with quotas. Generally governments expand import quotas and reduce import taxes on grains.

A few examples of what happened in 1997: in Asian states like Pakistan and the Philippines, grain prices were escalating. In Sudan grain prices rose by 150 percent, and in several Latin American countries like Brazil and Venezuela, prices reached record levels. The population in Bolivia and El Salvador was confronted with spiraling bread prices, and both governments did away with import taxes on grain to facilitate distribution and to make prices cheaper. Mexico also eliminated taxes on imported wheat and corn and expanded the import quotas for grains. In June 1995 Mexico liberalized prices completely, but price levels of meal skyrocketed by 400 percent. The problem of malnutrition and hunger is becoming more and more a distribution problem and less of a supply problem.

## Rising Food Prices: The Snowball Starts Rolling

Low-income private households ask themselves often: "Are we going to make it until the next monthly salary?" On a global level, we must ask the question: "Are we going to make it to the next harvest?"

Governments, industry, and consumers are not very impressed if Mother Earth becomes only "a little more" polluted. The best proof of this is the fact that very few countries are respecting the decrees of the Berlin Climate Conference in which all participating countries promised to keep the carbon dioxide ($CO_2$) levels in 2000 at the same level as in 1990. The large majority of countries have a lethargic attitude and do not perceive the seriousness of the problem. Especially the majority of Asian countries think short term, and they have little respect for their environment. Their main goal is to make money, but *the worsening ecological state of Asia is backfiring on their economies.*

Politicians who depend on their voters have assured me that ecological matters are not very popular issues to win votes. Where is the Green Party USA? Al Gore would be the perfect person to get an American party based on ecological issues going. But in the United States the time is not yet ripe.

Only when food prices rise sharply, or new epidemics erupt, or billions of dollars of tax money need to be spent to help people suffering from catastrophes will everyone wake up, including the politicians. These phenomena will be the catalysts that will hopefully lead to ecological decisions for a sustainable balance between food supply and human consumption. It will make the headlines of the newspapers, and everybody will feel it in their wallets. The magnitude of the problem among all groups of society will be heightened, just like AIDS today.

## Oil and Grain: OPEC and Grainpec

The Organization of Petroleum Exporting Countries (OPEC) has a fairly good grip on oil prices. Many oil-producing nations belong to the oil cartel, and they regulate the supply of oil pretty well.

As far as grains are concerned, people do not realize that around a hundred countries today are dependent on grain imports. The breadbasket of the globe is controlled by only a handful of exporting countries—United States, Argentina, Brazil, Canada, European Union (EU) countries like France and Germany, Australia, and South Africa—all in all, a kind of "Grainpec." In 1996 and 1997 American grain crops were abundant. But when an American crop turns bad in the future because of heat or cold, drought or flood, the global supply can become very shaky.

## CONSUMER DEMAND: A LESSON IN DEMOGRAPHICS

### Exponential Population Growth

Exponential population growth is best compared to compounded interest in a bank account. In the beginning, capital grows slowly, but because the interest income is continuously added, capital growth *accelerates*. Or to come back to humanity, if you take today's population growth of 1.7 percent per annum, global population will double in 40 years. If you are under 40 years of age, the probability is high that twice as many people will have to find a place to live on this earth with you by the time you are 80. Certainly, your children with a longer life expectancy will have to deal daily with this phenomenon.

The dynamics of exponential growth are a slow increase in the beginning and accelerating increases in a later stage. Humanity multiples itself faster than ever before in history. We beat the rabbits. Just in the 1990s, 1 billion people will be added, which is a whole China extra. One year goes by, and we have another 80 to 90 million people on this earth. The gross national product (GNP) of China is growing at 8 percent a year, and the GNP of India at 7 percent. Then there is Russia, which came out of the doldrums very fast and has positive economic growth now. (It had the biggest stock market rise in 1997—222 percent.) Take these three countries, and you are talking about half the world's population. And everybody will need to eat better, to drink more, and to have a place to live.

Economic growth and population growth were hampered in the first half of this century by two world wars. Since the 1950s, world population has been growing by an annual average of 2 percent. Between 1955 and 1995 global population grew by 105 percent to 5.7 billion people (see Figure 3-1). I am a typical example of the postwar generation. I was born in 1949 when there were about 2.4 billion people in this world. Today twice as many people live on this earth, and it is projected that by 2000,

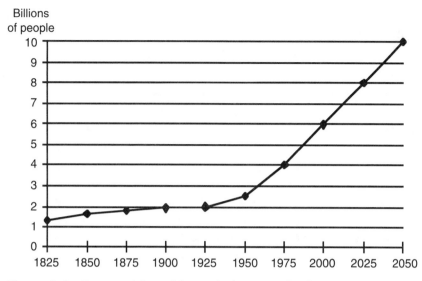

**Figure 3-1** Exponential world population growth. (*Source:* W. Nentwig, "Humanökologie," Springer, 1995, p. 77.)

there may be as many as 6 billion people. By 2050 the population will have doubled again.

> **A 100 percent increase in population between 1949 and 1995 means 2.5 billion more people. A 100 percent increase in population between 1995 and 2050 means 5 billion more people.**

When my children are 50, twice as many people will surround them as there are today.

Since 1975 the global population has grown by 2 billion people every 25 years. Is there enough space for all these people? Will they have enough to eat and to drink? Will there be an infrastructure, and will they all have jobs? And last but not least: What will the pollution be?

The present world population is around 5.7 billion people, of which 4.4 billion people live in developing countries. About half the world's population, 2.3 billion people, is younger than 20. Many of the people who live in the least developed countries—

total population of 556 million—are very young, and population is increasing rapidly.

We live in an age in which technology is transferred to developing nations at a breathtaking tempo. The 4.4 billion people in developing nations are working hard to improve their standard of living. This causes a huge *additional* strain on demand for raw materials. Simultaneously global stocks of many commodities such as oil, grains, and some nonferrous and some precious metals are being drawn down more and more.

**This demand explosion is one of the main reasons why you must be invested in natural resources before the next boom starts. As in any investment cycle, you make the most money in the beginning of the new cycle.**

## Growth of Gross National Product

In analyzing natural resources it is very significant to quantify how large the demand for commodities is. But it is even more important to recognize where the demand comes from. Figure 3-2 illustrates very well the average GNP growth rates in developed countries and emerging markets. Many developed countries are in sync and have an average annual growth rate of 2.41 percent. The emerging markets altogether grow twice as fast, at a pace of 5.09 percent. *And 80 percent of the global population now and in the future live in these emerging markets.* That is the area where the growth and the demand for natural resources occur.

## Population Growth and Grain Crops

Luckily food production has not grown arithmetically but has increased threefold since the 1950s. Since 1995 however, global

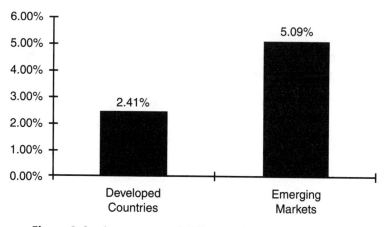

**Figure 3-2** Average annual GNP growth. (*Source:* Orbitex.)

grain production *has stalled or increased minimally at best, while the global population grows exponentially.* That is the reason why the gap between population and food production is widening (see Figure 3-3).

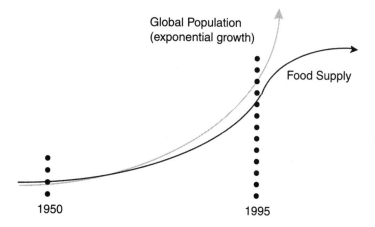

**Figure 3-3** The gap between population growth and food supply is widening.

## Global Urbanization

Some appalling facts are given by the World Health Organization (WHO) in Geneva:[2]

Today:

- 1.5 billion people live in megacities.

- 500 million children live in megacities.

- 125 million to 250 million people worldwide do not have clean water or sanitary facilities.

- 100 million people in megacities are homeless.

- In many megacities 50 percent of the people live in slums and shantytowns.

In the year 2000:

- 50 percent of the world population will live in megacities of 5 million people or more.

- 75 percent of the megacities will be in developing countries.

- 30 percent of the garbage will not be collected.

- 100 million children will be homeless.

- 10 percent of the city population will suffer from mental or neurological diseases, such as alcoholism or drug addiction.

**My Opinion:   We will be confronted with rapid dispersion of infectious diseases for which there is no cure.**

Especially in Asia, industrialization and urbanization are spreading like wildfire, and prime agricultural land is being converted at breathtaking speed into office buildings, roads, housing, and so on. City councils are permanently under pressure to deliver the necessary infrastructure, like energy, housing, transportation systems, railroads, bridges, and drainage systems, and all projects are claiming a lot of agricultural land.

The energy consumption in the megacities is rising dramatically, and if the global population continues to grow exponentially, our world will not be able to come to grips with the resulting pollution. In developing countries especially, questions about energy are asked continuously, for example: Where do we get our energy from? Which kinds of energy are we going to develop and provide to our population? Is it coal, oil, or maybe the sun, wind, and water?

A lot of land is still available in Africa and South America. Not so in Asia. Especially in the most densely populated countries, such as Hong Kong, Taiwan, Singapore, and South Korea, the disposable agricultural land is shrinking. Between 1980 and 1984 and again between 1990 and 1994, the agricultural land shrank 5 percent.[3]

In Java, Djakarta, Bangladesh, and Bangkok, agricultural land also shrinks at an alarming rate. China today has more than 100 cities with a population of over 1 million, and due to the industrial revolution of the past 10 years, more than 200 new cities have been built.

## Skyscrapers

This chapter is meant to give you a concrete idea of the demand for building materials (copper, aluminum, lead, zinc).

Of the 100 tallest buildings in the world, 35 are outside the United States. Half of the non-American buildings are in Asia. In Beijing alone, there are plans for 180 skyscrapers. For the past 20 years, the Sears Tower in Chicago was the world's tallest building. Now the tallest skyscrapers are the twin towers of the oil company Petronas in Kuala Lumpur, built by the famous American architect Cesar Pelli. The towers are 1,482 feet high, 29 feet higher than the Sears Tower, and look like two modern pagodas. More people work there than in the twin towers of the World Trade Center in New York. In the near future the Petronas record will certainly be surpassed, probably in Taiwan, Singapore, Djakarta, or Shanghai. The inclination in Tokyo to build skyscrapers is somewhat subdued because of the earthquakes.

## The Great Mall versus the Great Wall

Malaysia has grandiose plans. Malaysia not only built the *tallest* building in the world but also plans to build the *longest* building in the world—a 1¹/₄-mile-long, snake-like office complex, KL LinearCity, along the main Kelang River flowing through Kuala Lumpur. The complex would follow all the curves of the river and cost 4 billion dollars to build. The project reflects Malaysia's growing wealth and ambitions. The government is in the process of giving the building permits for the construction, which will take 24 years. The plans might be put on the back burner because of the economic crisis, but as soon as the Malaysian economy gets going again, construction should start on LinearCity. Malaysia will surely be beaten in terms of the tallest construction in the world, but it will take a while to beat the record of The Great Mall.

## Megacities

Table 3-1 illustrates the number of people who were living in megacities in 1990 and projections for the year 2000. For cities like Mexico City, Sao Paulo, Shanghai, and Calcutta, the figures are approximations because nobody knows how many people are really dwelling in city houses, streets, and garbage belts.

TABLE 3-1    Population of Megacities (in millions)[4]

|  | 1990 | 2000 |
|---|---|---|
| Mexico City | 20.2 | 25.6 |
| Sao Paulo | 17.4 | 22.1 |
| Tokyo | 18.1 | 19.0 |
| Shanghai | 13.4 | 17.0 |
| New York City and suburbs | 16.2 | 16.8 |
| Calcutta | 11.8 | 15.7 |
| Bombay | 11.2 | 15.4 |
| Beijing | 10.8 | 14.0 |
| Los Angeles | 11.9 | 13.9 |
| Djakarta | 9.3 | 13.7 |

## Population Growth in China

In 1959 one-half billion people lived in China. In only 21 years China added another half-billion people, totaling 1 billion inhabitants. Today 1.2 billion people live in China. If you take 1980 as a starting point, another half-billion people will be added by 2020. Luckily the Chinese growth rate will slow down from 2030 onwards, as Figure 3-4 shows. This of course

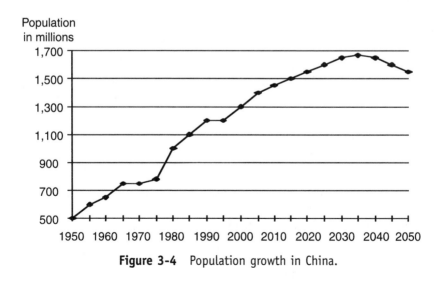

**Figure 3-4**    Population growth in China.

is due to the successful implementation of the "one child per family" legislation.

Three hundred million people live in the urban coast provinces, and by 2010 population will have doubled. China has 21 percent of the world population, but it has only 7 percent of the global agricultural land. It holds five times the population of the United States, but it has less agricultural land. According to the latest forecasts, China in 2005 will have a population of 1.4 billion people. *Without the family planning, total population would have been 2 billion.*[5]

## Comparison between China and India

As is shown in Figure 3-5, Indian population was 400 million people in 1960. It doubled in only 31 years, and several organizations estimate that by 2000 the population will surpass 1 billion people. The temporary peak will be around 2019 with a population of 1.9 billion people.

Between 2000 and 2020 India will surpass China and become the most densely populated nation on earth. Those two nations will contain 40 percent to 45 percent of the world's population.

Figure 3-5 also shows that India has a much higher birth rate than China. China has executed the world's most successful program to reduce population growth. Our Western moral standards object to curbing the right to reproduce oneself. But don't forget that the next generation has the right to survive and live decently, too.

## Conclusions

Today's demographics are characterized by two main facts:

1. World population is exponentially exploding.

2. Living standards of the *majority* of the population are rapidly improving.

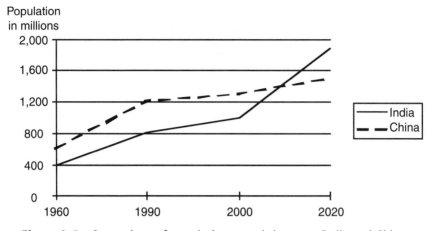

**Figure 3-5**  Comparison of population growth between India and China.

The net result will be an unprecedented rise in the demand for natural resources like grain, metals, and energy.

Countries like China will turn from a *population* explosion to a *consumption explosion,* buying such items as refrigerators, television sets, portable telephones, and better food. The only thing that counts in Asia is making money. Go to Hong Kong, Singapore, or Shanghai, and judge for yourself. Young people in Asia take very little vacation. Despite an economic crisis, their mood is very upbeat. They are extremely competitive, and they have one goal in mind: to get rich as soon as possible.

The Chinese are earning more and changing their eating habits. Asia was never a continent of carnivorous people, but now meat demand is soaring in Asia. Therefore, I project food demand not to rise by 40 percent in the year 2025 but to *double.* The actual global grain crop is about 1.8 billion tons. Mother Earth does not have enough space and healthy soil to double the crop in 20 years to 3.6 billion tons of grain without health risks to humanity.

We are heading to a situation where the strain of the demand for food will continue to intensify and where grain will rise in price to unprecedented levels. Expensive grain priced in expensive dollars will become unaffordable for vast numbers of people.

# 4

## CHINA, THE SWING FACTOR

### STATUS QUO

The three most important factors in the global commodity markets are China, China, and China. Because of its sheer size, enormous population, and impressive economic development, China is the "swing factor," the hinge on which many economic factors turn. This means commodity prices can be pushed much higher when Chinese demand really comes into play.

Until 1994 China was a net exporter of grain. In 1995 China started to import, and in the future a good or a bad grain crop will be the determining factor of the Chinese import volume. Because China's economy is booming, 1.2 billion Chinese are improving their eating habits and can cause great constraints on the world's grain markets.

The United States is the biggest energy-user on earth. The United States has only 5 percent of the global population, but until recently, it was consuming about one-third of the world's resources. We are now coming to a point where China's booming economy and growing population will soon put more demands on the earth's resources than the United States, according to the World Watch Institute in Washington.

In several areas China now consumes more than the United States does. It already consumes more grain and red meat, it uses more fertilizers, it produces more steel and burns more coal. Its current emissions of carbon dioxide are one-tenth of the world's total. Of course the per capita consumption in China is far less than that in the United States, but China is catching up fast. For instance, a Chinese person now consumes 66 pounds (30 kilos) of pork a year, compared with 68.3 pounds (31 kilos) in the United States. And the upward trend in meat consumption is rising fast. If each Chinese person were to consume as much *beef* as an American does—99 pounds (45 kilos) per year—according to World Watch, it would take 343 millions tons of grain, or entire U.S. harvest, to feed the cattle to make up the difference.

Although China is the third-largest country on earth, its surface consists largely of mountains, plains, and other sorts of land that cannot be used for agriculture. So 22 percent of the globe's population must feed itself on only 7 percent of the globe's arable land.

The following *supply factors* are crucial for China's position on the world's grain markets:

- China's grain production is expanding but not increasing fast enough to feed 1.2 billion hungry mouths. China's population and improvement of taste are growing faster than China's grain production.

- The surface of China's agricultural land is not increasing but decreasing.

- The average Chinese citizen does not have any respect for the environment. The pollution is colossal, and this will have disastrous consequences for future crops.

On the *demand side*, China has the following characteristics:

- Population keeps on increasing.

- China's economic growth has been over 50 percent in the past five years. Incomes are rising, and people can afford better nutrition and incorporate more and more meat into their diets. The Chinese move into modern houses, and they buy refrigerators, televisions, cars, portable telephones, and so on. China is becoming a consumer society, and one of the most popular programs on Chinese television is "Baywatch." In this program the Chinese see the good life in the United States: big cars, big houses, big kitchens, big Harley Davidsons, and other physical components that have been made artificially bigger in Silicon Valley. The whole world will feel the effect of the Chinese consumption boom.

Domestic prices of grain and oil can go much higher in the future, and carbon emissions will continue to soar.

## INFRASTRUCTURE DEMAND

Let's take Shanghai as an example of what is happening. Shanghai today has 14 million inhabitants and 22,000 construction sites. It is a city like Sao Paolo, Rotterdam, or Milan: a trade city and very efficient. Shanghai has an obsession: to build a huge number of buildings, roads, factories, and harbors as fast as possible. On the other side of the Huangpu River on the Pudong peninsula, a new business quarter, Lujiazhui, will become the financial center of Shanghai. It is the biggest construction site in the world. Total office space is 1.97 million square yards, which is half of the office space of Singapore. The total city on Pudong will have a planned surface of 200 square miles. One hundred skyscrapers are under construction, plus 125 miles of highway. In total, 3,000 foreign companies have an office or are planning to open an office in Pudong. The total investment volume is $8.4 billion. The whole new city should be completed in 2010, including an airport, subways, bridges, tunnels, and so on. Over 1.5 million people will live there. Chinese construction fever has caused a temporary over-supply of offices, and rental prices have come down. It will take some time before demand is outstripping supply again.

Another impressive example: in August 1995 a new highway ring was completed around the center of Shanghai. The length is about 19 miles. How long does it take in western Europe to construct a highway of 19 miles? 2 years? 3 years? 4 years? From the expropriation of land until the opening, the Chinese did it seven months.

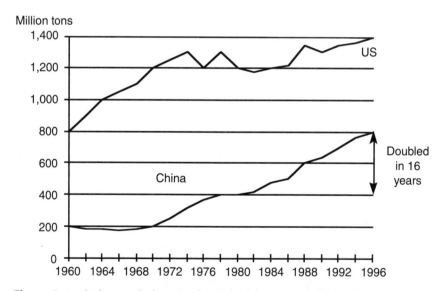

**Figure 4-1** Carbon emissions in the United States and China. (*Source:* Brown and Flavin, "China's Challenge to the United States and to the Earth," September/October 1996, *World Watch Magazine*. Reprinted with permission.)

## POLLUTION

Pollution in China is soaring. Figure 4-1 illustrates the disturbing trend in China and the United States.

Analyzing the chart, the following can be said:

- Oil consumption and carbon emissions in the United States are at an all time high. The trend is increasing instead of declining.

- Today the United States emits eight times as much carbon per person as China.

- China, however, in the past 16 years doubled their carbon emissions, and the trend is firmly increasing at a rate faster than in the United States. China today contributes 11 percent to global emissions.

- In the past 10 years, carbon emissions in the United States increased by about 16 percent.

It is also not a surprise that the densest population on earth also has one of the biggest water problems. According to China's National Environmental Protection Agency, 79 percent of China's population drinks contaminated water. The Yangtze River is being polluted with 40 million tons of industrial and sewage waste a day.

## BEER

What are the Chinese drinking when they eat a chicken leg or a slice of pork? For a hundred million households, the answer is beer. The Chinese do not want to eat rice and drink tea anymore. They want to eat chicken and have a beer! Today the Chinese beer market is about 15 times bigger than it was in 1980. This market is growing so fast that China now has overtaken Germany in beer consumption, becoming the world's second largest beer consumer after the United States. In 1995 China imported 1.5 million tons of barley for beer production.

## CHINA'S GRAIN PRODUCTION

China's agriculture is confronted with the following problems:

- Arable land is not increasing but decreasing.

- The gap in incomes between rural China and urban China is widening.

- 100 million farmers are leaving or have left their land and are migrating to the big cities.

- Climate factors are deteriorating the crops.

Figure 4-2 shows that China has increased its grain production in 45 years—1950 to 1995—from 100 million tons to 465 million tons. In 1996 China produced 480 million tons, which is a very good result. However, China has increased its grain output in the past five years by only 3 percent. Some analysts forecast a 20 percent lower grain output in 1998 due to the El Niño effect. El Niño causes draught, floods, and hurricanes. The probability that China will have to import large quantities of grain in the future is therefore high.

For the year 2000 China wants to produce 500 million tons of grain. I have strong doubts that China will reach this goal because of El Niño's influence in 1998, the shrinking and erosion of arable land, the farmers' migration to the big cities, the pollution, the floods, the heat waves, and the lack of water. The industrialization and urbanization will claim more and more arable land. One year of an abundant crop may very well be followed by a year with disastrous crops.

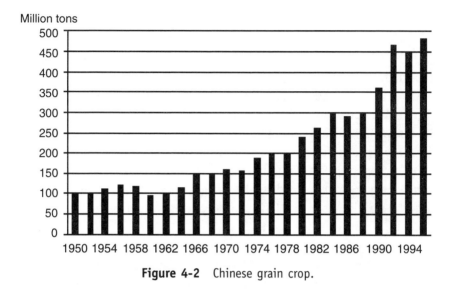

**Figure 4-2** Chinese grain crop.

On the demand side, estimates vary. *The Economist* thinks that China at the beginning of the twenty-first century will consume 600 tons of grain.[2]

The Chinese themselves estimate that their demand by 2010 will not be higher than 550 million tons. They give these relatively low figures to give the grain trade the impression that their import requirements will be no more than 5 percent of their grain production. The Chinese think they can raise output significantly because their present yields leave room for improvement and because there are unnecessary losses before crops reach end users.[3]

A longer term forecast was given by Jikun Huang, the director of the Centre for Chinese Agricultural Policy, during a farming conference in Oxford, England, in January 1998. He estimated Chinese consumption at 594 million tons by 2020. This is 44 percent higher than consumption levels of the mid-1990s.[4]

## CHINA'S GRAIN IMPORTS

In 1995 China advanced to the second largest grain importer in the world.

In 1995 China's grain imports were 16 million tons (see Figure 4-3). Although China has a trade surplus with the United States of $35 billion, one bad crop can wipe out this surplus, and China would be forced to import and pay for a greater quantity. The Chinese market is so vast that a small change in consumption habits can have a destabilizing effect on world grain markets. As an example, the Chinese consumption of instant noodles, biscuits, and bread is rising fast.

China will remain one of the biggest importers of world grain in the future. This import scenario is more and more accepted by many Chinese leaders as well. Take, for instance, Kang Xiaoguang, an economist at the state-run Chinese Academy of Sciences. He stated that simple economics suggest another solution, because China has to feed 22 percent of the global population with 7 percent of the world's arable land, some of

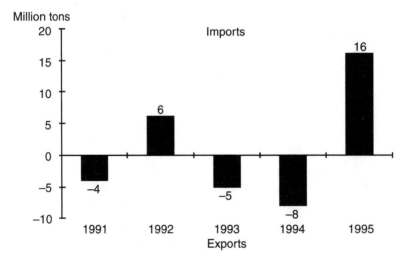

**Figure 4-3**  China's grain imports.

which is quickly giving way to industry, housing, roads, and so on, China should use its comparative advantage to export industrial goods and import grain. Mr. Kang adds: "It is absurd to pretend China does not need to import grain. China should import."[5]

Jikun Huang estimates that Chinese imports will rise to between 25 million and 27 million tons by 2005. Imports would take the form of feedgrain for animals, which is projected to rise from 22 percent of total grain consumption today to 44 percent by 2020. This means that the Chinese appetite for meat is rising fast and will double.[6]

**My Opinion: Personally I believe that a more pessimistic Chinese crop scenario is more likely and that China will be forced to import larger quantities in the future.**

## ECONOMIC GROWTH

China is experiencing a tremendous economic growth. Never in human history have 1.2 billion people increased their gross national product (GNP) by more than 50 percent in five years. This means in simple terms that the Chinese are improving their standard of living and increasing their demand for long-term consumer goods and nourishment. In fact the economy in the past few years was overheating, and inflation was rampant. For the near future the Chinese government is planning an annual growth rate of between 8 and 9 percent. The Chinese GNP in 1995 was $660 billion. By 2000 the GNP should grow to $1,000 billion. In the next eight years, the Chinese economy will double again.

How do the Chinese make their money? On a recent trip through the United States, I saw a good example of Chinese consumer-goods-production hard at work. As a European I love the United States, but I do enjoy spotting differences from other continents as well. As I got off the plane in Miami in December 1997, I noticed that, apart from airline  personnel, nobody is wearing leather shoes anymore. Everybody was wearing Nike, Reebok, and Adidas jogging shoes. Ordinary shoes are not even called just shoes any more. They are called "dress shoes." And it is not so easy to find a good shoestore in Florida. And who produces all those jogging shoes for the 300 million Americans? You guessed it—the Asians, and in particular the Chinese. We don't realize how fast America is turning into a service sector society and how strong the Asian grip is on cheap production of American consumer goods. That is the area where the Asians make their money. The Americans are world champions in creating brands and merchandising the goods around the world. The Chinese are the cheap volume producers of these brands.

By the way, prices in the service sector in America—hotel rooms, fitness-clubs, car rentals, airline tickets, restaurants and coffee shops, golf-course-green fees, ski-lift tickets, and tuition fees—are rising pretty fast and are not sufficiently reflected in the American consumer price index. Many economists argue that the inflation rate is even too high, that it should be lower, and that we live in a deflationary period. I don't agree. I think that the service sector is underweighted in the consumer price index and that the true inflation rate would be higher if the weightings were more realistic.

If we take China and India as one entity and the industrialized countries of the United States, Europe, and Japan as a second entity, two differences strike us the most:

1. The populations of China and India continue to increase and are very young. In the industrialized countries, population growth is stable. In the United States every two minutes somebody turns 50.

2. Economic growth in China and India is phenomenal: 2 billion people are climbing the social ladder fast. In the industri-

alized states, economic growth is positive but no more than 2 to 3 percent per annum at best.

Sometimes it is difficult to imagine the magnitude of China's population. But it can be put in perspective if China is compared with other countries: if, for instance, every Chinese drank 2 additional glasses of beer per year, a grain crop as large as that of Norway would have to be reserved to produce all that extra beer.[7] If China had the same beer consumption as that of Germany, the total global grain crop would have to be reserved for brewing purposes. And we have not talked about food yet. If the Chinese ate as much fish as Japan does today, the global fish catch of 100 million tons would all go to China.

Out of every hundred Chinese, only six have a car. A Chinese citizen consumes only 118,800 gallons of water a year and pumps only 2 tons of carbon dioxide into the air. But because of the huge population in China, any slight increase in individual use of energy, water, food, and so on, has a huge effect on overall statistics, causes a strain on natural resources, and will cause prices to rise. Pollution and consumption statistics are increasing rapidly.

**My Opinion:   The rapid demand increase in China is a long-lasting, accelerating megatrend. Already this phenomenon is enough reason to be invested in natural resources.**

# 5

# THE INFLUENCE OF OUR ECOLOGY ON NATURAL RESOURCES

## DETERIORATING ECOLOGY

The deteriorating ecology of our planet reduces the long-term supply of natural resources. This long-term trend is one of the main arguments why 10 to 15 percent of your assets must be invested in this area.

Our planet faces unprecedented difficulties to produce enough food, energy, water, and base metals for humanity. Greenhouse gases, urban smog, acid rain, overfishing, and depletion and pollution of ground and surface water are depriving future generations of access to already limited natural resources. Humanity is on a total collision course with ecology. Ecological disasters already take place all over the world and in places where people never had any trouble of this kind. If we do not take radical action and start by changing our own personal behavior toward our environment, the probability increases every day that a squeeze in natural resources will develop and that a food or energy disaster will strike this earth in the first quarter of the third millennium. According to the latest forecasts, this planet will have to feed 3 billion additional people by the year 2030. Will the earth be able to produce 75 percent more grain without destroying the natural resources and the ecology on which we and our children all depend? I do not believe so, and it will force the prices of basic nourishment to go up.

This world must produce more raw materials every year to meet a growing demand. World stocks of several commodities, like grains, coffee, and several metals, have dwindled to dangerously low levels, which is pushing up export prices substantially. Food supplies are very fragile, and this will also be the case in the new century.

Important factors that lead to rising prices and to an eventual ecological disaster also relate to demand: an explosion in world population, a huge increase in global demand for raw materials, global pollution leading to climate change, and a stubborn refusal of Homo sapiens to face reality and change his course.

## GLOBAL WARMING AND THE GREENHOUSE EFFECT

What is the greenhouse effect? Natural sunlight passes through the atmosphere and warms the earth. Radiant heat is emitted back to the atmosphere, and some of it is absorbed by such atmospheric gases as methane and carbon dioxide ($CO_2$). When there is too much $CO_2$ in the air, it functions as a shield around the globe holding in the heat. Subsequently this radiation is remitted back to earth. The more $CO_2$ and methane there are in the air, the more they act like a shield, trapping more heat and sending it back to the earth, causing further global warming. This heat trapping is known as the greenhouse effect. It is easy to understand this heat trapping if you think of a car that stands in the sun the whole day. The heat is trapped in the car. It is the same with Mother Earth.

Atmospheric $CO_2$ is now about 360 parts per million, or a total of 25 million tons, and the number keeps going up (see Figure 5-1).

Burning of fossil fuels coupled with massive deforestations emits about 6 billion metric tons of carbon annually into the air. Since the beginning of the Industrial Revolution, 170 billion tons of carbon have been emitted. One to two billion tons a year are being absorbed by rain forests and oceans, and the balance of these emissions end up in the atmosphere, contributing to global warming. So we need the rain forests as the lungs of the earth, but our children will inherit a world with less than 20 percent of the original global forests intact.

The greater the greenhouse effect, the greater the global warming. Under the United Nations Framework Convention on Climate Change, nations in principal agree to reduce and stabilize greenhouse emissions. So far the politicians prescribe what everyone should be doing, but the net result is that very little is

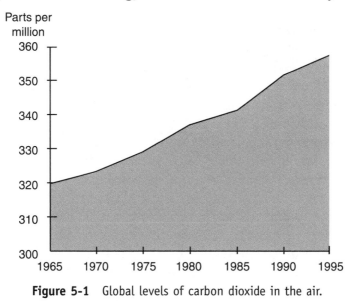

**Figure 5-1**  Global levels of carbon dioxide in the air.

being done. The end of the thick polluted air is not in sight. On the contrary: *all economic trends point to a pollution twice as great by 2050.*

Meanwhile temperatures are rising: the hottest three years in the century occurred in the last decade, and the warmest year so far was 1995. The scary fact is that the climate change has barely started and that the worst is still to come.

Forecasting global warming models point to temperature increases anywhere from 1 degree Celsius (1.8 degrees Fahrenheit) to 5 degrees Celsius (59 degrees Fahrenheit) by the end of the next century. Many scientists' forecasts predict further melting of the polar ice caps, a consequent rise in sea level, and floods that will submerge cities like New York, Bombay, and San Francisco.

## CONFLICTING INTERESTS

We are heading for an international conflict that pits the global environment against the industrial giants and the forces in global infrastructure development. Prosperous nations of the north tell poor nations of the south not to pollute. Emerging-market nations defend their laissez-faire policy by stating that present pollution levels are caused by the Western world.

A simple example: India already suffers from a lack of energy. On any given day machines in factories stop working, irrigation pumps in agricultural fields run dry, and lights go out in offices. Power cuts are a daily routine of life. India's population is growing exponentially, and it will need to double its energy capacity in the next decade. How can India increase its energy supply, and what are the priorities? The cheapest way to double energy supply is to dig more coal out of the nationalized mines. But coal is also the dirtiest form of energy. So the second most densely populated country in the world will have to pollute more. This country does not want to give up economic growth for clean air. They put the blame for the existing pollution on the Western world.

The United States is the most polluting country on earth. It is the source of 22 percent of emissions worldwide. The Rocky Mountain Institute in Colorado has calculated that the United States wastes $300 billion of energy a year. This amount is more than its entire defense budget. The United States must reduce its energy usage by 30 percent or more by 2008 to 2012 to return to the 1990 level of carbon emissions.[1]

But President Clinton has not taken drastic measures to curb pollution. The power of the big American industries is too great, and environmental measures would certainly cost votes and a lot of money. American industry must understand that customers will gladly choose products and technologies that help safeguard the global environment as long as these products and technologies are available and affordable. This is a paradigm shift already well underway in industries like cosmetics and automobiles.

Because the United States is the most polluting country and a domestic change in environmental policies is required to induce the rest of the world to follow suit, in general, reproaching other nations over their polluting habits has turned out to be futile. In politics it is the same as with human beings: *we cannot change each other, we can only change ourselves*. Like the ancient Chinese resonance principle, if we change ourselves first and set a good example, we will induce others to change themselves as well. Environmental aides of Clinton favor more drastic action against pollution, but economic aides fear that environmental taxes and cuts in emissions will provoke a downturn in the economy. For instance, a 50-cent gasoline tax would not be very popular with investors. But implementing these forms of eco-taxes would be the right thing to do because the American consumer would look for a car with high gas mileage. By doing so, Clinton would show strong leadership, but the Democrats are afraid to lose votes.

**My Opinion:    I think that Clinton betrays the next generation by cutting emissions only by 10 percent stretched over 15 years.**

India and China are still behind the United States in polluting: China emits 11 percent of pollution and India 3 percent. But the *rates of change* are the biggest in India and China: if they keep on polluting at the same rate, they will surpass the United States in less than 30 years.

For years now climatologists have warned that a doubling of $CO^2$ in the air would be possible and likely. Today it appears that it will be virtually impossible to avoid a doubling of the $CO^2$ content. If this probability turns into reality, the average temperature of the globe would be raised between a minimum of 3 degrees Fahrenheit and a catastrophic 8 degrees Fahrenheit. This would distort the globe's climate completely, and sea levels would rise because of melting polar ice. Low-lying coastal areas and small island nations would be inundated. Some climatologists think cities like San Francisco would disappear. Such a temperature increase would cause severe floods and droughts and a shift in natural ecosystems and climatic zones.

In general, resolutions taken at climate conferences have not been binding for the attending countries, and the ecological improvements have been minimal. Even before the Kyoto conference started in December 1997, the mood of the attendees was not very optimistic. Jerry Mahlman, director of the National Oceanic and Atmospheric Administration's Geophysical Dynamics Laboratory at Princeton University, formulated it as follows: "What Kyoto will do, almost predictably, is produce a small decrease in the rate of increase.[2] His comments turned out to be very realistic.

The present and future states of the world can be summed up as follows:

- Today 6 billion tons of $CO^2$ are being pumped into the air annually.

- About 2 billion tons of greenhouse gases are being absorbed by rain forests and the world's oceans.

- The next couple of decades will produce unprecedented changes in climate with all the negative consequences for our environment and the availability of natural resources.

- As the global temperatures are warming, the absorption capacity of the rain forests is declining, resulting in extra tens of billions of tons of greenhouse gases being released into the air. This phenomenon could intensify the warming process.

- The ozone layer is being destroyed more and more. Ozone is a relatively thin shield of gas that absorbs the sun's ultraviolet rays and thus protects the earth against radiation. In one level of the atmosphere, the ozone layer is practically destroyed, according to the United Nations Weather Agency.[3]

An important effect of global warming is the prolonged dry spells. Already 80 countries with 40 percent of the world's population have a chronic lack of water, according to a study by the World Bank.[4]

If global temperatures keep on rising, the quantity of arable land will continue to shrink. Global warming also promotes the promulgation of epidemics and diseases for mankind, animals, and nature in general. Scientists believe that temperatures will rise by 9 degrees Fahrenheit by the latter half of this century due to greenhouse gas emissions and atmospheric changes.

## EL NIÑO

A lot has been said and written about El Niño, and a lot of jokes are being made about this weather phenomenon. One of NBC television's meteorologists now calls himself "Al Niño." And in the New York press, an article appeared called "El Niño or El Nonsense?" But, on a more serious note, we know now that this change in weather has very serious consequences for our ecology and crops.

El Niño is Spanish for "the little boy," which refers to "the Christ Child." It is the nickname for a quasi-periodic appearance of warm surface seawater in the central and eastern equatorial Pacific Ocean (off the coast of Peru). The reason why it is called Christ Child is the fact that this warming often starts in the beginning of December, close to Christmas. There are minor and major El Niños. A minor El Niño occurs every two or three years, and a major El Niño occurs every eight to eleven years. Some scientists believe the major cycle is getting shorter—that a major El Niño will occur every four to seven years. Other pessimistic scientists even believe we are heading for a *permanent* El Niño weather pattern.

With a minor El Niño, seawater rises by only a few degrees *over a relatively small surface of water*. A major El Niño spreads over a *large* expanse of the equatorial Pacific. The greater the surface affected, the greater the destructive impact of El Niño.

El Niño is also associated with changes in sea-level pressures at locations on opposite sides of the Pacific Basin. Sometimes a change in sea-level pressure close to Darwin (Australia) is accompanied by a seesaw pressure at the opposite side of the globe and vice versa. When the pressure is high on one side, it is low on the exact opposite side. This phenomenon is referred to as the "southern oscillation." It is like daytime on one side of the globe and nighttime on the other side. Or like high tide and low tide. Or like yin and yang.

In an El Niño year two weather patterns occur. Warm air rises, which creates clouds, and the clouds lead to *increased rainfall*. But also cold air descends, which *inhibits* cloud formation. This second part of the process causes *long dry heat spells*. The consequence is excessive rainfall and hurricanes in areas that are normally dry (Western Mexico, west coast of South America, California, and Florida) and long heat spells in areas where there has been sufficient rainfall in normal times (Indonesia). El Niño's influence on the global weather system is gaining enormous steam. This is the growing consensus among scientists.

The 1982–1983 El Niño caused $13.6 billion in damage. In the last quarter of 1997, El Niño caused hurricanes in Acapulco, France, and Spain and floods in the former East Germany, Poland, California, and so on. The temperature rise in 1997 was at least as great as in 1982, and according to scientists it is only a matter of time until the effects of this El Niño on grain, coffee, rice, cocoa, and sugar crops will be devastating.

El Niño is the cause for heat waves in Asia that aggravated jungle fires in Malaysia and Indonesia. Logging and deforestation continued there, as if there was no ecological tomorrow. Kalimantan, the Indonesian portion of the island Borneo, is the site of the globe's largest deforestation. It is a money machine for Indonesia's real estate tycoons and, simultaneously, an ecological disaster. Experts estimate that by 2015, two-thirds of Kalimantan's forests will be gone. No fewer than 278 logging companies have a permit to log in Kalimantan.[5]

If you try to walk through the smoke-filled forests in Indonesia, it feels like you are at the end of the world. The sun has disappeared behind a haze of smoke, the air is grey, cars are driving with their headlights on, and the earth is on fire. Dr. Keith Bentley, a consultant for the World Health Organization, described very graphically the severity of the smog hanging over Sumatra and Kalimantan: "If you use a yardstick of 10 cigarettes per 100 milligrams, a pollution level of 6,000 is equivalent to smoking 600 cigarettes a day."[6]

## EL NIÑO DAMAGE

El Niño caused the following damage to commodity crops during the autumn of 1997 with more to come in 1998:[7]

1. Malaysia
   - 40 to 50 percent drop in cocoa production, totaling 120,000 tons.

   - 2.2 percent drop in palm oil production, and palm oil prices rallied sharply in 1997 (see Figure 5-2).

   - 60,000 fewer tons in the natural rubber crop.

2. Philippines
   Substantial reduction in domestic rice crop requiring extra imports of 850,000 tons of rice as buffer stocks.

3. Thailand
   More than 276 million acres of cropland have been damaged, reducing sugar and rice crops. A reduction of 38 percent in rice is forecast.

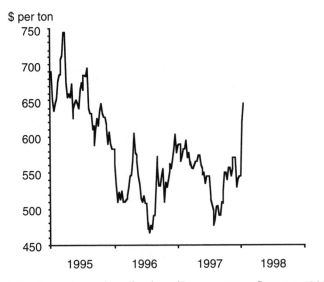

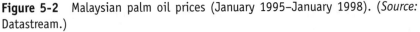

**Figure 5-2**  Malaysian palm oil prices (January 1995–January 1998). (*Source:* Datastream.)

4. Indonesia
   - 40 percent drop in robusta coffee beans.

   - Reduced palm oil crop. Palm oil plants need at least five hours of sunshine per day, and due to the smog, they did not get it in 1997. So the palm oil pits did not receive enough sun to grow.

5. Peru
   A reduced fish catch, resulting in a sharp reduction in fish-meal and fish-oil production and in rising prices (see Figure 5-3).

6. India and Ceylon
   Sharply reduced tea crops. Tea prices nearly doubled in the past two years (see Figure 5-4).

7. China
   Several analysts predict that the Chinese summer in 1998 will be long, hot, and dry. Because an El Niño cycle

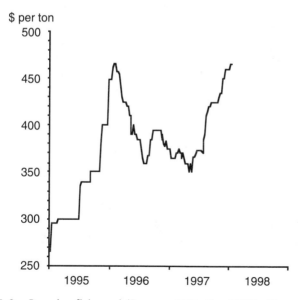

**Figure 5-3**  Peruvian fish meal (January 1995–May 1998). (*Source:* Datastream.)

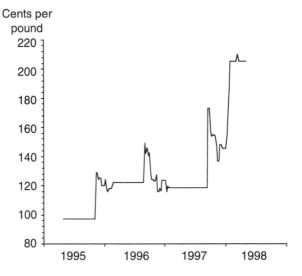

**Figure 5-4**  London auction prices for Indian tea. (*Source:* Datastream.)

lasts for 12 to 18 months, the influence of the 1997 El Niño on Chinese weather might cause a 20 percent reduction in the 1998 Chinese corn crop. If indeed the impact of El Niño on the Chinese corn crop turns out to be substantial, the probability is high that China will again have to import large quantities of grain from Western sources. Coupled with a long, hot, dry 1998 summer in the United States, this could be the root for spikes in grain prices.

Grain markets are already anticipating what is to come. In April 1998, the price of American soybean oil hovered around 29 cents per pound. This was the highest price paid since late 1996, and further price rises are likely. Chapter 12 explains how you can profit from a price rise in grains by buying warrants on the Goldman Sachs Agricultural Index.

# Part Two

## UNNATURAL PROFITS IN NATURAL RESOURCES

# 6

## INVESTING IN
## NATURAL RESOURCES

### CRITERIA

Natural resources is an investment area with vast opportunities, ranging from buying the material itself to buying shares of industries that drill, pump, mine, process, trade, or distribute natural resources. Excellent investment opportunities also exist in companies that service the natural resource industry, for example, oil service or agricultural service industries. A vast new investment area is opening up in so-called alternative natural resources, such as solar energy, wind power, fuel-cell production, and hydrogen technology. And last but not least, interesting venture capital projects that offer good returns on investments are sprouting up in natural resources, such as water-purifying projects in Malaysia.

Basically there are nine ways to invest in natural resources. You can:

1. Trade or stockpile physical commodities.

2. Participate in commodity squeezes.

3. Trade or buy precious metals in a metal account with a Swiss or Liechtenstein bank.

4. Trade commodity futures.

5. Invest in commodity futures funds.

6. Invest in resource-producing companies.

7. Invest in natural resource stock funds.

8. Invest in certificates on natural resource indexes.

9. Invest in natural resource development projects.

All the above investment possibilities are explained separately in Part Two. But before you invest one dollar, Euro, Swiss franc, or yen, you must do more homework and do some self-analysis.

The goal of this process is to determine which of the nine investment categories fits you best.

Ask yourself questions like:

• *How much money do I have available for natural resources?*
You must invest in good mutual funds to build up your own old-age private-pension plan. You should continuously invest 5 to 10 percent of your assets in natural resources. Think long term, and don't be distracted by short-term market gyrations.

• *Am I well diversified in other asset classes when I invest this amount in natural resources?*
Generally it is very important to *diversify* your investments. If you do your homework with brokerage and bank reports, search machines on the Internet, and newspapers and literature, you will come across excellent investment funds that show first-class returns over a number of years. I favor international

*sector* funds, like global brands, technology, communication, biotechnology, or sport funds. Within each sector I have a preference for the hedge funds because they can go long and short. I shall explain this later. I have less sympathy for regional or national funds, like "the India fund" or "the Thailand fund." Cross-border industry sector funds offer better returns. I prefer a fund manager to pick one excellent stock in Brazil and mix it with stocks of the same sector in a different country. In investing we do not have borders any more. Don't buy a country, but invest in a sector like oil or food and then buy the best stock in that sector or go with the best investment manager in that sector.

The new European currency, the *Euro,* will have an extremely positive effect on Greater Europe. Europe will offer great investment opportunities as economies of scale will enhance profits of large European companies. Especially for American retail and institutional investors, Europe will become much more liquid and transparent, and billions of American dollars will flow to European stock exchanges. There will be no more pesetas on the stock exchange in Madrid or lires in Milan. Whether you trade in Amsterdam, Frankfurt, or Paris, you will be buying shares in Euros. I think Europe is going to be the place to invest, and European natural resource companies will profit from this positive investment climate.

• *Am I going to make my own investment, or am I going to buy a product?*

It all depends on your investment style, expertise, and costs. It is certainly a lot cheaper if you don't pay for services of fund managers and do it all yourself. The bottom line is the following: Is my net return better when I pay the higher fees for outside advice, or do I earn more when I make all investment decisions myself and pay discount commissions to a discount brokerage house? One style does not exclude the other one. Do yourself what you know best. Pay for advice and buy into good funds where your expertise is limited. For instance, if you are a doctor, you might have special knowledge of medical industries and products. You could handle investments in this field yourself. But for all other fields, let your investments be managed by the best investment manager you can find. Pay for financial advice, but do your homework to find the best advice available.

• *How much time do I have to monitor my investments?*

If you are very busy with your career, you should at least reserve sufficient time to select excellent investment products and investment managers. There is one bit of advice I want to give you if you are an investor who makes his own investment decisions: don't go on holidays with big open positions. Innumerable times I have witnessed investors who were sitting on big paper profits only to have it all wiped out while they were having a good time on the beach in South Africa or on the ski slopes in Vail or Gstaad, completely out of touch with the financial markets. Close out your positions when you go on holiday. I repeat: this advice counts only for investors who handle their own decisions and not for investors who diversify their holdings through a number of public funds.

• *Do I have the flexibility to broaden my horizon and to invest in currencies and countries other than my own?*

Don't confine yourself to the borders of your own country. There are fabulous investment opportunities in other countries, and you must select investment managers or fund products that invest cross-border. I know many Europeans who have missed the surge and profit opportunities in Wall Street, and I know many Americans who are missing fabulous stock markets in western and eastern Europe. If your advisor or institution is only nationally oriented, you are going to miss a lot of profit opportunities. Many American institutions and funds confine themselves to American stocks, and fund managers do not research international stocks and do not speak other languages to interview board members of first-class companies outside the United States. Often it is even spelled out in the fund rules and regulations that the fund can invest only up to, for instance, 20 percent in "foreign" stocks, restrictions I don't like very much. There aren't any borders when you invest in today's global village.

## LEGAL AND FISCAL ASPECTS

Investing has legal and fiscal consequences. This book cannot give extensive legal or fiscal advice simply because investment laws differ from country to country. But I do want to raise some questions that you should answer yourself before you invest. If you want to invest outside of your home country, it might very well be that you are legally forbidden to do so—incredible but true in today's small world. Some countries, in my opinion, have excellent communications but outdated investment laws (like the United States and Germany). You must seek the best legal and fiscal advice and inform yourself about the consequences of your dealings.

Before you invest, ask yourself questions like:

- Do the investment laws of my home country allow me to make any investment anywhere in the world, or must I take special steps to accomplish what I want?

- Is the fund of your choice sold publicly in your country? If it is not, you must get active and let your money cross national borders.

- Am I going to invest in my name?

- Is it better to transform my assets into a company?

- Is it advisable to form a trust or a foundation and protect myself against political, fiscal, or even family pressures?

- What happens to the money when I die? Who are the beneficiaries? Did I take the necessary steps to accomplish what I want?

- Do I have to pay taxes on profits? If so, how much and where? Are losses deductible?

- Do I have to declare my foreign dealings to the domestic tax authorities?

From my perspective in Europe, an investment in an American Fidelity Fund is just a phone call away. But just as I can take a plane and open an account with Citibank in New York or Singapore, an American citizen can take a plane as well and open an account with a financial institution outside the United States. We live in a global village, and if you want to invest in a certain product, there is always a way to go about it and follow the development of your investment on the Internet. It is a matter of connections, a good network, and paying for good advice. You must deal with an institution or advisors who are connected globally. More importantly, the person who is handling your money within the institution you choose should have time for you, and his or her investment horizon should be broader than his or her national borders.

Mutual funds in the United States are regulated and controlled by the Securities and Exchange Commission (SEC). Only mutual funds that are registered with the SEC can be offered in the United States to the American public. American mutual funds have low minimum investment levels—like $2,500—and are meant for a large number of retail investors. Limited partnerships—as the term already says—are not meant to be distributed among thousands of investors. Legally they are not public funds; the circle of investors is much smaller than in a mutual fund, and the investment minimum is usually higher—from $250,000 to $5,000,000. The managers handling these pools can go long and short the markets, which is a great advantage. The managers often learned their skills in big institutions and set up their own shops afterward. The investment quality of these limited partnerships is often very good.

So *officially* an American citizen cannot invest in a Dutch or an English mutual fund or in an offshore product because the fund is probably not registered in the United States with the SEC. Every country has different fund laws, and these can be modern or antiquated. I regard the United States as the most efficient and most modern country on earth, but this laudation does not apply to America's antiquated fund legislation.

Before you invest in a limited partnership or mutual fund of your choice anywhere in the world, you must check with your banker, broker, lawyer, or accountant on how you should proceed.

## LIECHTENSTEIN

I have my residence in Liechtenstein, and this is my story: the Principality of Liechtenstein is situated in the heart of Europe, between Switzerland and Austria, about a 1½-hour car drive southeast of Zurich's airport. Liechtenstein is independent, but it is linked with Switzerland by many treaties. Passport controls between Liechtenstein and Switzerland do not exist. Just cross the Rhine bridge, and you are in Liechtenstein. Liechtenstein is unique in Europe: it has an offshore character because Liechtenstein lawyers and trust companies can set up foundations, trusts, and establishments for customers who need confidentiality. The name of such a legal entity plus the trust company or lawyer representing the legal framework are filed in the registry of Liechtenstein and published in the local newspaper. *The names of the real owners and beneficiaries remain sealed and secured in the vaults of the trust company and are not published.*

The lawyer usually opens an account for the foundation or trust with a bank in Liechtenstein or Switzerland. This means in practice that the bank does not know the real identity of the owner of the account. If, for instance, the bank has a trust as an account in its books, the trust can discreetly invest in stocks, funds, bonds, and so on. The real owner of the trust can stipulate in the trust deed that a fixed amount is paid out yearly to a beneficiary. Trust law is English law, and trusts are as old as the house of Windsor.

Liechtenstein has only 30,000 inhabitants, but it has around 75,000 trusts and foundations. It is estimated that around 200 billion deutsche marks and Swiss francs are invested discreetly through Liechtenstein this way. These vehicles are perfectly legal and are set up when a customer wants protection against political, fiscal, or even family pressures. Liechtenstein offers bank, legal, and trust company secrecy; discretion; and utmost confidentiality.

Liechtenstein is like a giant safety deposit box. The Swiss franc is the official currency, and taxes are extremely low. It is a true fiscal oasis. The people in Liechtenstein say, "When there is an oasis, there must be a desert around it." In November 1996 the American rating company Standard & Poor's gave a triple A rating to the Principality of Liechtenstein.

## INVESTMENT STRATEGIES

### Physical Commodities

Unless you deal with commodities professionally, you should stay away from filling up your garage with grain, sugar, barrels of oil, and so on. Almost all, 99.9 percent, of private investors should not hold a stockpile of physical commodities on their own.

But when you are a professional with special knowledge, the picture looks different. A farmer knows grains and livestock; a purchase manager of bulk goods might have special knowledge of silk or metals; and if you are a wine connoisseur, the 1996 premier grand cru wines in your cellar certainly have gone up in value. In general, physical commodities are expensive to finance, and you block a lot of capital. Stockpiles are not liquid investments; they are difficult to sell; the difference between the buyer's bid and the seller's offer can be large; and with the exception of diamonds, commodities can take up a lot of room. Investing in physicals is suitable for professionals with special knowledge and for the super rich. I know an investor who has a Lear Jet permanently filled with gold, and he is always prepared to take off. If you are not in this league, stay away from stockpiling physical commodities.

## Commodity Squeezes

What is a commodity squeeze? A *commodity squeeze* is a market situation in which demand is very high and supply of the material is very small. There are real squeezes and artificial squeezes. I think in the future we will see real squeezes in some commodities. Artificial squeezes are orchestrated: one or a few financially powerful groups buy large quantities of a certain commodity and reduce the supply. They buy discreetly and constantly at every opportunity on different markets because they want to drive up the prices. If the price is high, they need to keep it high and prevent it from falling *before* they cash out. So they need to support the prices and keep on buying. They literally "sit" on a commodity and are very reluctant to sell the goods to others. When demand is big enough and restrictive exchange rules do not interfere with the free market, prices rise further. The buyers are prepared to pay any price for the goods, and they are not in a hurry to accommodate other buyers and sell. This drives prices even higher. When the squeeze is perfect, the holders of the material try to unload their holdings discreetly at exorbitantly high prices.

When the squeezed market is topping out, articles appear in the tabloids shouting that you now must absolutely buy the material. Or to put it differently, when the cleaning lady starts reading about it and telling you what she is going to buy, you have a clear *sell signal* at hand.

In most cases, exchanges or governments then start to intervene and to regulate and restrict the free markets. As a consequence, prices start to fall rapidly. The speed of falling markets is always faster than the gradual tempo of rising markets. The speed of the declining prices takes everybody by surprise. When the squeeze is over and markets drop like stones, the holders "run after the market" and try to sell at any price. Now the buyers hold back and don't buy any more. Very often the holders of the material are too late to sell, and they lose a fortune instead of making one. Most of the artificial squeezes have failed sooner or later.

Here are four squeeze examples:

1. Holland is a trading nation and in the Middle Ages, way before they started to trade spices in the seventeenth century, the Dutch speculated in tulips. The first futures market in the world was in Amsterdam, and it traded tulip bulbs. A squeeze occurred, and Amsterdam had its so-called tulip mania. There was pandemonium on the futures market, and tulip bulbs were trading for 1,000 florins apiece. Eventually the air got out of the balloon, prices fell like stones, and most speculators lost a fortune. Even today the Dutch are the largest flower exporters in the world. Today the supply is huge, and tulip mania will be history forever.

2. During the great grain robbery in 1972, when the Russians were buying 20 million tons of grains, the large grain companies in the United States and Europe signed contracts with the Russians to sell grain at a certain price. The orders were so big that most grain companies did not have enough grain in their bins to honor the contracts. Prices on the cash and futures markets kept on skyrocketing, and the grain merchants had *to buy physicals at any price* they could get. A squeeze was developing. The Russians were courted by several grain houses belonging to the "Seven Sisters" (the nickname for the seven big privately held grain merchants of that period). The best entertainer of them all was the president of Continental Grain, Michel

Fribourg, who went out of his way to surround the Russians with all the earthly pleasures this world can offer. The only problem was that he did not have the grain the Russians wanted. He had to buy physicals and futures for nearby delivery, which drove up grain prices dramatically. Cargill just sat back on its huge grain stocks. The Russians and competitive grain merchants did not have any other place to go but to Cargill. The higher the grain prices went, the more profit Cargill made. Finally Cargill dictated the prices and sold the major part of the 20 million tons, cashing in huge unnatural profits. Because Cargill is a privately held company, exact profits are not disclosed. But with soybean prices going from $6 a bushel to $10 a bushel, I can imagine Cargill made a total dollar profit of nine or even ten figures. This was a perfect *real* squeeze.

3. In 1997 one of the best investment performances was delivered by Julian Robertson, the manager of the Tiger hedge fund. Next to his large *short* positions in the Asian stock markets, his profits also came from his large *long* positions in palladium. He held a massive amount of the rare white metal, and he sought to become a stable supplier to palladium users, along with the Russians. Tiger Management has tried to squeeze the palladium market and simultaneously establish long-term selling contracts in Japan. It is widely believed that Tiger Management started to buy palladium when prices were at around $135 per ounce and accumulated 1.5 million ounces of palladium, which represents 20 percent of world demand. (This is to illustrate that the large hedge funds are turning to natural resources for big profits and we will see much more of this in the future.) Julian Robertson drove up prices and profited handsomely. Palladium is a relatively small market, and it only takes a few billion to corner the market.

4. Contrary to the falling price of gold, the price of silver rose substantially, by 35 percent, in 1997. And the outlook for further price rises in the white metal is excellent. The funda-

mentals have never been better since the Hunt days. Industrial demand is large, and silver is not hampered by central bank sales. Orders from the photographic, jewel, and silverware industries are soaring. The metal is particularly popular in Mexico and India. Consumption is estimated to rise by 3 percent annually to around 730 million ounces a year, or 160 million ounces above supplies.[1] So inventories are being drawn down on a grand scale.

In Chapter 2, I described the silver dealings of Warren Buffett. Mr. Buffett considered his silver purchases to be strategic investments. Because he has revealed quite openly in which period and to what extent he made his silver purchases, I do not believe it is his intention to squeeze the silver market. But he certainly has the means to do it. The silver market has returned to quieter waters, but the basis is excellent for higher prices.

**My Opinion:   As a private investor you cannot participate in a commodity squeeze without taking big risks. But if you invest in a good fund, you might participate in a squeeze when your fund manager is smart and knows what is going on. This is a matter of building up a good network. As far as participation in precious metal squeezes is concerned, go to the next item—metal accounts.**

## Metal Accounts

You can profit from the rising prices of precious metal by opening a metal account with a large Liechtenstein or Swiss bank. I think of silver, palladium, and platinum, rather than gold. You can hold the account in Swiss francs or U.S. dollars. If, for instance, you buy silver, you do not receive physical silver bars in a vault; the value of the silver is credited to your account in the currency of your choice. It is a liquid investment because the bank will always buy the metal back from you at market prices. You do not leverage your investment this way, but you do participate when further price rises occur—and you will sleep better. I think it is an excellent strategy to buy silver, palladium, and platinum in a metal account in Switzerland or Liechtenstein. The metals are priced in dollars, and if dollars are your home currency and you hold the material in dollars as well, you do not speculate in currencies. If you hold it in Swiss francs, your value also depends on the currency fluctuations between the dollar and Swiss franc. Buy dollars, pay cash for the metal, and just hold on to it for a few years. You might realize unnatural profits faster than you think.

## Trading Commodity Futures

When you are a private investor, I advise you not to speculate in commodity futures markets, unless you have the following six qualifications:

1. A net worth of at least $5 million.

2. Nerves of steel.

3. Enough discipline to take losses.

4. An entrepreneurial spirit.

5. The willingness and the time to monitor the commodity markets day and night.

6. A trading mentality.

If you have these six qualities and enjoy the kick of success, the commodity futures markets might be the ideal marketplace for you. If you have a different profile and if you want to sleep well at night, don't touch these markets yourself because in the long run as an individual you have no chance against the professionals on the trading floors and the big hedge funds with the smart money. I have been a futures broker with highly reputable American brokerage firms for many years, so I have an in-depth knowledge of markets and participants. Statistically over 90 percent of all private speculators lose their money in futures when they trade themselves. Sure, I have witnessed fabulous success stories, but they all had one thing in common: the clients started out with a *substantial* amount of capital. In Switzerland I witnessed an investor in the 1980s who turned $5 million into $80 million in two years by riding long-term falling trends in interest rates futures markets.

I advise anybody who contemplates trading commodity futures to visit the Commodity Exchanges in Paris (Matif), London (LIFFE), New York (Commodity Exchange in the World Trade Center), or Chicago (Chicago Mercantile Exchange or Chicago Board of Trade). The exchanges in Chicago are the biggest in the world and the atmosphere is like that at the Super Bowl or a Champions League football match in Europe. If you are lucky and know a broker, you might even have access to the exchange floor instead of being in the spectator's gallery behind glass. The trading noise is the same as in a stadium, and as a spectator you will understand why brokers communicate with hand signals. So watch what you are doing with your hands. Don't gesticulate because you just might find that you have bought a railroad car full of pork bellies.

Basically *leverage* means trading on credit. If you invest $100 and have a leverage factor of 10, you are in fact responsible for an investment of $1,000. Profits can be mind-boggling, but so can the losses. *Futures* are leveraged investments. If, for instance, you want to buy gold on the New York Comex Exchange, you do not have to pay the full value of a gold contract. With a 10 percent deposit (or *margin*), you can trade a gold contract that has a value 10 times higher. In other words, if you put up $3,000, you can trade gold worth $30,000. Usually brokers require you to make larger initial deposits because the risks with small deposits for yourself and the brokers are too high. Suppose the gold price moved down 10 percent. You would lose 10 percent of the $30,000, which is $3,000, your entire investment. So leveraged trading is only suitable for well-capitalized investors. With small amounts, you cannot afford big risks, and you should stay away from any leveraged investment vehicles.

## Commodity Futures Funds

Despite the fact that commodity futures exchanges have existed for over a hundred years, not many good, long-term, profitable commodity futures funds are being offered to the public. Most of the time these funds are a mixture of financial futures, currencies, and commodities. Pure good commodity funds are rare, and I think therein lies a great future. I have described the good commodity funds with good potential and very capable managers in Chapter 7.

Very few commodity futures fund managers can produce a consistent winning track record of 10 years with low volatility. And very often the star of one year who makes 100 percent is the loser of the next year. Many track records are very volatile, and not every investor can take a temporary loss of 40 percent. What counts in investing is consistency and achieving a satisfactory *compounded rate of return* instead of a flash-in-the-pan success of 100 percent in one year. In this industry, you see many new products, hypothetical and "pro forma" track records. The only thing you can believe when somebody wants to sell you a futures fund is a track record that has been *audited* by one of the big auditing firms. This gives a true picture of the kind of net performance left for the investor after deduction of all fees, expenses, and commissions.

## Resource-Producing Companies

If you invest in stocks yourself, take a look at companies that produce natural resources or that distribute finished consumer goods worldwide. It is a great investment area, and many resource companies have reduced their costs greatly and operate with healthy profit margins. Don't limit yourself to oil, mining companies, and grain merchants, but investigate companies engaged in solar and wind energy as well. You will find a selection of good companies with the potential of unnatural profits in Chapter 13.

## Natural Resource Stock Funds

These funds invest in securities of companies that mine, process, or distribute natural resources. There are natural resource funds that specialize in one sector, such as in energy or precious metals resource funds, and that invest mainly in American resource stocks and very few good *international* resource funds. A selection of the good funds are described in the next chapters.

## Commodity Certificates

The price and your profits of commodity index certificates depend directly on the price levels of the commodity futures represented in the underlying index. I advise you to read Chapter 12 on commodity price certificates before you invest.

## Natural Resource Development Projects

Instead of buying stock of a natural resource company, you can participate in venture capital projects, varying from investing in greenhouses in the Ukraine to water-purifying projects in Malaysia. Chapter 13 will go into more detail.

# 7

# COMMODITY FUTURES FUNDS

## COMMODITY FUNDS VERSUS NATURAL RESOURCE STOCK FUNDS

The fall of 1997 brought a tidal wave in many natural resources. The Asian crisis had a very negative effect on prices of commodities in general, natural resource stocks, and natural resource stock funds. The prices of oil and industrial metals like copper sank substantially, and diverse commodity indexes, like the Commodity Research Bureau (CRB) Index and the Goldman Sachs Commodity Index (GSCI) Total Return Index, closed 1997 with a negative performance. Performances of natural resource funds, which are heavily weighted in the oil sector, were negative in the last quarter of 1997. Traditionally American mutual funds are long-only funds, which means that the fund manager buys stocks and hopes and prays that the stock price goes up. But when stocks decline, the performance turns negative very quickly.

The situation with commodity future funds, offshore funds, and limited partnerships is entirely different. The fund managers can go long and short the commodity or the stock, which means selling the commodity or the stock first and hoping for lower prices. When prices subsequently fall, the fund manager buys the stock back later at a lower price.

> **My Opinion:** An investment in good commodity funds or limited partnerships can be an excellent decision, especially in times when the general price level is dropping. The managers have much more flexibility to profit from this scenario and can reverse course from long to short when prices go down. The performance of the good commodity funds in the last quarter of 1997 was far superior to the performance of the natural resource funds, which could not hold on to the impressive gains they made in the first half of 1997. The negative influence of the Asian crisis on commodity prices had run its course by mid-1998. Commodity prices have stabilized, and many commodities are now at excellent, relatively cheap buying levels.

## ACTIVELY AND PASSIVELY MANAGED COMMODITY FUNDS

The next two proposed funds—Sabre and Northern Light—didn't have stellar performances in 1997. The funds are rather passively managed, and the investments are diversified over a wide spectrum of commodities. They buy oil, grain, metals, orange juice, meat, and so on. The difference in these funds is that they can only go long the commodity, which means the manager buys the commodity when there is reason to believe that an uptrend is under way. So these funds do not make money for you when prices are depressed. Both these funds, however, are excellent investments when commodities are rising on a broad basis. You don't have to judge if wheat will rise more than copper because the fund acts as a kind of benchmark and you will have long exposure in many commodities. Their performances were not good in 1997 due to falling prices, not due to bad management.

Trading now at low levels, these funds are very good products, not to speculate but to get a general long exposure in natural resources.

Actively managed commodity funds are, for instance, De Tomasso, Finagra, and Fundamental Futures. These funds can have a very good performance in times when commodities prices, for whatever reason, go down. The managers have the possibility to go short the commodity in times of oversupply and slack demand. In other words, these funds can make money for you (and they do) when prices go up or down.

## SABRE COMMODITY RECOVERY FUND

Sabre Fund Management Company Ltd. in London promotes the Sabre Commodity Recovery Fund.[1] This is a long-only fund that participates in bull markets of commodity futures. The fund is not going short and does not have exposure in commodity markets that are in a down trend. The fund has existed since May 1993 and has risen since then over 60 percent (see Figure 7-1). The fund is an offshore fund, Bermuda based, and the minimum investment is $50,000. There are weekly dealings, and the fund is listed on the Irish Stock Exchange.

An offering memorandum can be requested at:

Sabre Fund Management Ltd.
Windsor House, 55 St. James's Street
London SW1A 11A
England
Phone 44-171-316-2801
Fax 44-171-316-0180

**My Opinion: The Sabre Commodity Recovery Fund is still waiting for the great recovery. When new bull markets come, this fund will be very well positioned. The fund does not take long positions**

when commodities are not in a clear up trend. The fund broke even in 1997, and I think the fund can produce great returns when commodities recover. The fund covers the energy sector, the grain markets, nonferrous and precious metal markets, cotton, and soft commodities like coffee, cocoa, and sugar. It is a good product to mix with a traditional stock portfolio.

## NORTHERN LIGHT COMMODITY FUND

### Investment Profile

If you want to invest in a *basket* of commodities, such as wheat, corn, soybeans, copper, and crude oil, the Northern Light Commodity Fund is a very good instrument to achieve this goal.[2] The fund holds continuous long positions in physical, unleveraged commodity futures contracts. The fund is not speculative; it is nearly a passive investment and it is an excellent diversification in commodities. The fund's net asset value (NAV) depends on the development of the commodity prices: when commodity prices

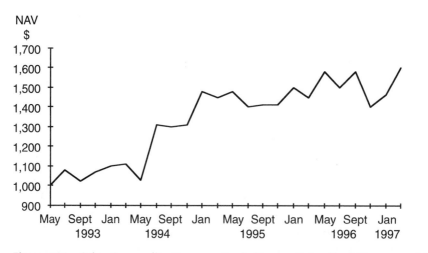

**Figure 7-1**  Sabre Commodity Recovery Fund. (*Source:* Sabre Fund Management.)

rise, the fund will go up in price. When commodity prices at a given moment are down because of an Asian crisis, the fund will be down as well.

The Northern Light Commodity Fund does invest in futures, but it will not leverage the fund capital. This means that when the fund has $10 million in assets, the total contract value of the futures will not be more than $10 million. The basis of the investments is the underlying value of the futures. The Northern Light Commodity Fund is going long only (buys futures) and blends several market sectors and individual commodities to create a well-balanced portfolio. The fund trades only nearby future contracts to benefit from spot premiums. Only exchange-listed futures are traded to ensure maximum liquidity, flexibility, and market transparency.

Weightings by market sector as of December 31, 1997, were as follows:

| | |
|---|---|
| Precious metals: | 6% |
| Grains: | 13% |
| Livestock: | 12% |
| Soft commodities: | 13% |
| Base metals: | 12% |
| Energy: | 44% |

These weightings are by no means static; they can vary according to market strategy.

## Structure

Northern Light Funds Limited is incorporated in the British Virgin Islands as an open-ended investment company with limited liability. The company can issue and redeem shares weekly, at a price based on the net asset value.

The share is listed on the Irish Stock Exchange.

## Fund Facts

| | |
|---|---|
| Investment manager: | Servisen Holding AB |
| | Birger Jarlsgatan 6 |
| | S 103 90 Stockholm |
| | Sweden |
| Trading adviser: | Northern Light Management AB |
| | Birger Jarlsgatan 6 |
| | S 103 90 Stockholm |
| | Sweden |
| | Phone 46-8-701 0910 |
| | Fax 46-8-701 0844 |
| Cash management: | Horizon Cash Management |
| | 325 West Huron |
| | Chicago, IL 60610 |
| | USA |
| Custodian bank: | Citibank N.A. |
| | 111 Wall Street |
| | New York, NY 10005 |
| | USA |
| Administrator and placing agent: | Custom House (Commodities) Ltd. |
| | 31 Kildare Street |
| | Dublin 2 |
| | Ireland |
| | Phone 353-1-661-3400 |
| | Fax 353-1-661-3601 |
| Clearing broker: | Cargill Investor Services Inc. |
| | 233 South Wacker Drive |
| | Chicago, IL 60606 |
| | USA |
| Auditors: | KPMG Peat Marwick |
| Minimum initial investment: | $100,000 |
| Reuters: | IE0646727.1 |
| Bloomberg: | NTHLCFI (equity) (go) |

## Performance for 1997

The fund has the passively managed GSCI Total Return Index as a benchmark. The fund seeks to outperform the GSCI and has succeeded so far. The fund ended the year down 13.7 percent with an average risk of about 12.5 percent. The GSCI Total Return Index was down 15.6 percent (inclusive of costs) with an average risk of about 15.5 percent (see Figure 7-2).

You can order an offering memorandum with subscription forms from Northern Light Management AB in Sweden or from the placing agent, Custom House (Commodities) Ltd., in Ireland.

## Fees

A sales commission is charged up to 2.5 percent, and the management fee is 1.25 percent per annum. In addition, the fund is

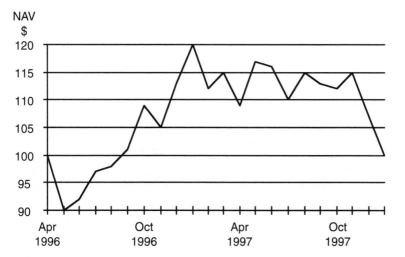

**Figure 7-2**  Northern Light Commodity Fund, 1996–1997. (*Source:* Northern Light Management.)

charged around 1 percent for brokerage commissions, cash management, custodial services, and administration.

**My Opinion:   I believe that commodity prices will experience a substantial rise in the years ahead, and consequently the Northern Light Commodity Fund will rise as well. Commodity spot prices are now at the same level as in 1992–1993, which positions the fund well for the future.**

**I recommend this fund as a diversification next to stocks and bonds, especially for institutional portfolios.**

## DI TOMASSO EQUILIBRIUM FUND

### Goal of the Fund

The Di Tomasso Equilibrium Fund invests in commodity futures and options that are generally restricted to tangible commodities, such as grains, meats, metals, energy products, and soft commodities.[3] The program has the following two fundamental and distinctive characteristics:

1. Di Tomasso has a longer-term, value-oriented perspective. It calculates the intrinsic value each commodity and identifies those that are the most under- or overvalued and that thereby offer the most profit potential. The company has collected and analyzed selected data over a 75-year period in order to calculate each commodity's long-term intrinsic value. The current price of each commodity is compared to its calculated intrinsic value in order to determine each commodity's risk/reward relationship. Only those commodities with attractive risk/reward ratios are bought and held in the program. Short positions are taken

only when a commodity is overpriced relative to its intrinsic value.

2. Di Tomasso implements sound trading strategy that enables it to translate the mispricing of these commodities into profits by:

- Using option valuation models.

- Disciplined execution to minimize option time decay.

- Implementing rigorous risk controls and management.

The fund normally invests approximately 5 percent of assets in margin on futures contracts and roughly 20 percent in costs of options purchased. So the main trading vehicles of the program are options on commodities. The total underlying value of the net forward and futures positions plus the total net costs of the option purchases does not exceed twice the net assets under management.

## Philosophy of the Di Tomasso Group

The Di Tomasso Group has observed that the general level of inflation-adjusted commodity prices is currently near a historically low level. In fact, tangible commodities, generally speaking, are currently trading near their lowest real prices in the past 150 years. Di Tomasso Group anticipates that various market forces affecting the supply of and demand for certain tangible commodities will bring a resolution to this disequilibrium, resulting in generally higher commodity prices. In order to take advantage of this opportunity, the Commodity Trading Programs are invested in a diversified portfolio of tangible commodity contracts, while reducing the risk of loss of capital through the implementation of prudent risk controls.

## Fund Facts

Trading and
administration:          Di Tomasso Group Inc.
                         5325 Cordova Bay Road, Suite 250
                         Victoria B.C.
                         Canada V8Y 2L3
                         Phone 250-658-3650
                         Fax 250-658-3690
                         e-mail: ditom@islandnet.com
                         Internet access:
                         www.traderscan.com
Fees:                    25 percent management fee plus
                         18 percent incentive fee
                         OR
                         1 percent management fee plus 25
                         percent incentive fee

Figure 7-3 illustrates that the volatility of the Equilibrium Trading Program has been perfectly acceptable for investors and

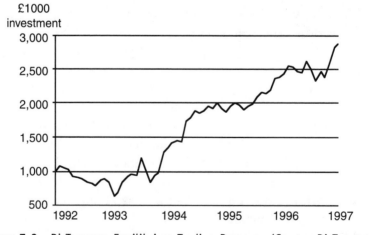

**Figure 7-3**   Di Tomasso Equilibrium Trading Program. (*Source:* Di Tomasso.)

TABLE 7-1    Equilibrium Trading Program Compared to CRB Index

|  | Returns | | | | |
|---|---|---|---|---|---|
|  | 1993 | 1994 | 1995 | 1996 | 1997 |
| Equilibrium Program | 52.2% | 57.7% | 8.6% | 8.6% | 18.7% |
| CRB Index | 34.8% | 13.7% | 8.3% | −4.4% | −13.1% |

Source: Data from offering memorandum and monthly reports, Di Tomasso, Victoria, Canada.

that DiTomasso is a good risk manager. Table 7-1 shows that the Equilibrium Trading Program has outperformed the Commodity Research Bureau Index (CRB Index) every year from 1993 to 1997. The CRB Index, which is a basket of the most important commodity and financial futures contracts, ended 1996 and 1997 with a negative performance. The Equilibrium Trading Program ended both years positively. I think that the performance of this program will be even better when the CRB Index starts the next upward trend.

The Equilibrium Trading Program is leveraged three times. This means that for every dollar invested, positions worth three dollars are being traded.

**My Opinion:  Many commodity trading programs have short-term trading strategies with a turnover of 5,000 to 6,000 futures contracts per $1 million assets. This program has only 500 to 1,000 transactions per $1 million and has a five- to six-month holding period. This is very positive. Total leverage is relatively low. (Hedge funds sometimes leverage their assets 10 times.)**

**The program had a pretty rough start and did not make money from January 1992 until June 1993. Since option trading was introduced in 1994, the performance has been very good, and what is**

much more important, the risks are under much better control. From June 1993 to March 1997, a $1,000 investment increased nearly threefold. I share the same commodity philosophy with this trading adviser, and when commodity prices rise, this program will certainly benefit from it. Di Tomasso sends his performance punctually at the beginning of the month via e-mail to you. The fund is highly recommended.

## FUNDAMENTAL FUTURES INC.

### Profile

Fundamental Futures Inc. (FFI) primarily trades agricultural futures and options like soybeans, wheat, and corn.[4] FFI looks at factors that affect the supply and demand of a particllar commodity in order to predict futures prices. As an example, some of the fundamental factors that affect the supply of a commodity include the acreage planted; crop conditions, such as drought, El Niño, floods, and disease; strikes affecting the planting, harvesting, and distribution of the commodity; and the previous year's crop carryover. The demand for commodities such as corn consists of domestic consumption and exports and world economic conditions. FFI reviews historical and seasonal patterns that might indicate the direction in which the market could move in the future.

Such technical factors as the price of a commodity in relation to its price during previous months, open interest, and volume are taken into consideration as well. These factors are generally used by FFI to assist in determining when to liquidate positions.

## Fund Facts

Trading and
administration:                 Fundamental Futures Inc.
                                9669 Jourdan Way
                                Mrs. Melinda Goldsmith, Partner
                                Dallas, TX 75230
                                Phone 214-368-2500/515-223-3783
Fees:                           Management Fee—4%
                                Performance Fee—20%
Internet access:                iasg.com./report/cta/
                                fundamental.html
                                www.traderscan.com

**My Opinion:  This program invests in stocks of
energy or food industries, not in grains like soybeans, corn, and wheat, traded on the futures markets in Chicago.**

**This trading adviser company is one of the old-
est in the futures advisory business. It has a very
respectable track record and offers a good program. The company specializes in asset management in grain futures. They have managed money
this way since 1976. Each $1,000 invested with FFI
in 1976 was worth close to $150,000 in April 1997
and around $135,000 in March 1998 (see Figure 7-
4). The  majority of commodity trading advisers
(CTAs) trade according to their designed "technical or statistical trading system." But in the end, a
commodity moves on supply-and-demand factors
(fundamental factors), and this is exactly the fundamental basis on which this adviser trades. With
El Niño causing a 9-degree Fahrenheit increase in
water temperatures off the coast of Peru, staple
commodities like grains, sugar, coffee, and cocoa
can be in for a big move, and FFI will certainly**

catch these trends. Consider an engagement with FFI as long-term diversification of your portfolio. As a standalone product, you must be prepared for some volatility but the long-term rewards can be "unnatural."

## FINAGRA MANAGEMENT INCORPORATED

### Investment Profile

If you want to invest in physical commodities, Finagra Management Incorporated (FMI) has a very impressive track record and acts primarily as a merchant in physical cocoa, coffee, and sugar on a worldwide basis.[5] The principal of the company, Mr. S. W. Glover, made a career in physical-commodity trading for such companies as Volkart Brothers in London and New York, V. Berg International Inc., and Lonray Cocoa Inc. In August 1992, he established Finagra Futures Inc.

Finagra's trading program is called HYCAP, which stands for high yield commodity arbitrage program. Under the program, physical commodities are bought from producing coun-

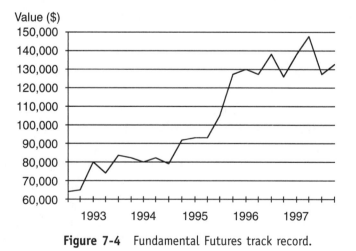

**Figure 7-4** Fundamental Futures track record.

tries. Price exposures are hedged on the futures markets, and finally the commodity is sold and delivered to commodity industrial clients in the United States and Europe.

The goal of the program is to deliver more than 20 percent net annual returns on a consistent basis, characterized by low drawdowns and stable monthly returns. So-called "directional" strategies (buy a commodity, hope and pray the price goes up, and sell) are avoided. In other words the strategy does not seek to capture profits from price movements or developing market trends. The program concentrates on arbitrage strategies (strategies that capture price disparities between or within markets).

A $1,000 investment in January 1993 was worth around $2,900 at the end of 1997 *without major drawdowns* (temporary big losses). (See Figure 7-5.)

FMI has developed proprietary software and compares soft commodity prices (cocoa, sugar, coffee) with its own calculated valuations. In the event of a significant discrepancy between the actual and calculated value, the arbitrage trading proposal is reviewed through a variety of money management, correlation,

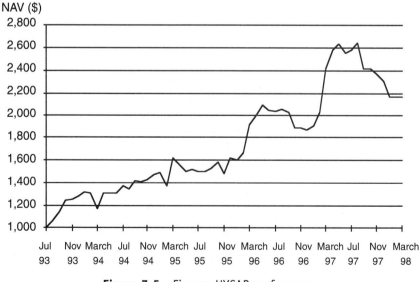

**Figure 7-5**  Finagra HYCAP performance.

and risk/reward filters. The firm's positions fall into two categories: short-term price discrepancies, usually the result of sharp
changes in the outright price affecting the nearby trading months;
and long-term value realignments, in which the firm identifies a
clear fundamental variance between the one- or two-year trading positions and forecast fundamentals.

## Performance

| | |
|---|---|
| 1993: | +49.34% |
| 1994: | +15.29% |
| 1995: | +9.88% |
| 1996: | +15.35% |
| 1997: | +34.42% (Year to date, January–September) |

## Fund Facts

| | |
|---|---|
| Trading and administration: | Finagra Management LLC c/o AIGIAM 1281 E. Main Street Stamford, CT 06902 USA Phone 203-324-8444 Fax 203-324-8467 Mr. Simon Glover Ms. Joelle Marciconi |
| Internet access: | http://iasg.com/report/cta/finagra.html |
| Minimum investment: | $250,000 |
| Round turn trades per million dollars: | 1,000 |

Commission limit:          $40
Fees:                      Management Fee—2%
                           Incentive Fee—20%

**My Opinion:   Finagra is doing a serious job. The program is nondirectional, and this always comes in handy when markets turn down and all traditionally managed long-only funds lose money. The background of the trading manager, S. Glover, is pure commodities, and this is a great advantage. He has been a physical-commodity trader himself, and he has a great affinity with the markets. Nondirectional programs are never spectacular, but they often deliver steady returns in both up and down markets. I recommend an investment with Finagra.**

# 8

## MINING AND METAL FUNDS

### U.S. GLOBAL STRATEGIES FUND LTD.

The umbrella fund, U.S. Global Strategies Fund Limited, is registered and administered in St. Peter Port, Guernsey.[1] This fund has one single subfund, which is the U.S. Precious Metals & Natural Resources Portfolio. The fund specializes in small mining stocks in emerging markets and has done very well, with the exception of the last half of 1997.

### Performance of U.S. Precious Metals & Natural Resources Portfolio (as of December 31, 1997)

Since inception (September 2, 1993):     +877.30 %
1997:                                    −16.56%

### Fund Investments

The company invests primarily in shares of companies that mine gold and precious metals worldwide, but it may also invest a portion of its assets in gold bullion. When, in the investment adviser's opinion, the prices of gold and precious metals mining shares are overpriced and vulnerable to a decline in price, the company may invest all or a portion of its assets in shares of companies that mine base metals and in shares of companies that mine, produce, fabricate, or sell natural resource products including but not limited to timber, hydrocarbons, minerals, and metals such as platinum, uranium, strategic metals, gold, silver, diamonds, coal, oil and phosphates. The adviser will at such times choose the areas of mining and energy that he or she believes to be less risky or to have more growth potential at that time than gold and precious metals mining shares. For hedging purposes or to enhance the company's yield, the company may purchase and sell options and futures contracts and may enter into swaps and options on swaps.

## Fund Facts

| | |
|---|---|
| Management: | U.S. Global Investors (Guernsey) Limited<br>P.O. Box 211<br>Roseneath<br>The Grange<br>St. Peter Port, Guernsey GY1 3NQ<br>Channel Islands<br>Phone 01481-720-321<br>Fax 01481-716-117 |
| Secretary, registrar, administrator: | Butterfield Fund Managers (Guernsey) Limited<br>P.O. Box 211<br>Roseneath<br>The Grange<br>St. Peter Port, Guernsey GY1 3NQ<br>Channel Islands |

|  |  |
|---|---|
|  | Phone 01481-720-321 |
|  | Fax 01481-716-117 |
| Registered office: | Butterfield House |
|  | The Grange |
|  | St. Peter Port |
|  | Guernsey GY1 3NQ, |
|  | Channel Islands |
| Custodian: | Bank of Butterfield International |
|  | (Guernsey) Limited |
|  | P.O. Box 25 |
|  | Roseneath |
|  | The Grange |
|  | St. Peter Port, Guernsey GY1 3NQ |
|  | Channel Islands |
|  | Phone 01481-711-521 |
|  | Fax 01481-714-533 |
|  | e-mail: buttfund@guernsey.net |
| Investment adviser: | U.S. Global Investors, Inc. |
|  | 7900 Callagan Road |
|  | San Antonio, Texas 78229 |
|  | USA |
|  | Phone 210-308-1234 |
|  | Fax 210-308-1230 |
|  | Mr. Frank E. Holmes |
| Auditors: | Price Waterhouse |
|  | Barclaytrust House |
|  | Les Echelons |
|  | St Peter Port, Guernsey |
|  | Channel Islands |
| Eligible advisers: | The fund is only accessible for |
|  | non-U.S. investors. |
| Minimum investment: | $25,000 |
| Initial offer price: | $10.00 |
| Net asset value: | Bid price per December 31, 1997: |
|  | $97.73 |

|                        | Offer price per December 31, 1997: $101.64 |
|------------------------|--------------------------------------------|
| Fees:                  | The difference in bid and offer is the sales commission (4%). |
| Management fee:        | 2% per annum |
| Performance fee:       | 20% above high watermark |
|                        | In addition there are custodian and accounting fees. |
| Dealings:              | Weekly; on Wednesday, the net asset value is calculated. |
| Currencies:            | Investors can buy shares in British pounds, Deutsche marks, U.S. dollars, and Italian lire. |
| Price publication:     | *London Financial Times*, Offshore and Overseas Section. *International Herald Tribune* Bloomberg: symbol: USAGPMI OS Micropal: US GSF Prec. Met & Nat Res OS |

**My Opinion:  Of course the fund had a magnificent performance in the first 2½ years (see Figure 8-1). This fund has delivered unnatural profits during this period. All of the positive performance has been realized with a relatively small amount of assets under management. Since April 1996 the fund did not make any money due to declining precious-metals prices. Out of 30 funds, this fund won the one- and three-year Micropal Award 1996 for best Commodity and Natural Resources Offshore Fund.**

**The specialty of the fund is to invest in small mines in emerging markets, that are in a launch state and not listed yet on a stock exchange. It is turning more and more into a venture capital fund, so it is quite risky. I publish this fund to show that**

**Figure 8-1**  U.S. Global Strategies Fund Ltd.

indeed unnatural profits have been made in the past in natural resources, and this might very well come back in the future.

Also the fees are quite high: if you invest $100 and you pay a 2 percent management fee, 4 percent sales commission, and a 20 percent performance fee in your first year, assuming the fund advances 10 percent in value, you pay a total of 8 percent in fees; so you more or less make only 2 percent net in your first year. Therefore you need a long breadth in this fund, but it might very well profit from a squeeze in one of the precious metals.

## THE METAL OMNI FUND

### Investment Profile

The Metal Omni Fund is a creation of Metallgesellschaft Ltd. (MG Ltd.), one of the most well-established and oldest trading companies on the London Metal Exchange.[2] The objective of the fund is to profit from Metallgesellschaft's experience in base metal trading on the London Metal Exchange (LME), such as in copper, lead, zinc, aluminum, and tin. The fund also trades precious metals on the London Bullion Market, commodity-based derivatives, and other commodities. Metallgesellschaft Ltd. is a subsidiary of Metallgesellschaft AG in Germany, a major public quoted company. Investors in the fund gain from the skill and expertise of MG Ltd. and its ability to draw on the Metallgesellschaft metals group in managing a direct exposure to the metal markets.

The fund offers three classes of shares to accommodate the temperament of the investor:

1. A Shares:    Will not use leverage.

2. B Shares:    May leverage the assets up to three times.

3. C Shares:    May leverage the assets in excess of four times.

An investment in this fund is only suitable for high-net-worth individuals and institutional investors: the minimum is $250,000. So the fund is not very retail oriented. The charges are not cheap: an annual fixed management fee of 2 percent, an annual "sponsor" fee of 1 percent, and a profit-sharing fee of 20 percent per annum on new net profits. Subscriptions and redemptions can be made every two weeks.

The Metal Omni Fund is an offshore fund: the fund was incorporated in the British Virgin Islands on June 19, 1996. An investment in metals managed by metal professionals is a good strategy for well-to-do investors. Many commodity funds are "system" trading funds. This means that buy and sell signals are generated by computers without human influence. The Metal Omni Fund is traded purely on fundamental factors: buy and sell decisions are based upon demand and supply factors in the metal markets and based upon the expertise of Metallgesellschaft in the metal business. From inception in July 1996 through October 1997, the fund gained 35.7 percent. The fund is not correlated to the equity and bond markets with their current volatility. It also benefits from an investment approach that does not rely entirely on system trades.

Metallgesellschaft (MG Ltd.) has an impressive track record trading metals for their own account and for customers' accounts. They are one of the largest metal traders in the world, and they have an average audited, pretax return on capital of over 30 percent per year over the past 14 years, from 1983 to 1996 (see Table 8–1). An investment of $100,000 with MG Ltd. in 1983 would be valued at more than $3 million today.

It trades cash metals and metal derivatives on the London Metal Exchange and associated interest and exchange rate hedging transactions, transactions in gold and silver bullion, and warehousing activities of its wholly owned subsidiary Henry Bath and Son Limited. The fund profits from Metallgesellschaft's

**TABLE 8-1   Trading Results MG Ltd.**

| Year | Return on Capital Employed (pretax) |
|------|-------------------------------------|
| 1983 | 33% |
| 1984 | 31% |
| 1985 | 24% |
| 1986 | 5% |
| 1987 | 15% |
| 1988 | 18% |
| 1989 | 19% |
| 1990 | 18% |
| 1991 | 22% |
| 1992 | 28% |
| 1993 | 31% |
| 1994 | 85% |
| 1995 | 50% (provisional) |
| 1996 | |

Source: Data from Offering Memorandum, Internet, and performance tables, Magnum Global Investments, Ltd., Nassau, Bahamas.

experience and information on mining, engineering, and world-wide marketing. They trade commodities, ores, chemicals, and ferrous and nonferrous metals.

Figure 8-2 shows the trading results of the Metal Omni Fund.

## Fund Facts

| | |
|---|---|
| Management: | Metallgesellschaft Ltd. |
| | Manager: Craig Young |
| | London |
| | United Kingdom |
| Sponsor and prospectus: | Magnum Global Investments Ltd. |
| | Mr. Dion Friedland |
| | P.O. Box SS 5539 |
| | Windermere House |
| | 404 East Bay Street |
| | Nassau, Bahamas |

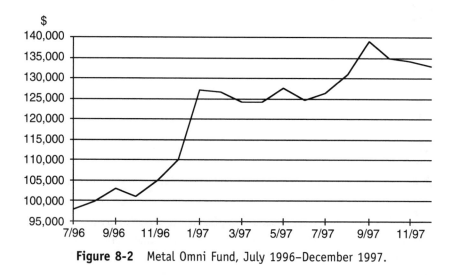

**Figure 8-2**   Metal Omni Fund, July 1996–December 1997.

Internet access:
Phone: 242-394-2547
Fax: 242-394-3284
www.magnumfund.com

**My Opinion:** The Metal Omni Fund is developing an impressive track record. But what is even more impressive is that so far, the fund does not have big drawdowns. The fund jumped more than 15 percent in January 1997 and managed to consolidate the profits. The fund has been short in gold and has used option strategies to capitalize on short-term trades. The Metal Omni Fund was ranked by Micropal as the number-one commodity and natural resources fund in the world for the 12 months ending October 31, 1997, published in the December 1997 issues of *Portfolio International* and *FT Magazine* "The International." In times of slackening demand, it is a big advantage to be invested in a fund that not only goes long but, at times, can also go short the metals. The fund is highly recommended.

# 9

## DIVERSIFIED NATURAL RESOURCES EQUITY FUNDS

### VAN ECK GLOBAL HARD ASSETS A

#### Investment Profile

The Van Eck Global Hard Assets A invests at least 65 percent of assets in hard-asset securities.[1] These include equities of companies involved in exploring for, producing, or distributing any of the following: precious metals; ferrous and nonferrous metals; gas, petrochemicals, or other hydrocarbons; forest products; and real estate. It also invests in securities with values linked to the price of hard-asset commodities or commodity indexes. It may invest without limit in foreign securities.

The fund offers three classes of shares:

1. A shares: Have front loads.

2. B shares: Have deferred loads, higher 12b-1 fees, and conversion features.

3. C shares: Have level loads.

## Performance as of March 31, 1998

Tables 9-1, 9-2, and 9-3 give the cumulative and the average annual total returns and the historical performance, respectively (data from Internet, Van Eck Global Hard Assets).

**TABLE 9-1   Cumulative Total Returns**

|  | No Load | S&P 500 |
|---|---|---|
| Year to Date | −2.45% | 13.94% |
| 1-month | −2.09% | 5.12% |
| 3-month | −2.45% | 13.94% |
| 6-month | −13.65% | 17.21% |
| 1-year | 11.43% | 47.96% |

**TABLE 9-2   Average Annual Total Returns**

|  | Load Adj. | No Load | S&P 500 |
|---|---|---|---|
| 1-year | 6.13% | 11.43% | 47.96% |
| 3-year | 20.78% | 22.75% | 32.79% |
| Life | 19.67% | 21.4% |  |

**TABLE 9-3   Historical Performance**

|  | Total Returns | Net Assets (millions of dollars under management) |
|---|---|---|
| Year to Date | −2.45% | 56.7 |
| 1997 | 14.39% | 58.0 |
| 1996 | 45.66% | 24.7 |
| 1995 | 20.09% | 3.6 |
| 1994 | N/A | 1.4 |

## Fund Facts

| | |
|---|---|
| Management company: | Van Eck Global Funds |
| | Phone (USA):    800-826-1115 |
| Manager: | Derek S. Van Eck |
| Morningstar symbol: | GHAAX |
| Internet access: | www.quicken.com— |
| | click Mutual Funds |
| | www.personal.fidelity.com/funds |
| Fees: Expenses and minimum purchase: | Expense Ratio:  0.72% |
| | Maximum Front Load: 4.75% |
| Management fee: | 1.00% |
| Minimum initial purchase: | $2,500 |
| Holdings: Asset allocation (as of March 30, 1998): | |
| Domestic equities (American): | 40.00% |
| Foreign equities: | 42.40% |
| Cash: | 11.20% |
| Top ten holdings (as of December 31, 1997): | Cali Realty |
| | Alcoa |
| | Patriot American Hospitality |
| | Prentiss Properties Trust |
| | KCS Energy |
| | Tubos de Acero de Mexico |
| | Canadian Fracmaster |
| | Capstar Hotel |
| | Placer Dome |
| | Saint Laurent Paperboard |

Figure 9-1 gives the performance of Van Eck Global Assets compared with the S&P500.

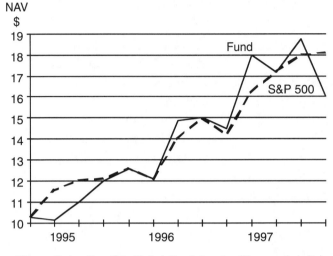

**Figure 9-1**  Van Eck Global Hard Assets. (*Source:* Intuit.)

**My Opinion:** The Van Eck Global Hard Assets Fund is still a young fund. Derek Van Eck is an original stock picker. From 1995 to the third quarter of 1997 he proved that he can deliver decent returns. Like most natural resource funds in the fourth quarter of 1997, the Van Eck Global Hard Assets Fund did not come out of the Asian crisis unscratched. The fund is cheap now, and the effect of the Asian crisis is waning. So this is the right moment to buy. It is one of the better American natural resources retail funds and well positioned to take advantage of the coming boom. I do miss exposure in the major European resource stocks.

## STATE STREET RESEARCH GLOBAL RESOURCES FUND

### Investment Profile

The State Street Research Global Resources Fund—Class A seeks long-term growth of capital.[2] The fund normally invests at least 65 percent of assets in equity securities issued by energy and natural resources companies located in at least three countries. It may invest the balance of assets in debt securities of varying maturities, up to 10 percent of which may be rated below investment grade. The fund is nondiversified.

The fund offers four classes of shares:

1. A shares: Have front loads.

2. B shares: Have deferred loads and higher 12b-1 fees.

3. C shares: Available to institutional investors only.

4. D shares: Have level loads.

## Performance as of November 30, 1997

Tables 9-4, 9-5, and 9-6 give the cumulative and the average annual total returns and the historical performance, respectively (data from Internet, State Street Research Global Resources).

**Table 9-4   Cumulative Total Returns**

|          | Load Adj. | No Load  | S&P 500 |
|----------|-----------|----------|---------|
| 1997     | 6.42%     | 11.44%   | 31.10%  |
| 1-month  | −14.79%   | −10.78%  | 4.63%   |
| 3-month  | −11.93%   | −7.78%   | 6.67%   |
| 6-month  | 0.79%     | 5.54%    | 13.57%  |
| 1-year   | 9.05%     | 14.19%   | 28.50%  |

**Table 9-5   Average Annual Total Returns**

|         | Load Adj. | No Load  | S&P 500 |
|---------|-----------|----------|---------|
| 1-year  | 9.05%     | 14.19%   | 28.58%  |
| 3-year  | 29.73%    | 31.73%   | 31.03%  |
| 5-year  | 21.94%    | 23.07%   | 20.13%  |
| Life    | 9.43%     | 10.08%   |         |

**Table 9-6   Historical Performance**

|      | Total Returns | Net Assets (millions of dollars under management) |
|------|---------------|---------------------------------------------------|
| 1997 | 11.44%        | 116.3 |
| 1996 | 70.25%        | 57.4  |
| 1995 | 22.63%        | 23.9  |
| 1994 | −4.45%        | 26.6  |
| 1993 | 32.08%        | 30.3  |
| 1992 | 6.78%         | 19.2  |

Figure 9-2 shows the performance of the State Street Research Global Resources Fund.

## Fund Facts

| | |
|---|---|
| Management company: | State Street Bank |
| | Phone (USA): 800-882-0052 |
| Fund manager: | Daniel J. Rice (with State Street Research since 1984) |
| Morningstar symbol: | SSGRX |
| Internet access: | www.quicken.com—click Mutual Funds |
| | www.personal.fidelity.com/funds |
| Expenses and minimum purchase | |
| Expense ratio: | 1.75% |
| Front load: | 4.50% |
| Deferred sales charge: | 0.00% |
| Minimum initial purchase: | $2,500 |

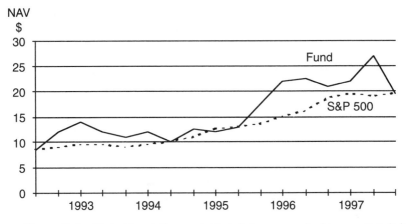

**Figure 9-2**  State Street Research Global Resources A. (*Source:* Intuit.)

| | |
|---|---|
| Redemption fee: | 0.00% |
| 12b-1 fee: | 0.25% |
| Holdings: | |
| Asset allocation (as of September 30, 1997): | |
| Domestic equities (American): | 62.90% |
| Foreign equities: | 34.20% |
| Cash: | 2.9% |
| Top ten holdings (as of September 30, 1997): | KCS Energy |
| | Seagull Energy |
| | Ocean Energy |
| | Nuevo Drilling |
| | Noble Drilling |
| | Atwood Oceanics |
| | Trans Texas Gas |
| | Ranger Oil |
| | OMI |
| | Barrett Resources |

**My Opinion (as of May 1988):    The State Street Research Global Resources Fund is in fact an energy fund. The manager of the fund, Daniel Rice, who has managed the fund since its inception, realized a 70.4% return in 1996. He prefers small-cap energy and offshore drilling stocks. Most of the other resource funds have a bigger-cap orientation. The fund has always been pretty volatile and was hit hard by the slackening Asian demand in the fourth quarter of 1997. Rice himself as an energy sector manager is not so optimistic. He finds oil values attractive at $12 or $13 a barrel. (In May 1998, oil was trading at $14.50 a barrel.) Rice is sticking with the majority in exploration and production, and he is not diversifying much in other natural resource areas. It is a big American retail fund with $250 million in assets. This fund will do very well again when the Asian crisis fades away.**

## T. ROWE PRICE NEW ERA

### Investment Profile

One of the oldest natural resources funds in existence is the T. Rowe Price New Era Fund.[3] The fund started trading on January 20, 1969. The fund has $1.6 billion under management. The fund seeks long-term capital appreciation by investing primarily in the common stocks of companies that own or develop natural resources and other basic commodities and in the stocks of selected nonresource growth companies. The fund focuses on U.S. and foreign companies whose earnings or tangible assets are expected to grow faster than the rate of inflation. The minimum investment is $2,500. T. Rowe Price, one of the largest fund management groups in the United States, has a program whereby you automatically invest a fixed amount of money every month in one of their funds. This is very good: by investing the same amount every month, you have paid over time the lowest average price of the fund. If you invest everything at the same time and your fund all of a sudden takes a nosedive, you can be faced with a sudden 20 percent loss in your account. This automatic investing is a perfect way to build up your own pension plan. Not every fund management company offers this service, but T. Rowe Price does.

## Performance as of March 31, 1998

Tables 9-7, 9-8, and 9-9 give the cumulative and the average annual total returns and the historical performance, respectively (data from Internet, T. Rowe Price New Era). Figure 9-3 represents the NAV development in graphic form.

**TABLE 9-7  Cumulative Total Returns**

|  | No Load | S&P 500 |
|---|---|---|
| Year to Date | 7.9% | 13.94% |
| 1-month | 6.22% | 5.12% |
| 3-month | 7.9% | 13.94% |
| 6-month | −2.25% | 17.21% |
| 1-year | 20.28% | 47.96% |

**TABLE 9-8  Average Annual Total Returns**

|  | No Load | S&P 500 |
|---|---|---|
| 1-year | 20.28% | 47.96% |
| 3-year | 18.33% | 32.79% |
| 5-year | 15.51% | 22.38% |
| 10-year | 11.76% | 18.93% |

**TABLE 9-9   Historical Performance**

|  | Total Returns | Net Assets (millions of dollars under management) |
| --- | --- | --- |
| Year to Date | 7.9% | 1382.5 |
| 1997 | 10.96% | 1492.7 |
| 1996 | 24.25% | 1467.7 |
| 1995 | 20.76% | 1090.4 |
| 1994 | 5.17% | 979.5 |
| 1993 | 15.33% | 752.6 |
| 1992 | 2.08% | 699.6 |

## Fund Facts

| | |
| --- | --- |
| Management company: | T. Rowe Price |
| Phone (USA): | 800-638-5660 |
| Manager: | Charles M. Ober |
| Morningstar symbol: | PRNEX |
| Internet access: | www.quicken.com/Investment— click Mutual Funds www.personal.fidelity.com/funds |

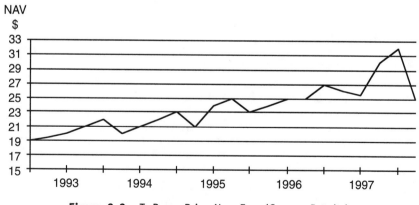

**Figure 9-3**   T. Rowe Price New Era. (*Source:* Intuit.)

Holdings
Asset allocation (as of
December 31, 1997):
Domestic equities
(American):                    68%
Foreign equities:              27.08%
Convertibles:                  0.66%
Cash:                          4.26%
Top ten holdings (as of
December 31, 1997):            Mobil
                               Royal Dutch Petroleum (ADR)
                               Wal-Mart Stores
                               Newmont Mining
                               Atlantic Richfield
                               McDermott International
                               British Petroleum (ADR)
                               Camco International
                               EI duPont de Nemours
                               Burlington Northern Santa Fe

**My Opinion:   It is a good middle-of-the-road fund with a good but not spectacular track record. Theoretically it can invest up to 35 percent in "foreign" securities. If you are a small investor with an average risk/return profile, this fund is suitable for you—this is a very reputable fund management company.**

**Morningstar gives an overall two-star rating to this fund, but the fact remains that a gap between the steadily climbing S&P 500 and the slowly increasing T. Rowe Price New Era fund is widening. Although the performance is not spectacular, the fund certainly did a lot better than its peers during the fourth quarter of 1997. The fund has not been heavily affected by the Asian crisis. The size of the**

fund is huge—it moves like an oil supertanker. An average annual return over 10 years of 11.76 percent (as of March 30, 1998) might be perfectly acceptable for you, but the average annual rate of return of the broad stock market (S&P 500) in the same period was 50 percent higher.

# 10

## ENERGY FUNDS

### EASTERN NATURAL RESOURCES

#### Investment Profile

One of my favorite investments in natural resources is Eastern Natural Resources (ENR).[1] ENR invests in a diversified portfolio of securities of companies with substantial activities in the natural resources industry in Russia and other newly independent states (NIS). It also invests, within certain limits, in debt instruments, physical commodities, and privatization vouchers. As of September 30, 1997, 55 percent of the portfolio was invested in the Russian oil and gas industry. The fund also seeks investment opportunities in less liquid, smaller capitalization companies, such as pipe manufactures, fertilizer plants, and the steel sector. Investments as of this date were further made in electric utilities (12 percent), followed by investments in steel, tube and pipeline producers (11 percent), and a further 6 percent in pulp and paper mills.

ENR is a product of MC Securities in Geneva, Switzerland. MC Securities was set up by Hans-Jörg Rudloff, who has been a board member for many years of Credit Suisse, one of the three large Swiss banks. He set up his own company and now concentrates on fund products investing in central and eastern Europe.

ENR is quoted on the Zurich Stock Exchange. The performance was very good in 1997 (see Figure 10-1), but gave back substantial gains in the first quarter of 1998.

## Fund Facts

| | |
|---|---|
| Board of directors: | Hans-Jörg Rudloff, Chairman |
| | Robet Pennone, Vice-Chairman |
| | Jean-Paul Aeschimann, Secretary |
| | Martin Pestalozzi, Member |
| Investment manager: | NRM Natural Resources |
| | Management Ltd. |
| | 14, Rue Etienne-Dumont |
| | 1211 Geneva, Switzerland |
| | Phone 4122-732-0707 |
| | Fax 4122-311-08-28 |

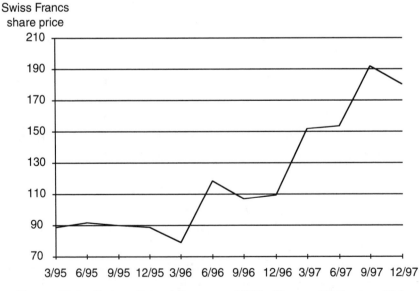

**Figure 10-1**  Eastern Natural Resources (ENR). (*Source:* MC Trustco, SA.)

| | |
|---|---|
| Fund manager: | Gustav Stenbolt |
| Investment advisers: | MC Trustco |
| | Axiom Advisory Service SA |
| | Vulcan Petroleum Ltd. |
| Custodian: | ING Bank Eurasia |
| Administrator: | L & S Conseil |
| Auditors: | Atag Ernst & Young |
| Fees: | Management: 2% per annum of the average stock market capitalization |
| | Performance: 15% of the amount by which the share price increase exceeds an annual return of 10%, and 20% of the amount in excess of an annual return of 20%. |

Top ten investments (as
of December 31, 1997):

| Registered Shares | % of Assets |
|---|---|
| Surgut Holdings | 20.4 |
| LUKoil Holding, ADR | 10.6 |
| Sakhalinmorneftegaz | 8.3 |
| Red Square Debt Fund | 5.7 |
| Surgat Neftegaz | 5.3 |
| Yuganskneftegaz | 3.5 |
| United Energy System | 3.0 |
| Noyabrskneftegaz | 3.0 |
| Irkutsk Energo—ADR | 2.5 |
| Samara Energo | 2.2 |

| | |
|---|---|
| Publication listing: Net asset value (NAV) publication: | *Finanz & Wirtschaft*— Switzerland (twice a week) |
| | *The Financial Times* (once a week) |
| | Reuters (MCSY daily) |
| Internet: | www.trustnet.co.uk./funds/59057.html |
| Monthly report: | Available upon request at the company. |

| Listing: | Swiss Stock Exchange |
| --- | --- |
| Ticker symbol: | Bloomberg: ENR SW |
| | Reuters: ENR.S |
| Security number: | Bearer Shares 347.166 |
| | Warrants 347.167 |

Here you see a clear difference between investments of plain vanilla American natural resources funds and the new Eastern world. Portfolio managers of American funds can tell you everything about Amoco and Exxon, but huge companies like Sakhalinmorneftegaz remain underresearched in America and are not part of American natural resource fund portfolios. But for me, this is the exciting area. Of course, it is fair to say that several American majors will participate in the coming Russian oil boom. So if you buy an American fund and your fund holds, for instance, Atlantic Richfield & Co (ARCO), the stock price will reflect the coming profits in countries like Kazakhstan and Siberia.

Personally I am very bullish on central and eastern Europe, and I prefer a direct engagement. Russia's credit standing is improving steadily, and natural resource companies are in the middle of a huge clean-up-and-merge process. They attract foreign capital to pay back taxes, modernize management, and make production more efficient. Their capital needs are huge, and they run in the billions of dollars. But because Russia has gained access to the international debt markets, it continues to place bonds at attractive rates. So foreign capital is flowing into the natural resource industry. For instance, LUKoil's recent $350 million convertible bond issue was largely subscribed for by ARCO, which bought $250 million of the bonds as a strategic investor. The Russian oil industry is undergoing a period of restructuring, the likes of which has not been seen since the time of the Rockefellers and the breakup of Standard Oil in the United States earlier this century. In Russia companies are being formed whose reserves are equivalent to those of Exxon and Shell. In the near future they will control the drilling, the distribution, and the retailing of oil and gas, just like in the Western world. In time, their cash flows will dwarf those of Western companies. Did you know that LUKoil recently opened its first gas station in the United States and that it plans to open a hundred more in the coming years? So if you do not feel comfortable buying into Russia, you can start by buying gas at the LUKoil gas station in Altamira, Virginia. If your car is still running and you feel more confident, you can also buy the LUKoil stock on the NASDAQ.

The world's largest oil and gas industry, which was run under the communist regime by the Ministry of Fuel and Energy, has now split up into more than a dozen integrated oil companies, the pipeline operator Transneft, the world's biggest natural gas producer Gazprom, and a number of geological and technical companies. The demand for natural gas is rising so fast that in 10 to 15 years Europe will be dependent largely on natural gas suppliers from outside Europe. After the year 2010, 60 percent of the European demand will be met by Russia. And Gazprom is the biggest supplier of them all. Gazprom intends to expand its pipelines all over Europe and Asia. Billion-dollar investments are involved. In the coming five years, a major effort will be made to access one of the greatest natural gas reserves in the world, which is the Yamal gas field in Siberia. Not the gas price itself but the distribution factor will largely influence the price of natural gas. Holland, a trading nation for centuries, has signed a letter of intent with Gazprom. Holland wants to become the "natural gas banker" for Europe—importing Russian gas from 2001 onward and storing it for other nations. The Germans do not like this development and do not want to see the business go to Holland. But the Germans' biggest company—Ruhrgas—does not have the huge storage capacities that the Dutch do.

There are a number of large companies in the natural resource sector scheduled to be sold off in the coming months and years. These can be very attractive investment opportunities because, in the past, prices paid in auctions have been significantly lower than on the open market. ENR will participate in the auctions.

Table 10-1 shows which stakes are for sale among Russian oil and gas companies.

## Russia's Natural Resources

As in the Middle East, Russia has abundant natural resources. This will become a key economic factor in the coming years. Compare it with the Middle East: As soon as oil started to flow, the Arabs got very wealthy. This will happen to Russia, too.

Russia holds 34 percent of world gas reserves and exports 40 percent of total world exports (see Figure 10-2).

Russia also holds 5 percent of the world's oil reserves and produces 9 percent of total world oil production (see Figure 10-3).

Russia's share in the world's production of precious metals is 6 percent for gold and 16 percent for platinum (see Figure 10-4).

Lastly, Russia is a big producer of nickel and palladium: it

**TABLE 10-1   Stakes for Sale at Russian Oil and Gas Companies**

| Company | 1996 Production | Stake for Sale | Minimum Bid Price (in millions of US $) |
|---------|-----------------|----------------|------------------------------------------|
| Tyumen Oil | 152m bbl | 49.00% | to be announced |
| Eastern Oil | 81m bbl | 85.00% | 1.300 |
| Lukoil | 432m bbl | 6.60% | 1.030 |
| Slavneft | 91m bbl | 59.93% | 217.0 |
| Ohrenburgneft | 55m bbl | 85.00% | 154.0 |
| Novolipetsk Steel | 7 million tons | 14.90% | to be announced |
| Zab-Sib Steel | 4 million tons | 14.30% | 52.0 |

(m = million, bbl = barrels)
Source: Data from offering memorandum, Internet, and quarterly reports, Eastern Natural Resources, Geneva, Switzerland.

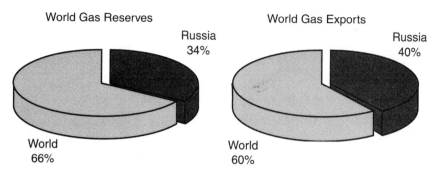

**Figure 10-2** Russia's gas share. (*Source:* MC Trustco, SA.)

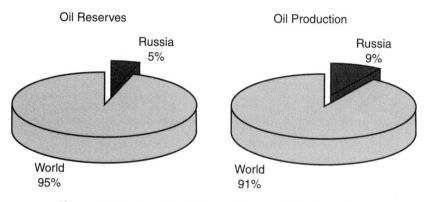

**Figure 10-3** Russia's oil share. (*Source:* MC Trustco, SA.)

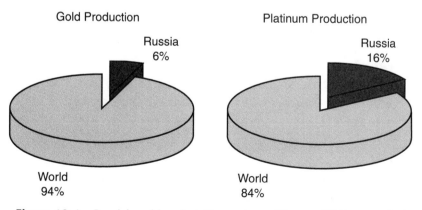

**Figure 10-4** Russia's gold and platinum share. (*Source:* MC Trustco, SA.)

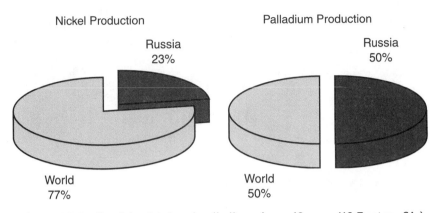

**Figure 10-5**  Russia's nickel and palladium share. (*Source:* MC Trustco, SA.)

produces 23 percent of the world's nickel and 50 percent of the
world's palladium (see Figure 10-5).

> **My Opinion:  Make a long-term investment and
> buy this stock on the Zurich Stock Exchange. Check
> back after five years, and the chance is real that
> you will have more than doubled your money.**
>
> **The essence of the story is that if you want to be
> invested in natural resources, you should invest in
> Russia, the country with the greatest natural re-
> sources in the world. You are not alone: George
> Soros has stated publicly that Russia is the
> most exciting emerging market in the world. He is
> now one of the biggest investors there. And a lot of
> wealth is being created in Russia. Do you know
> how many millionaires (in U.S. dollars) are living
> in Moscow alone? Three hundred thousand, as of
> mid-1998. I know people in the Kiev (Ukraine) who
> make a million dollars a week in steel trading. The
> best way for private investors is not to buy rubles
> and Russian stocks but to invest in Russia through
> a safe, hard currency like Swiss francs. If you buy
> ENR on the Zurich Stock Exchange, you make a**

**liquid investment in Russia, which you always can sell if you need the money. If you plan to buy a large block, you should contact MC Securities in Geneva directly. They might be able to sell you the net asset value of ENR at a discount of the stock price.**

## Russian Weddings

In November 1997 Boris Yeltsin lifted a 15 percent cap on foreign investments in Russian oil companies. This decree paved the way for alliances between the large Russian oil and gas companies and Western resource companies with capital and know-how. "Big Oil" is now buying oil reserves in Russia instead of trying to drill for oil themselves.

1. Royal Dutch Shell, the world's largest publicly quoted oil company, announced their marriage with Russian Gazprom and an investment of $1 billion in a Gazprom convertible bond issue in 1998.

2. British Petroleum (BP) announced they would buy a 10 percent stake in AO Sidanco, Russia's fourth-largest integrated oil company. The deal is worth $571 million. BP would also acquire a minority stake in Siberian gas fields controlled by Sidanco. This represents an investment of $172 million.

These two and other future marriages will propel the Russian oil companies into the spotlight as attractive investment partners for Western oil majors. Western oil companies will now accelerate their investments in eastern Europe, and the Russian majors who own the world's largest gas and oil reserves will now benefit from Western capital and technology. We can expect a modernization of the oil industry in Russia on a very grand scale. Russian oil reserves are estimated to be between 60 and 80 million barrels.

## Cheap Russian Oil

Do you want to buy cheap oil or expensive oil? If you buy Russian oil, you buy cheap oil. As an investor in ENR, you have a splendid opportunity to participate in this new development and reap the benefits.

Why is Russian oil cheap? Imagine you are the chairman of a well-capitalized Western oil company with decent oil reserves. You now buy a stake in a relatively *small capitalized* Russian oil company with *huge* oil reserves. You are now buying cheap oil.

Figure 10-6 compares the undercapitalized Russian companies and their huge reserves with Big Oil in the West. You see that the price of a barrel of oil is much cheaper in Russia than in the Western world. You buy value for money.

In the North Sea, you have to drill for oil. That is not the case in Russia—the production already exists.

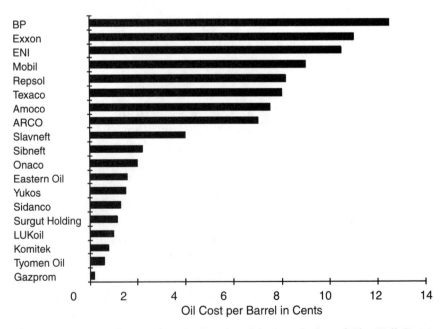

**Figure 10-6** Pennies per barrel. (Reprinted by permission of *The Wall Street Journal*, © 1997 Dow Jones & Company, Inc. All rights reserved worldwide.)

This situation is manna from heaven. In terms of supply, not much new oil has been found in the last 30 years, with the exception of the reserves in the Caspian Sea. And now Western oil companies get access to Russia's oil at discount prices.

In past years, Big Oil was rather arrogant and thought it could do everything itself: drilling, refining, and distributing. But now Big Oil is a "strategic investor" and accesses the oil through partnerships.

The newlyweds are eyeing China as a new customer. BP and Sidanco want to supply China with gas from eastern Siberia. And Shell and Gazprom want to sell oil and gas to China, Europe, South Korea, and Japan. "This is truly a global alliance," said Jeroen van der Veer, Shell's group managing director.[2] Gazprom is the world's largest gas producer, with more than a fifth of the world's gas reserves. Gazprom also has condensate oil reserves of 14.3 billion barrels.

## EXCELSIOR ENERGY & NATURAL RESOURCES

### Investment Profile

Excelsior Energy & Natural Resources Fund seeks long-term capital appreciation.[3] The fund normally invests at least 65 percent of assets in equity securities issued by companies from which management expects availability, development, and delivery of secure hydrocarbon and other energy sources. It typically invests at least 25 percent of assets in the crude oil, petroleum, and natural gas industries. The fund may invest in American depository receipts. Fund shares may be purchased at the net asset value (NAV) by registered investment advisers and fee-based financial planners. The fund had different names in the past, such as UST Master-Long-Term Supply of Energy Fund and Excelsior Long-Term Supply of Energy Fund.

## Performance as of March 31, 1998

Tables 10-2, 10-3, and 10-4 give the cumulative total and the average annual total returns and the historical performance, respectively (data from Internet, Excelsior Energy & Natural Resources). Figure 10-7 shows the NAV from May 1996 until November 1997.

### TABLE 10-2   Cumulative Total Returns

|              | No Load  | S&P 500 |
| ------------ | -------- | ------- |
| Year to date | 2.76%    | 13.94%  |
| 1-month      | 5.41%    | 5.12%   |
| 3-month      | 2.76%    | 13.94%  |
| 6-month      | −5.64%   | 17.21%  |
| 1-year       | 25.17%   | 47.96%  |

### TABLE 10-3   Average Annual Total Returns

|        | No Load  | S&P 500 |
| ------ | -------- | ------- |
| 1-year | 25.17%   | 47.96%  |
| 3-year | 24.99%   | 32.79%  |
| 5-year | 16.79%   |         |

### TABLE 10-4   Historical Performance

|              | Total Returns | Net Assets (millions of dollars under management) |
| ------------ | ------------- | ------------------------------------------------- |
| Year to date | 2.76%         | 43.4                                              |
| 1997         | 18.51%        | 44.5                                              |
| 1996         | 38.38%        | 33.8                                              |
| 1995         | 20.11%        | 24.0                                              |
| 1994         | −2.7%         | 13.5                                              |
| 1993         | 14.69%        | 4.8                                               |

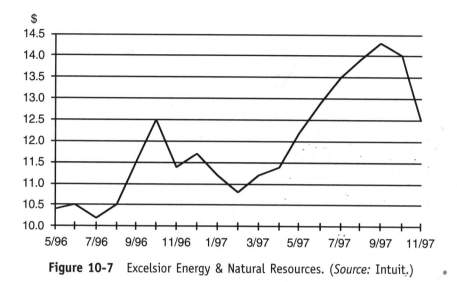

**Figure 10-7**   Excelsior Energy & Natural Resources. (*Source:* Intuit.)

## Fund Facts

| | |
|---|---|
| Management company: | U.S. Trust |
| Phone (USA): | 800-446-1012 |
| Fund manager: | Michael E. Hoover—since 1996 |
| Morningstar symbol: | UMESX |
| Internet access: | www.quicken.com— |
| | click Mutual Funds |
| | www.personal.fidelity.com/funds |
| Expenses and minimum initial purchase: | |
| Expense ratio: | 0.96% |
| Front load: | 0.00% |
| Deferred sales charge: | 0.00% |
| Minimum initial purchase: | $2,500 |
| Fees: | |
| Redemption fee: | 0.00% |
| 12b-1 fee: | 0.00% |
| Management fee: | 0.55% |

Holdings:
Asset allocation (as of
December 31, 1997):
Domestic equities
(American):                 84.68%
Foreign equities:           8.99%
Cash:                       6.3%
Top ten holdings (as of
September 30, 1997):        Exxon
                            Royal Dutch Petroleum (ADR)
                            British Petroleum (ADR)
                            Mobil
                            General Electric
                            Amoco
                            AES
                            Falcon Drilling
                            Schlumberger
                            Atwood Oceanics

**My Opinion: Although for an American energy fund the composition of the top ten holdings is fairly classic, consisting of American energy blue chips, the overall performance as of November 1997 has been fair to good. The fund gave back quite some profits in the latter half of 1997 but is now at attractive levels to buy. It is a typical "long only" fund.**

**The fund is also fairly small, which I think is an advantage. The fees are low, and the fund is well positioned to profit from an upswing in natural resource stocks. It is a promising investment for American investors who wish to have dollar exposure in domestic natural resource equities.**

## FIDELITY SELECT ENERGY PORTFOLIO

## Investment Profile

The Fidelity family of funds offers several investment possibilities in the natural resources sector.[4] The Fidelity Select Energy Portfolio invests mainly in equity securities of companies
in the energy field, including the conventional areas of oil,
gas, electricity, and coal and newer sources of energy such
as nuclear, geothermal, oil shale, and solar power. The fund
has existed for 10 years, and investors who put money in this
fund in the beginning have made nearly 300 percent.

Figure 10-8 represents a hypothetical investment of $10,000
made in 1987. The development includes reinvestments of dividends and capital gains. It does not include sales charges or
redemptions fees.

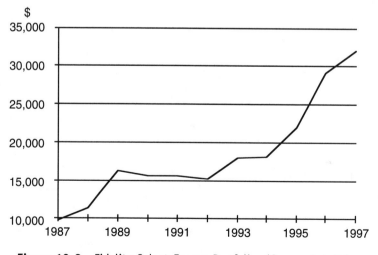

**Figure 10-8**  Fidelity Select Energy Portfolio. (*Source:* Intuit.)

## Performance as of March 31, 1998

Tables 10-5, 10-6, and 10-7 give the cumulative total and the average annual total returns and the historical performance, respectively (data from Internet, Fidelity Funds).

## Fund Facts

| | |
|---|---|
| Management company: | Fidelity Group of Funds |
| Phone: | 800-544-8888 |
| Fund manager: | Lawrence Rakers (since January, 1997) |
| Morningstar symbol: | FSENX |
| Internet access: | www.quicken.com— click Mutual Funds, enter FSENX www.personal.fidelity.com/funds |

**TABLE 10-5   Cumulative Total Returns**

| | With Load | No Load | S&P 500 |
|---|---|---|---|
| Year to Date | 1.86% | 5.01% | 13.95% |
| 1-month | 1.62% | 4.76% | 5.12% |
| 3-month | 1.86% | 5.01% | 13.95% |
| 6-month | −6.11% | −3.2% | 17.22% |
| 1-year | 19.06% | 22.74% | 48.00% |

**TABLE 10-6   Average Annual Total Returns**

| | With Load | No Load | S&P 500 |
|---|---|---|---|
| 1-year | 19.06% | 22.74% | 48.00% |
| 3-year | 19.07% | 20.29% | 32.81% |
| 5-year | 13.2% | 13.89% | 22.4% |
| 10-year | 11.24% | 11.58% | 18.94% |

**TABLE 10-7   Historical Performance**

| | Total Returns | Net Assets (millions of dollars under management) |
|---|---|---|
| Year to Date | 5.01% | 161.4 |
| 1997 | 10.28% | 158.2 |
| 1996 | 32.47% | 239.7 |
| 1995 | 21.38% | 131.5 |
| 1994 | 0.41% | 96.7 |
| 1993 | 19.15% | 82.5 |
| 1992 | −2.39% | 68.8 |
| 1991 | 0.04% | 72.1 |
| 1990 | −4.49% | 96.4 |
| 1989 | 42.83% | 90.5 |
| 1988 | 15.94% | 75.1 |

Fees and expenses:
Maximum sales charge:   3.00%
Expense ratio:   1.57%
Redemption fee:   $7.50 or 0.75%, whichever is less
Holdings:
Asset allocation (as of
September 30, 1997):
Equity:   93.5%
Cash/other:   6.5%
Major market sectors:
Energy:   85.2%
Basic industry:   3.2%
Other:   12.6%
Geographical spread:
UK:   5.6%
US:   66.4%
Canada:   8.5%
France:   9.7%
Netherlands:   3.2%

Top ten holdings (as of
March 31, 1998):

Total B Spon ADR
USX-Marathon Group Common New
Texaco Inc.
British Petroleum PLC ADR
Mobil Corp.
Coastal Corp.
Elf Acquitaine Sponsored ADR
Transocean Offshore
Royal Dutch Petroleum
Noble Drilling Corp.

**My Opinion:   Fidelity is doing a good job with the Select Energy Portfolio. It is one of the oldest funds in the energy sector. Until the third quarter of 1997, the fund had a good performance. The Asian crisis was the reason why the net asset value fell back from $26 to $20 a share. But by May 1998, the losses had already recuperated by 40 percent.**

**As you can see from their top ten holdings, the fund also has a substantial exposure in the oil exploration and oil service industries. More and more fund managers use the track record of this 10-year-old fund as a benchmark in energy portfolio management. The fund is very good for small investors: it has turned a $10,000 investment into $34,408 in 10 years' time.**

## INVESCO STRATEGIC PORTFOLIO ENERGY

### Investment Profile

The Invesco Strategic Portfolio Energy invests at least 80 percent of assets in the equities of companies principally engaged in

the energy field, including those that explore for, develop, produce, or distribute known energy sources.[5] These issuers may
also provide related transportation, distribution, or processing
services or those that engage in the research or development of
energy-efficient technologies. The fund may invest up to 25
percent of assets in non-American securities. It may also purchase ADRs and Canadian issues.

## Performance as of March 31, 1998

Tables 10-8, 10-9, and 10-10 give the cumulative total and
average annual total returns and the historical performance,
respectively (data from Internet, Invesco Strategic Portfolio
Energy).

**TABLE 10-8    Cumulative Total Returns**

|              | No Load   | S&P 500 |
| ------------ | --------- | ------- |
| Year to date | 0.5%      | 13.94%  |
| 1-month      | 7.48%     | 5.12%   |
| 3-month      | 0.5%      | 13.94%  |
| 6-month      | −13.38%   | 17.21%  |
| 1-year       | 23.17%    | 47.96%  |

**TABLE 10-9    Average Annual Total Returns**

|         | No Load | S&P 500 |
| ------- | ------- | ------- |
| 1-year  | 23.17%  | 47.96%  |
| 3-year  | 24.63%  | 32.79%  |
| 5-year  | 12.64%  | 22.38%  |
| 10-year | 8.0%    | 18.93%  |

**TABLE 10-10   Historical Performance**

|  | Total Returns | Net Assets (millions of dollars under management) |
|---|---|---|
| Year to date | 0.5% | 173.6 |
| 1997 | 19.09% | 212.1 |
| 1996 | 38.84% | 233.1 |
| 1995 | 19.80% | 98.5 |
| 1994 | −7.25% | 46.9 |
| 1993 | 16.71% | 49.2 |
| 1992 | −13.23% | 13.0 |

## Fund Facts

| | |
|---|---|
| Fund management company: | Invesco |
| Phone (USA): | 800-675-1705 |
| Fund manager: | John Segner, vice president of Invesco Trust Company since early 1997. |
| Morningstar symbol: | FSTEX |
| Internet access: | www.quicken.com—click Mutual Funds, enter FSTEX www.personal.fidelity.com/funds |
| Expense ratio: | 1.30% |
| Front load: | 0.00% |
| Deferred sales charge: | 0.00% |
| Minimum initial purchase: | $1,000 |
| Fees: | |
| Redemption fee: | 0.00% |
| 12b-1 fee | 0.00% |

Holdings:
Asset allocation (as of
September 30, 1997):
Domestic equities
(American):                77.97%
Foreign equities:          12.70%
Preferreds:                2.77%
Cash:                      6.56%
Top ten holdings (as of
September 30, 1997):       Repurchase Agreements
                           Gulf Canada Resources
                           Baker Hughes
                           Sonat
                           Noble Drilling
                           EI duPont de Nemours
                           Patterson Energy
                           Apache
                           NS Group
                           Philips Petroleum

**My Opinion:   The Invesco Strategic Portfolio Energy started trading in January 1991. The fund's performance matched the S&P 500 pretty well during the first 5¹/₂ years (see Figure 10-9). From October 1996 until October 1997, the fund has outperformed the S&P 500 very clearly.**

**A new fund manager, John S. Segner, took over the portfolio management of the fund in February 1997. Targeted industries are stocks in oil; natural gas; coal; uranium; geothermal, solar, or nuclear power; and new energy sources. The fund has a large exposure to American, internationally operating oil companies, exploration and production companies, and oil service companies.**

**The fund has given back many profits due to the Asian economic crisis, which has resulted in**

**substantial reductions of the fund's assets. If you can live with volatility, you can buy this fund at relatively cheap levels.**

## ENERGY SERVICE FUNDS

A fascinating aspect of natural resources is not only the oil or the oil drilling but the *servicing* of the oil industry. Why is this industry so profitable?

To recapitulate, if you want to invest in the energy sector, you have the following possibilities:

1. Investing in the commodities themselves. Your success or misfortune depends on the fluctuations of oil and gas prices. They are pretty volatile and sometimes unpredictable. Even among professionals, not too many oil traders make money from buying and selling oil futures.

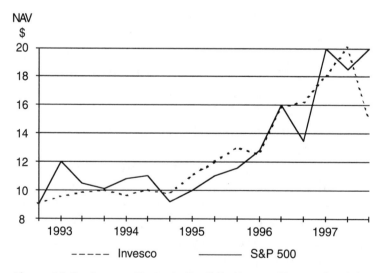

**Figure 10-9** Invesco Strategic Portfolio Energy. (*Source:* Intuit.)

2. Investing in exploration and production companies. They are also heavily dependent on oil and gas prices, so their revenues are also rather unpredictable and volatile.

3. Investing in the oil-field service companies. Their revenues are more *independent* of oil and gas prices. Because the volume of the oil and gas industries is expanding, the demand for oil-field service companies, their revenues, and their profit is increasing all the time.[6]

What do oil-field service companies offer?

- Geophysical services.

- Drilling services/tool rental.

- Offshore drilling.

- Offshore construction.

- Offshore transportation.

- Environmental services.

- Production and well services.

- Equipment manufacturing.

Revenue and profit developments of several oil and gas service firms are increasing sharply (see Table 10-11).

Why is the trend firmly up? In the 1980s, demand for oil was met by just turning the taps of existing reservoirs. But today demand can only be met by increased oil-service activity. As we have seen before, the consumption of oil has the potential to expand significantly in the future. Increasing global-energy demand requires finding, drilling, and servicing more oil and gas wells, both in developed nations and in smaller, deeper, and more complicated reservoirs, which are more lucrative to the oil-

**TABLE 10-11  Higher Revenues and Profitability of Oil and Gas Service Firms (in thousands of dollars)**

| Name | | 1989 | 1991 | 1993 | 1995 | 1996 |
|---|---|---|---|---|---|---|
| BJ Services | Revenue | 173.369 | 390.296 | 394.363 | 633.660 | 965.261 |
| | Profit | 10 | 24.422 | 14.561 | 9.889 | 40.486 |
| Ensco | Revenue | 59.355 | 101.300 | 246.235 | 279.114 | 468.800 |
| | Profit | −7.551 | −17.394 | 12.231 | 41.763 | 95.400 |
| Input/Output | Revenue | 21.411 | 36.006 | 54.205 | 134.698 | 278.283 |
| | Profit | 1.933 | 5.735 | 9.142 | 24.500 | 38.677 |
| Nabors | Revenue | 74.451 | 240.111 | 362.037 | 572.788 | 719.743 |
| | Profit | 5.497 | 27.057 | 34.263 | 51.104 | 70.500 |
| Pride | Revenue | 65.898 | 112.224 | 127.099 | 268.000 | 407.174 |
| | Profit | 544 | 3.519 | 5.940 | 15.200 | 22.728 |
| Schlumberger | Revenue | 4,685.995 | 3,847.645 | 8,696.845 | 7,621.694 | 8,956.200 |
| | Profit | 441.454 | 815.600 | 536.077 | 649.157 | 849.500 |
| Tidewater | Revenue | 182.700 | 455.804 | 475.500 | 584.608 | 643.447 |
| | Profit | −12.500 | 36.900 | 40.100 | 51.187 | 76.177 |
| Energy Ventures | Revenue | 107.927 | 178.015 | 246.017 | 351.587 | 539.000 |
| | Profit | 2.851 | 5.888 | 5.890 | 11.311 | 93.000 |

Source: Orbitex.

field service sectors. The fundamentals for the oil service industry will continue to be very positive and will provide solid revenue and profit-growth opportunities. Oil producers, like any other American industry sector, increasingly outsource production activities. The majors are moving toward a lean, just-in-time, energy-production system. There is plenty of oil and gas to supply global demand, but finding it and producing it strains the capabilities of the oil-field service industry. The industry is running out of spare capacity, and pricing and profitability should continue to rise, as should many of the stocks.

In addition to global demand increases, outsourcing services and supply constraints drive the growth of oil service companies. Just like in many other businesses (cars, computer manufacturing, etc.), companies in the oil business outsource many services to the oil service companies, while they concentrate on their core business. They also create more and more long-term alliances with oil service companies. In addition, prices of services have risen steadily for all in the past two years, increasing the profits of the service companies. A good example of how prices are going up in the oil service industry is the daily leasing price of an offshore drilling rig (see Figure 10-10). In 1994 you could lease

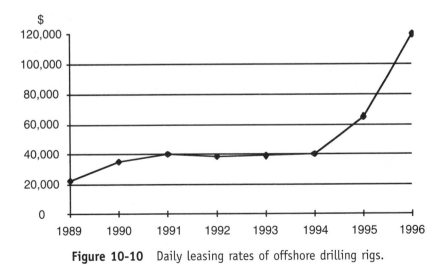

**Figure 10-10**   Daily leasing rates of offshore drilling rigs.

an oil rig for $40,000 a day. At the end of 1996, oil rig leasing companies fetched 300 percent more, or $120,000, a day. The same rise is taking place in the price of drill pipes, mud pumps, engines, offshore supply vessels, and other classes of oil service equipment.

## EASTGATE INTERNATIONAL

### Investment Profile

Eastgate Management Corporation has its full-time management devoted to researching and investing in oil service companies. They can be reached at:

Eastgate Management Corporation
504 North Fourth Street, Suite 104
P.O. Box 1305
Fairfield, IA 52556
Phone 515-472-4887
Fax 515-472-6929

Eastgate offers two classes of shares: for U.S. citizens and for non-U.S. citizens. Minimum investment is $500,000, although the company will accept lower subscriptions. The absolute minimum is $50,000. Investors can buy shares in Eastgate International Limited, an offshore fund based in the Bahamas.

A subscription memorandum can be requested at:

Eastgate International Limited
Charlotte House
Charlotte Street
P.O. Box N-9204
Nassau, Bahamas
Attention: Mrs. Dawn E. Davies
Phone 515-472-4887
Fax 515-472-6929

## Performance

Eastgate has delivered an impressive performance so far. Figure 10-11 shows the performance of Eastgate Fund Limited Partnership from its inception on March 1, 1995, through the end of 1996.

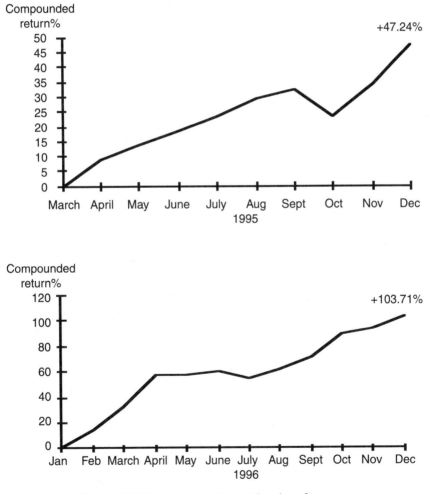

**Figure 10-11**   Eastgate International performance.

## Fund Facts

| | |
|---|---|
| Fund manager: | Harris Kaplan |
| | Eastgate Management Corporation |
| | 707 South Main Street |
| | Fairfield, IA 52556 |
| | Phone 515-472-4887 |
| | Fax 515-472-6929 |
| Fees: | |
| Management fee: | 2% per annum |
| Performance fee: | 20% of new net profits |

Mr. Kaplan spends a great deal of his time researching oil service companies. He regularly travels by helicopter to oil rigs in the North Sea. He does not kick the tires like a second-hand car dealer, but he turns the oil taps! From 1988 until 1995, Mr. Kaplan was involved in the corporate development of Nabors Industries, an oil-field service company whose stock is listed on the American Stock Exchange.

**My Opinion: This is an outstanding niche product from which you can earn unnatural profits in natural resources. Having worked in the oil service industry himself (Nabor Industries), Mr. Kaplan is a very knowledgeable connoisseur of this service sector. His performance in 1995 and 1996 was outstanding. I had the pleasure of participating in conference calls with other investors. He refers to service sector stocks as an "in the money option," meaning that your risk is very small. The worst things that could happen to oil service stocks are (1) global recession and (2) new global resource of energy for cars. Both scenarios are highly unlikely in the short term. Mr. Kaplan's personal benchmark is the Fidelity Select Energy Portfolio, which he has outperformed by far.**

Mr. Kaplan concentrates his efforts on finding the best trading opportunities and is not focused on marketing. He has a small organization, and his good performance will attract investors automatically. His fund is highly recommendable for professional investors, who can do their own allocation among the different sectors in natural resources.

## FORSTMANN-LEFF ENERGY SECTOR

### Investment Profile

The well-respected, New York–based, asset-management firm Forstmann-Leff Associates Inc. (FLA) offers a hedge fund product in the energy field: "Hedge Energy."[7] The fund invests in the securities and the derivatives of both domestic and foreign companies involved in the energy business. Forstmann-Leff divides the energy business up as follows:

- *Petroleum/natural gas industry:* Companies engaged in exploration, development, production processing, refining, gathering, transportation, storage, distribution, or marketing of petroleum, natural gas, or derived products.

- *Coal industry:* Companies involved in the extraction, mining, processing, transportation, or sale of coal.

- *Electric power:* Companies engaged in the generation, transmission, distribution, or purchase or sale of electric power.

- *Energy service:* Companies engaged in the provision of goods and services or support to petroleum or natural gas, coal, or electric power companies.

- *Nonconventional energy areas:* Nuclear power, geothermal, solar, or oil shale energy companies.

Figure 10-12 shows gross perfomance figures before fees.

## Performance

Summary of Performance Data:

### FL Hedge Energy

| 1994 Total Gross: | −1.37% |
|---|---|
| 1994 Total Net: | −2.37% |
| 1995 Total Gross: | 77.62% |
| 1995 Total Net: | 61.09% |
| 1996 Total Gross: | 133.35% |

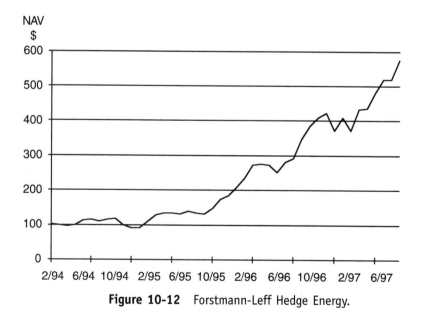

**Figure 10-12**   Forstmann-Leff Hedge Energy.

| | |
|---|---|
| 1996 Total Net: | 105.68% |
| 1997 (9-month) Total Gross: | 41.15% |
| 1997 (9-month) Total Net: | 32.17% |
| 45-month Gross: | 478.99% |
| 45-month Annualized: | 59.58% |
| 45-month Net: | 327.54% |
| 45-month Annualized: | 47.32% |

## Fund Facts

| | |
|---|---|
| Investment adviser: | Forstmann-Leff Associates Inc. 55 East 52nd Street New York, NY 10055 USA |
| Directors: | Peter A. Lusk John C. R. Collis Devandranauth R. Shastri |
| Minimum investment: | $500,000. Directors can accept subscription for lesser amounts. |
| Dealings: | Monthly, according to NAV. |
| Subscription charges: | Maximum 2%. |
| Redemptions: | Monthly, according to NAV of preceding month, with prior 30-day written notice. |
| Registration and listings: | The fund is offshore, Bermuda based, with a listing on the Irish Stock Exchange. |
| Fees: | |
| Management fee: | 1% |
| Performance fee: | 20% |

My Opinion:   Forstmann-Leff caters to institutions and high-net-worth individuals. Forstmann-Leff offers one of the best energy products I have come across. The FLA Hedge Energy is not your typical "long only" fund. It has a large exposure in derivatives, so it can also be profitable when the energy complex is going down in price. A 327.54 percent net increase in four years in the energy complex is a great performance. After slightly negative results in 1994, Forstmann-Leff delivered a stellar performance in the next three years. And what is even more remarkable, the performance has been achieved without major drawdowns.

This fund goes into the category of excellent management and unnatural profits in natural resources.

## CAMBRIDGE INVESTMENTS LTD.

### Investment Profile

Cambridge Investments Limited, a California corporation, manages assets in the oil and gas sector. The company has issued several limited partnerships, such as the Cambridge Energy L.P. and Cambridge Oil & Gas L.P., and public funds, such as the Cambridge Energy Fund International Ltd. and the Cambridge Oil & Gas International Fund.

Although the Cambridge Energy Fund International Ltd. is closed to new investors, I highlight the performance of this fund (see Table 10-12) to show the company's capabilities in the energy service sector. The fund may use options and short sales. Shares can only be sold to non-U.S. persons. The fund started on July 12, 1994, at $10 per Class B share.

**TABLE 10-12** Cambridge Energy Fund International Ltd. Annual
Performance

| | Net Asset Value per B Share | Change |
|---|---|---|
| 1994 | $8.55 | |
| 1995 | $13.97 | +63.4% |
| 1996 | $26.71 | +91.2% |

Source: Data from Cambridge documentation and performance updates, Cambridge Investments Ltd., San Francisco, 1997.


# Fund Facts for the Cambridge Energy Fund International Ltd.

Investment adviser:  Cambridge Investments Limited
600 Montgomery Street
27th Floor
San Francisco, CA 94111
USA
Phone 415-781-0866
Fax 415-781-0869
Principal: John R. Tozzi

Administrator:  Tremont (Bermuda) Ltd.
4 Park Road
Hamilton HM11, Bermuda
Phone 441-292-3781
Fax 441-296-0667
Contact: Joseph Soares

Minimum investment:  $250,000 (closed to new investors)
Fees:
Annual fee:  1.5%
Performance fee:  20% of new net profits earned

over the average three-month U.S. Treasury Bill rate plus 2%. Class C shares started in August 1996 (also closed to new investors) have a straight 20% performance fee.

## Investment Profile for the Cambridge Oil & Gas International, Ltd., Fund

Another fund product, the Cambridge Oil & Gas International, Ltd., Fund, is open for new investors. It started trading on March 1, 1997, and invests in the energy sector of the market both in the United States and overseas. The fund may use options and short sales. Shares in the fund can only be sold to non-U.S. persons. The performance is impressive (see Table 10-13).

## Fund Facts for the Cambridge Oil & Gas International, Ltd., Fund

| | |
|---|---|
| Investment adviser and administrator: | Same as for Cambridge Energy Fund International Ltd. |
| Minimum initial purchase: | |
| Minimum investment: | $500,000 (open to new, non-U.S. investors) |
| Fees: | |
| Annual fee: | 1.5% |
| Performance fee: | 20% of new net profits earned annually |

**My Opinion: The Cambridge Oil & Gas International Fund delivered a 67.28 percent performance in 1997 (see Figure 10-13). Cambridge offers an**

**TABLE 10-13   Cambridge Oil & Gas International, Ltd., Fund.**

| Date | NAV per Share | Monthly Net Return | Cumulative Return |
|------|---------------|--------------------|--------------------|
| March 1 | $100.000 | | |
| March 31 | $112.427 | 12.43% | 12.43% |
| April 30 | $110.386 | −1.82% | 10.39% |
| May 31 | $124.965 | 13.21% | 24.97% |
| June 30 | $162.034 | 20.63% | 62.03% |
| August 31 | $171.889 | 6.08% | 71.89% |
| September 30 | $195.799 | 13.91% | 95.80% |
| October 31 | $201.234 | 2.78% | 101.23% |
| November 30 | $175.232 | −12.92% | 75.23% |
| December 31 | $167.281 | −4.54% | 67.28% |

**excellent limited partnership and offers this product to international investors. Their overall track record is very impressive. They also manage a part of the Sabre Multi Manager Natural Resources Fund. I recommend this product highly, but you must be prepared for a fair amount of volatility.**

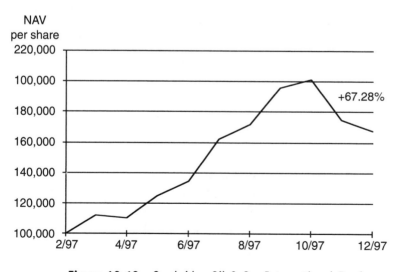

**Figure 10-13**   Cambridge Oil & Gas International Fund.

## FIDELITY SELECT ENERGY SERVICE PORTFOLIO

### Investment Profile

The Fidelity family of funds offers several investment possibilities in the natural resources sector.[9] The Fidelity Select Energy Service Portfolio (FSESX) invests at least 80 percent in equities of companies in the energy-services field. These include companies that provide services and equipment to the areas of oil, gas, electricity, and coal, as well as nuclear, geothermal, oil-shale, and solar power energy. The fund may invest up to 25 percent of assets in one issuer, and it may invest up to 5 percent in lower-quality debt. The fund is nondiversified.

### Performance as of March 31, 1998

Tables 10-14, 10-15, and 10-16 give the cumulative total and the average annual total returns and the historical performance, respectively (data from Internet, Fidelity Funds).

### Fund Facts

| | |
|---|---|
| Fund promoter: | Fidelity Group |
| Fund manager: | Robert D. Ewing |
| Phone: | 800-544-8888 |
| Minimum initial purchase: | $2,500 |
| Fund assets: | $975.6 million |
| Morningstar symbol: | FSESX |
| Interne access: | www.quicken.com—click Mutual Funds, enter FSESX www.personal.fidelity.com/funds |

**TABLE 10-14  Cumulative Total Returns**

|              | With Load | No Load | S&P 500 |
|--------------|-----------|---------|---------|
| Year to Date | −4.05%    | −1.08%  | 13.95%  |
| 1-month      | 4.27%     | 7.49%   | 5.12%   |
| 3-month      | −4.05%    | −1.08%  | 13.95%  |
| 6-month      | −11.91%   | −9.19%  | 17.22%  |
| 1-year       | 44.59%    | 49.06%  | 48.00%  |

**TABLE 10-15  Average Annual Total Returns**

|          | With Load | No Load | S&P 500 |
|----------|-----------|---------|---------|
| 1-year   | 44.59%    | 49.06%  | 48.00%  |
| 3-year   | 39.24%    | 40.66%  | 32.81%  |
| 5 -year  | 24.75%    | 25.51%  | 22.4%   |
| 10-year  | 14.8%     | 15.15%  | 18.94%  |

**TABLE 10-16  Historical Performance**

|              | Total Returns | Net Assets (millions of dollars under management) |
|--------------|---------------|---------------------------------------------------|
| Year to Date | −1.08%        | 975.6                                             |
| 1997         | 51.87%        | 1133.4                                            |
| 1996         | 49.08%        | 562.8                                             |
| 1995         | 40.87%        | 254.1                                             |
| 1994         | 0.57%         | 50.8                                              |
| 1993         | 20.96%        | 40.2                                              |
| 1992         | 3.43%         | 35.0                                              |
| 1991         | −23.48%       | 28.6                                              |
| 1990         | 1.75%         | 82.1                                              |
| 1989         | 59.44%        | 70.9                                              |
| 1988         | −0.40%        | 29.6                                              |

Expenses:

| | |
|---|---|
| Expense ratio: | 1.45% |
| Maximum front load: | 3.00% |

Fees:

| | |
|---|---|
| Redemption fee: | 0.75% |
| 12b-1 fee: | 0.25% |
| Management fee: | 0.70% |

Figure 10-14 compares the performance of the Fidelity Select Energy Service Portfolio with the S&P 500.

Holdings:
Asset allocation (as of March 31, 1998):

| | |
|---|---|
| Equity: | 93.2% |
| Cash: | 6.8% |

Major market sectors:

| | |
|---|---|
| Energy: | 81.4% |
| Construction and real estate: | 9.6% |
| Other: | 9.0% |

Geographical diversification:

| | |
|---|---|
| Panama | 2.5% |
| Others | 6.7% |
| France | 5.4% |
| United States | 85.4% |

Top ten holdings (as of March 31, 1998):

Cooper Cameron Corp.
Transocean Offshore Inc.
Schlumberger Ltd. NY Reg.
Halliburton Co.
R&B Falcon Corp.
Noble Drilling Corp.
Coflexip SA Spon ADR
Diamond Offshore Drilling
Western Atlas Inc.
Baker Hughes Inc.

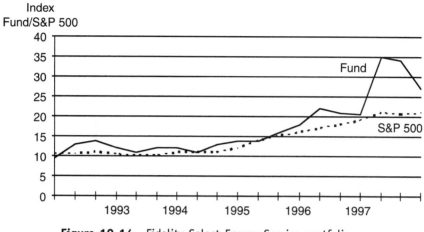

Index
Fund/S&P 500

**Figure 10-14**   Fidelity Select Energy Service portfolio.

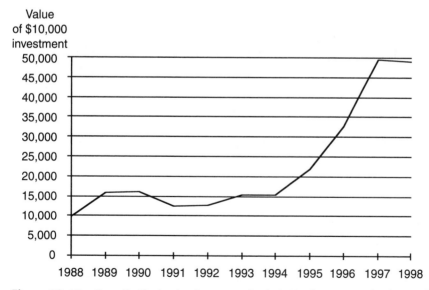

**Figure 10-15**   Hypothetical value increase of a $10,000 investment in the Fund in 1987. All dividends and capital gains are reinvested. Sales charges and redemption fees are excluded.

**My Opinion:** The service sector of the oil industry has been one of the most profitable investment sectors in 1997. Stocks in this category jumped during the year, sometimes more than 100 percent. The Asian economic crisis deflated the premiums, and fund stock prices dropped at the end of 1997 to substantially lower levels. This industry sector will benefit from the general consolidation process, and mergers are to be expected. By May of 1998, losses in the fund due to the Asian crisis had already been recouped by 50 percent.

This industry sector is maximizing profits due to the need of the oil majors to outsource activities as much as possible. Companies that were leasing oil platforms to the majors can do so at rates of $200,000 a day. This compares to rates of $40,000 a few years ago.

Fidelity Energy Service Portfolio has been the number-one retail mutual fund in the energy service sector for a number of years. An investment of $10,000 in 1988 was worth $49,085 in May of 1998. The biggest acceleration in the value increase took place between 1994 and 1998. If you are an American retail investor, you must be in this fund before oil prices start to rise again.

## WELLINGTON MANAGEMENT

### Investment Profile

Wellington Management is an independent Boston-based investment adviser that specializes in managing discretionary client assets.[10] The firm has extensive experience in the research and portfolio management of investments in the energy sector and related sectors and currently manages over $8 billion of securities in these sectors. Wellington Management currently has 52 partners and over 150 investment professionals.

The company offers the so-called Spindrift classes of shares: class A are offered directly to institutional and certain sophisticated individual investors, while class B are offered to financial intermediaries who purchase the class B shares on behalf of various investors and who will receive a servicing fee.

The partnership Wellington Management Investors (Bermuda), Ltd., seeks capital appreciation through investment primarily in securities of companies in the energy sector and related sectors worldwide. Opportunities to enhance capital appreciation are also pursued through the use of short positions, margin borrowing, derivative instruments, and other aggressive investment strategies. The partnership invests at least 75 percent of assets primarily in securities engaged in the production, transportation, and/or refining of crude oil and gas; companies that provide services to such companies; and electric and other utility companies. The primary investment strategy of the partnership is to take aggressive long positions in undervalued small- to medium-size companies, seeking investment opportunities created by general investor pessimism about the energy sector as well as market inefficiencies in the valuation of these companies. The partnership also seeks opportunities that result from market inefficiencies in the valuation of major oil companies and the valuation of non-U.S.-based energy companies relative to those based in the United States. The partnership may take further short positions in an effort to benefit from valuation distortions arising from the volatility of commodity prices, political and environmental pressures, excess optimism about exploration successes, and other factors. The portfolio will be generally net long.

## Fund Facts

| | |
|---|---|
| Minimum investment: | $500,000 |
| Fees: | Management fee—A shares:   1% |
| | Servicing fee: 0.5% extra for B shares |
| | Incentive fee: 20% |
| Subscriptions and withdrawals: | Quarterly |

Figure 10-16 shows the net asset value of Spindrift Investors. For a disclosure statement, contact:

Wellington Management
75 State Street
Boston, MA 02108
USA
Phone     617-951-5000
Fax       617-951-5250

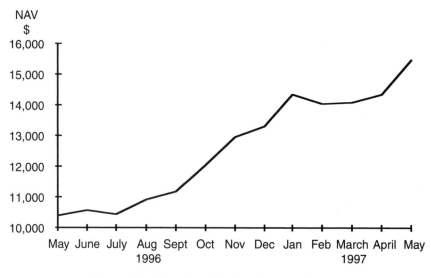

**Figure 10-16**     Spindrift Investors—A shares.

My Opinion: The A shares—with a minimum of $500,000—of Spindrift are meant for institutions and high-net-worth individuals. The B shares are sometimes bundled by intermediaries and sold to individual investors. Spindrift offers excellent capital preservation, and their performance in the energy sector is very good: +60 percent since May 1996. The performance history is still young, but the funds can be recommended. Unnatural profits.

## PEQUOT ENERGY OFFSHORE FUND

### Investment Profile

The Pequot Energy Offshore Fund is the product for international clients of Dawson-Samberg Inc.[11] This investment management firm was founded in 1981 and manages $2.8 billion. They manage $1.9 billion in six limited partnerships, $700 billion in tax-exempt client assets, and $100 million in individual, trust, and family group accounts.

| | |
|---|---|
| The principals are: | Arthur J. Samberg and Deborah W. Pratt. |
| They can be contacted at: | Dawson-Samberg Inc. 354 Pequot Avenue P.O. Box 760 Southport, CT 06490-0760 USA Phone 203-254-0091 Fax 203-255-2558 |

The firm is focused on investing in the United States equity market only. The research at Dawson-Samberg is an in-house fundamentally driven process. The investment staff visits approximately 200 companies a month.

The Pequot Energy Offshore Fund started trading on January 2, 1997. It is managed in a way similar to that of their domestic equivalent Pequot Energy Limited Partners.

The fund invests in energy exploration companies, as well as in the energy service sector. Stock selection is made in exploration and production of oil and gas onshore and offshore seismic drilling and production services for the petroleum industry. The fund also invests in pipeline transportation services, and the manufacturing of materials, tools, and equipment used in oil and gas drilling production. The fund will attempt to take advantage of fundamental changes in the industry by identifying supply-and-demand shifts, restructuring and consolidation, production innovation, application of new technology, lease availability, regulatory changes, and production-volume growth driven by successful exploration and development of hydrocarbon assets.

To hedge risks, the investment manager may use short sales of stock, stock commodity options (puts and calls), and commodity puts and calls. The fund will be hedged at all times.

Also Pequot states that the outlook for the energy industry as a whole is excellent. Service company performances have improved significantly because oil companies must make substantial expenditures to replace production from declining reserves. New exploration frontiers such as deepwater have become economical for downsized and rationalized companies using innovative technologies.

## Performance

The fund has a short performance history, but it had a very good 1997: The fund started on January 2, 1997, at $100 a share. The net asset value on January 15, 1998, was $130.50.

## Fund Facts

| | |
|---|---|
| Minimum Investment: | $500,000 |
| Subscriptions and Redemptions: | Quarterly |
| Fees: | |
| | Annual Management Fee: 1% |
| | Incentive Fee: 20% of new net profits |
| Registration: | British Virgin Islands |

**My Opinion:  Dawson-Samberg wants to make their services available to international customers. The fund is not retail oriented; it is suitable for institutions and high-net-worth individuals. The fund prices are published in the *International Herald Tribune*.**

# 11

# NUTRITION AND FOOD DISTRIBUTION

## FIDELITY SELECT FOOD AND AGRICULTURE PORTFOLIO

If you want to invest in the energy sector, you have quite a number of possibilities. However, if you want to invest in the food and agricultural side of natural resources, not many possibilities are available, *and it is the better sector*. I think having exposure in food production and food distribution is at least as important as having exposure in energy. The financial industry has not recognized this fact yet, and Fidelity is one of the very few fund management companies that made a very successful fund in the food sector.

One of my favorite funds overall is Fidelity's Select Food and Agriculture Portfolio.[1] The fund invests mainly in equity securities of companies engaged in the manufacture, sale, or distribution of food and beverage products, agricultural products, and products related to the development of new food technologies.

## Performance as of March 31, 1998

The long-term performance of the fund is really great: it has never had a losing year so far (see Tables 11-1, 11-2, and 11-3; data from Internet, Fidelity Funds).

**TABLE 11-1   Cumulative Total Returns**

|              | With Load | No Load | S&P 500 |
| ------------ | --------- | ------- | ------- |
| Year to date | 2.69%     | 5.87%   | 13.95%  |
| 1-month      | 0.72%     | 3.83%   | 5.12%   |
| 3-month      | 2.69%     | 5.87%   | 13.95%  |
| 6-month      | 10.32%    | 13.72%  | 17.22%  |
| 1-year       | 27.8%     | 31.75%  | 48.00%  |

**TABLE 11-2   Average Annual Total Returns**

|         | With Load | No Load | S&P 500 |
| ------- | --------- | ------- | ------- |
| 1-year  | 27.8%     | 31.75%  | 48.00%  |
| 3-year  | 24.00%    | 25.27%  | 32.81%  |
| 5-year  | 18.48%    | 19.21%  | 22.4%   |
| 10-year | 19.55%    | 19.91%  | 18.94%  |

**TABLE 11-3   Historical Performance**

|              | Total Returns | Net Assets (millions of dollars under management) |
| ------------ | ------------- | ------------------------------------------------- |
| Year to date | 5.87%         | 244.6                                             |
| 1997         | 30.34%        | 309.1                                             |
| 1996         | 13.35%        | 252.8                                             |
| 1995         | 36.64%        | 240.1                                             |
| 1994         | 6.09%         | 85.5                                              |
| 1993         | 8.82%         | 173.1                                             |
| 1992         | 6.03%         | 117.4                                             |
| 1991         | 34.09%        | 122.0                                             |
| 1990         | 9.33%         | 32.1                                              |
| 1989         | 38.87%        | 23.0                                              |

## Fund Facts

Fees:
Sales charge:            3%
Minimum investment:      $2,500
Management fee:          0.60%
Top ten holdings (as of
March 31, 1998):         Sara Lee Corp.
                         H.J. Heinz Co.
                         Bestfoods
                         Pepsico Inc.
                         Ralston Purina Group
                         Coca-Cola Co.
                         Hershey Foods Corp.
                         Campbell Soup Co.
                         Safeway Inc. New
                         Nabisco Holdings CL A

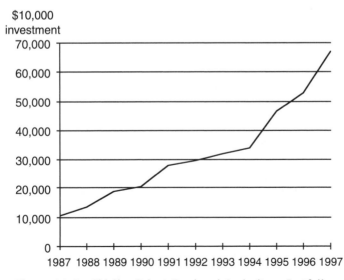

**Figure 11-1**  Fidelity Select Food and Agriculture Portfolio.

These holdings are 48 percent of the total portfolio. Since 1995 the fund has distributed capital gains and dividends.

Figure 11-1 represents a hypothetical investment of $10,000 in the fund in 1987. All dividends and capital gains are reinvested. Sales charges and redemption fees are not included.

**My Opinion: Fidelity recognized the exciting food sector 10 years ago, and they offer an excellent fund that invests in U.S. blue-chip food stocks that are really global brands. A $10,000 investment in 1987 grew into $67,513 as of May, 1998. The performance has been realized without great drawdowns or excessive volatility. The average net asset value increase has been over 20 percent a year, and this is an excellent result. This is a very good long-term investment, good for unnatural profits over time.**

# 12

## COMMODITY CERTIFICATES

### VALUE INVESTING: THE CASE FOR HARD ASSETS

When you invest, it is always prudent to take the long-term view. By analyzing inflation-adjusted or real commodity prices in the past 87 years, we can find compelling arguments for investing in commodities.[1] In stocks we know famed value investors like Warren Buffett, and Ben Graham, the original "value investor." His idea was "to buy low and sell fair." *Fair value* was defined as "the true, intrinsic worth of a security." His theory is based on "the reversion to the mean," which means that eventually prices come back to their long-term average.

We can also apply this value-investing theory in commodities. Inflation-adjusted prices have never been so cheap as they are today, and the relative value between stocks and bonds has never been so low. Stock markets experienced an extraordinary bull move from 1982 to 1997, but few people realize that commodities were in a bear market from 1980 to 1993. According to the value-investing theory, commodities will move back to their fair value in the near future.

Figure 12-1 tracks the inflation-adjusted price of an equally weighted portfolio of 25 commodities. The graph starts in 1921,

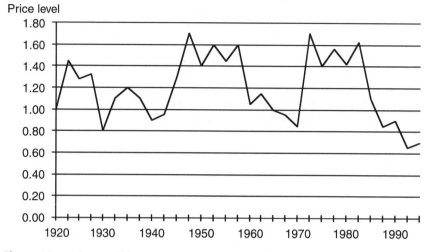

Price level

**Figure 12-1** Commodities in constant dollars (1921–1996). (*Source:* Di Tomasso.)

and the mean over time is around 1.2. With a present historical low mean of 0.7, there is considerable upward potential. If you buy natural resources now, you certainly buy at *very cheap historical levels.*

If you look at Figure 12-1, you see that life is organized in cycles and that the timing now is excellent to diversify a portfolio in commodities *at very cheap levels.* It is time again to own tangible hard assets. Other smart people think the same way. James Grant, editor of *Grant's Interest Rate Observer,* and Jim Rodgers, the astute investor who went around the world on his motorbike, have been touting hard assets for a long time. Peter Lynch, the legendary former asset manager of the Fidelity Magellan Fund, likes oil stocks. Their arguments are the same as those you find in this book: free markets are spreading around this world, and billions of low-income people are moving up the social ladder into the middle class. Demand for housing, fuel, and food is rising, while supplies of arable land give way for housing, offices, roads, and so on. In the 1970s, real estate was a great investment, and financial assets were terrible. Since 1982 real estate has been a bad investment, and financial assets have been going straight up. Just consider Citibank: nearly bankrupt 10 years ago, it is now one of the great retail banks in the world, and the stock shot up from $10 to $70. Now it has merged with Travelers to become the largest financial group in the world.

But now the hard-asset cycle is about to come back, and investments in natural resources, dealing in natural gas fields, agricultural land, art, and real estate can be excellent. Right now real estate is climbing fast in Europe, not only in London, for instance, but also in Spain, where plots and houses in Majorca and on the Costa del Sol after the recession from 1987 to 1994 are moving north again.

Chapter 13 explains how you can buy warrants on the Goldman Sachs Commodity Index-Total Return.

## GOLDMAN SACHS COMMODITY INDEX-TOTAL RETURN

This chapter is not so much a guide on how to realize unnatural profits with natural resources but more an illustration of what passive investments are and how risks can be reduced in a portfolio with natural resources. This chapter is meant more for institutional investors than for private individuals. Natural resources have some unique qualities that you do not find in other asset classes like real estate or bonds.

The American financial institution Goldman Sachs has an excellent research department in commodities and has developed a good commodity benchmark: the GSCI-TR (Goldman Sachs Commodity Index-Total Return). In the GSCI, Goldman Sachs has weighted the different commodities according to their production value. For instance, the value of the total crude oil production is higher than the platinum production. Therefore oil has a higher weighting in the index than platinum does. All in all, as of January 8, 1997, the GSCI contains 22 raw materials in five classes: energy—63.18 percent, agricultural products—18.91 percent, cattle—9.44 percent, industrial metals—6.27 percent, and precious metals—32.20 percent.[2] Figure 12-2 shows that this index rose from 2300 to 3700, or 60 percent, from mid-1995 until February 1997. Many natural resources like oil and non-ferrous metals were hit by the Asian crisis, and the GSCI-TR was trading around 2900 by the end of 1997.

It is important to understand the concept of *total return*. The GSCI-Total Return is the most widely used benchmark for commodities. There are two important differences between the GSCI-Spot Index and the GSCI-Total Return.

1. When a futures contract is bought, about 10 percent must be paid to the clearing house of the exchange as a down payment, or margin, and the rest (90 percent) can be invested in treasury bills or money market funds. This is exactly what happens in the GSCI-TR as well. Future contracts of underlying spot commodities of the GSCI Spot Index are bought on futures exchanges such as the Chicago Board of Trade. The margins are paid to the exchange, and the money market return of the balance is an essential extra revenue part of the GSCI-TR.

2. Relationships between spot prices and future prices fluctuate. When the supply of a commodity is limited and demand is

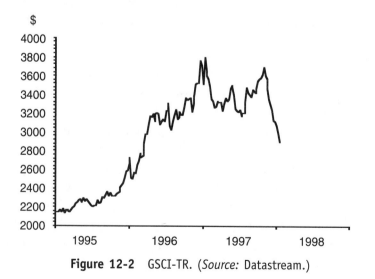

**Figure 12-2**   GSCI-TR. (*Source:* Datastream.)

high, everybody is prepared to pay a higher price for the spot commodity, and the spot is priced more expensive than the futures price. This spot premium over futures is called *backwardation*. When you own a futures contract that approaches expiration and you want to roll it over into the next future, you sell the expiring, more expensive futures contract and buy the next following future cheaper. For instance at the end of November you sell the (more expensive) December contract and buy the (cheaper) March contract. In this case you pocket the difference. This can happen also with the GSCI-TR. If the demand for the commodity is high, Goldman Sachs sells the expiring future at a premium and buys the next following futures contract cheaper. The profit is a part of the GSCI-TR. The opposite can happen as well. When supply and demand of a commodity are slack, spot prices are below future prices, and the new future must be bought at a premium to the spot price. In this case the investor loses the difference. The bottom line is that all these profits and losses go into the GSCI-TR.

And the difference between the GSCI-Spot Index and the GSCI-TR is huge: between 1970 and mid-1996, the GSCI-Spot Index rose 107 percent. This is an annual return of 2.8 percent. The GSCI-TR rose 2,840 percent, or an annual return of 13.76 percent. The lower the global stocks in commodities, the higher the capacity constraints, and the higher global demand for natural resources is, the more investors are paying higher prices for spot commodities and the bigger the backwardation between spot and futures prices becomes.[3]

## CORRELATIONS

What happens to the performance of your stock portfolio when you integrate commodities or natural resource stocks in your overall investment portfolio? In this stage it is important to understand the concept of correlations between the several asset classes. If your portfolio consisted only of stocks in the health care industry, your bottom-line performance would be very much dependent on the overall performance of the health care industry. When you start to mix stocks and bonds of other industry groups, your bottom-line performance will start to be more smooth and will be less volatile, because stocks in one asset class will go down in value while stocks in a different field might rise at the same time. It is like the old proverb: There are many ways leading to Rome. A temporary loss in one stock class will negate profits in stocks of another class. But after a couple of years, both asset classes will have risen significantly in value, with different paths of up-and-down movements. A perfect correlation is expressed by 1.00, a neutral correlation by 0.00, and a perfect negative correlation by –1.00. All asset classes are between 1.00 and –1.00.

Table 12-1 shows clearly that the Goldman Sachs Commodity Index[4] correlates negatively with all indexes.

## RISK AND RETURN

It is very possible to increase the return of the portfolio and to decrease the risk simultaneously by adding natural resource stocks to a conventional portfolio of stocks and bonds. The following charts illustrate a typical U.S. portfolio consisting of

**TABLE 12-1   Three-Month Correlations**

| Sector | S&P 500 | U.S. Bonds | Stocks— World | Bonds— World | Real Estate | GSCI |
|---|---|---|---|---|---|---|
| S&P 500 | 1.00 | 0.35 | 0.83 | 0.24 | –0.03 | –0.23 |
| U.S. Bonds | | 1.00 | 0.30 | 0.81 | –0.18 | –0.23 |
| Stocks—World | | | 1.00 | 0.45 | 0.00 | –0.25 |
| Bonds—World | | | | 1.00 | –0.19 | –0.09 |
| Real Estate | | | | | 1.00 | –0.09 |
| GSCI | | | | | | 1.00 |

stocks (60%) and bonds (40%). We now add the GSCI, and the net result of this exercise is an increase of the return (see Figure 12-3) and a lower volatility (see Figure 12-4).[5] We reach the same effect by adding natural resources stocks instead of the GSCI.

The following conclusions can be drawn:

• Commodities and stocks of natural resources correlate slightly negatively with stocks and bonds. By adding these commodities and natural resources stocks, the volatility in a portfolio is reduced and the rate of return is better. Therefore natural resources stocks and funds also function as risk minimizers and portfolio optimizers.

• The main reason why an investor should make an allocation in natural resources stocks is the fact that this asset class offers excellent returns when the world is in an economic upswing.

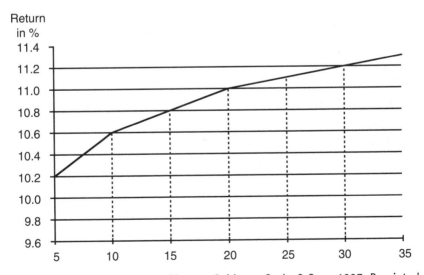

**Figure 12-3**  Adding the GSCI. (*Source:* Goldman, Sachs & Co. © 1997. Reprinted with permission.)

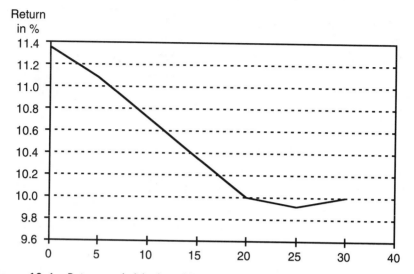

**Figure 12-4**  Return and risks by adding the GSCI. (*Source:* Goldman, Sachs & Co. © 1997. Reprinted with permission.)

## CERTIFICATES ON THE GSCI-TR

If you want to have exposure in the GSCI-TR, you can buy GSCI-TR *certificates* on the GSCI-TR.

You can buy and sell the certificates directly from:

Goldman Sachs International
London Branch
Fleet Street 133
London EC4A 2BB
England
Reuters Symbol: GSAF/GSCI-TR
Phone Derivatives Marketing Group: 0171-774-2897
Fax 0171-774-2020

Goldman has sold over $3 billion in these certificates to private and institutional investors. They make a market as liquid as high volume stocks traded on a stock exchange. The certificates track the GSCI-TR very well, and they are a passive allocation to commodities without ongoing administrative concerns. You can simply buy the certificate from Goldman Sachs and hold it in your portfolio. The securities are liquid, and their value is very transparent. The certificate is a two-year security issued by Goldman Sachs that tracks the GSCI-TR minus a hedge management fee of 1.5 percent per annum (or 3 percent over the full two-year period). The securities are unleveraged but are not principal protected. (The face value is not guaranteed.)

Goldman also issues certificates on their subindexes, such as the agricultural, petroleum, or industrial metals index. So if you have a strong opinion on grains or energy only, you can also buy those subindexes instead of the GSCI-TR.

Of course already existing certificates, with a shorter maturity, are traded as well: on January 16, 1998, you could buy July 1998 GSCI-TR certificates at \$2,877 or sell at \$2,855.

|                                         | Bid  | Ask  | GSCI Index |
|-----------------------------------------|------|------|------------|
| GSCI Listed Certificates (July 98)      | 2855 | 2877 | 2931       |
| GS Agricultural Certificates (July 98)  | 1235 | 1244 | 1277       |

For example, if you want to invest \$1 million, you can buy 347 GSCI-TR certificates at a price of \$2,877, for a total of \$998,319.

The security is denominated in U.S. dollars and settles in Euroclear/Cedel like a Eurobond. They are listed on the Luxembourg Stock Exchange. The minimum trading size is 10 certificates. Unfortunately these certificates may not be sold within the United States. Goldman Sachs effectively rolls the futures positions forward every month.

The GSCI consists of the following two main groups: Energy—56.80% and nonenergy—43.20%.

The *energy* group consists of the following four components:

1. Crude oil:          19.18%

2. Unleaded gas:       9.975%

3. Heating oil:        8.98%

4. Natural gas:        18.67%

The *nonenergy* group consists of the following four subgroups:

1. Industrial metals:  7.29%
   Aluminum:           3.43%
   Copper:             2.08%
   Lead:               0.31%
   Nickel:             0.45%
   Tin:                0.12%
   Zinc:               0.91%
2. Precious metals:    2.27%
   Gold:               1.89%
   Platinum:           0.16%
   Silver:             0.23%
3. Agricultural:       22.76%
   Wheat:              7.32%
   Corn:               4.76%
   Soybeans:           2.41%
   Cotton:             2.90%
   Sugar:              2.78%
   Coffee:             2.22%
   Cocoa:              0.38%
4. Livestock:          10.88%
   Cattle:             7.26%
   Hogs:               3.62%

**My Opinion:  An investment in GSCI-TR certificates is a passive investment. It tracks the GSCI, which means that there is not a portfolio manager who buys and sells commodities based on his own**

opinion. The certificates are not actively managed, and your performance does not depend on the skills of a portfolio manager. You have an exposure in a number of commodities, such as grains, metals, and oil. You must realize that the biggest weighting of the GSCI is in the energy complex (54 percent). I do believe that oil and dollar prices will rise in the coming years and that buying GSCI-TR certificates is therefore a good exposure in the energy complex.

Because of its negative correlation with other asset classes like stocks and bonds, the GSCI is an excellent investment to reduce volatility or risk. The absolute performance of the investment depends purely on the price development of natural resources. A further advantage is the fact that the investment is not leveraged; that is, if you invest $1,000, you really invest $1,000, and not $10,000. It is also a liquid investment: you can buy and sell from Goldman Sachs every day. Goldman Sachs has had huge success with this product. They have sold over $3 billion worth of certificates.

Big price increases can be expected in the agricultural complex. Grains are relatively underweighted in the GSCI-TR. If you want to have a substantial passive exposure in staple commodities like cocoa, sugar, cotton, and grains, you might additionally buy certificates of a subindex like the Goldman Sachs Agricultural Certificates.

# 13

## THE FULL INVESTMENT SPECTRUM

### INTRODUCTION

What can be concluded from the investment possibilities mentioned in Chapters 7 to 12?

1. Compared to other investment sectors, like the emerging markets, telecommunications, and high-yield bonds, **the natural resource area remains underresearched, and relatively few good investment possibilities are being offered to the general public**. This fact does not cease to amaze me because natural resources with all its problems and possibilities will become one of the very major investment themes in the twenty-first century. Because the public at large has not yet been made aware of the necessity to invest a part of its assets in the resources of Mother Earth, institutional and private investors can participate in this investment arena at relatively low prices. It is always best to start investing at the bottom—the arena where the biggest profits are made before the investing herd starts to follow suit.

2. Despite the lack of choice of a large variety among good natural resources funds, **investors are being made more and more sensitive to environmental problems that start to affect their lives daily**. Television and the press inundate the public with programs and articles concerning the environment. Many television channels around the world are broadcasting environmental programs about El Niño, pollution, deforestation, climate conferences, increased carbon dioxide ($CO_2$) output, and so on. The majority of the financial industry has failed to respond with proper products. Everybody is affected by a change in weather patterns the world over.

3. **The natural resources investment area has a great variety of opportunities.** Most of the natural resource products we have recommended specialize in certain aspects of the wide spectrum of natural resources. For instance, many funds invest in energy only; others invest nearly exclusively in American natural resource stocks; and other funds seek positive returns through investing in commodity futures only. Very few funds have a global strategy, and very few fund managers in natural resources have the experience and the global knowledge and do global research. Once I spoke to a manager of a $100-million natural resources fund in New York who could not name me a single Russian oil stock. His oil knowledge stopped at Exxon. This is not so bad, but he will miss many great opportunities.

4. **Blue chip food stocks in Europe will benefit greatly from the new currency, the Euro.** American institutional and private investors alike do not have to calculate their holdings anymore in pesetas, lires, or French francs. Currencywise it does not make any difference anymore whether you buy Unilever in Amsterdam, Danone in Paris, or Telepizza in Madrid. The valuations will all be in Euro. The transparency of European stocks will be greatly improved, and I expect a huge influx of

new American money to Europe. This will push European stocks much higher, so great investment opportunities in European natural resource stocks are being unfolded now.

## MAJOR INVESTMENT SECTORS

As the director of fund management at the Liechtensteinische Landesbank (LLB) in Liechtenstein, I offer customers investment opportunities that encompass all aspects of natural resources. I invest for customers not only in traditional natural resources but also in alternative natural resources, like solar and wind energy. Through diversification the investment risks are spread over many components of global resources.

You can learn more about our opinion on several natural resources and request a prospectus from the Liechtensteinische Landesbank through our Internet Web site (**www.llb.li**), or e-mail me directly at **r.jansen@llb-funds.li**.

I divide the full investment spectrum of natural resources as shown in Table 13-1.

Before I recommend several stocks, let me introduce you further to the 13 main subsectors:

1. *The Oil Majors*
One can invest in the major oil-producing companies around the world. The profitability of the majors has greatly increased through rationalization and is now much less dependent on rising or falling crude oil or natural gas prices.

2. *Energy Service Industry*
The demand for oil rigs, drilling tools, pipes, and so on has increased enormously, and so have the profit margins of this industry sector. The oil and gas service industry has been one of the best-performing investment sectors in the past three years.

**TABLE 13-1    The Full Investment Spectrum in Natural Resources**

| Oil and Gas | Metals |
|---|---|
| Oil Producers | Nonferrous Metal Mining and |
| Oil and  Gas Service Industry | Trading |
| Energy Futures | Precious Metals Mining |
|  | Physicals and Futures |

| Nutrition | Alternative Energy Sources |
|---|---|
| Food and  Beverage Producers | Solar Energy |
| Agricultural Service Industry | Wind Energy |
| Water Purifying Industry | Fuel-Cell Technology |
| Life Sciences | Hydroelectric Power Generation |
| Indexes, Warrants, |  |
|  Agricultural Futures |  |

**Venture Capital Projects**

Water Purifying
Agriculture
Alternative Energy Development

3. *Agriculture, Nutrition, Food Products, and Distribution*
Demand for affordable worldwide nutrition increases constantly.
The major seed- and food-producing companies are expanding
their global sales constantly. And companies selling or purifying
water boast very healthy profits as well.

4. *Agricultural Service Sector*
An often-overlooked sector is the service industry within the
agricultural sector. This sector has been in the doldrums since
the 1980s as prices were depressed and demand was slackening.
Today the big companies that produce farm machinery like tractors and combines enjoy a healthy demand for their products
and are very confident that they can double their turnover in the
coming five years. They transform agriculture from a low-tech
industry into an efficient high-tech business. Invest in farming
by satellite.

### 5. *Life Sciences*

Farmers' demand for insect- and disease-resistant seeds is constantly increasing. The 1997–1998 American soybean crop consisted of 11 to 13 percent genetically altered seeds. In 1999 this share is expected to go up to 25 percent.

### 6. *Certificates on Commodity Indexes*

Goldman Sachs not only issues certificates on the Goldman Sachs Total Return Index (GSCI-TR) but also on several subindexes, such as the energy, agricultural, and industrial metal indexes. These indexes do not correlate with general stock indexes such as the S&P 500 and therefore reduce the overall volatility in the portfolio. My investment program can invest in these certificates.

### 7. *Nonferrous Metal Mining*

Depending on stocks, consumption, and mining capacity, I can invest in nonferrous and precious metal mining producers.

### 8. *Precious Metals*

It is possible to hold precious metal accounts at the Liechtensteinische Landesbank AG. Without taking physical delivery, you can hold cash positions and be credited in several precious metals, like gold, palladium, silver, or platinum.

### 9. *Electricity*

In the alternative investment sector, I can invest in companies engaged in the building of hydroelectric power plants. The Three Gorges Dam is the best example of how huge the demand for electrical power is.

### 10. *Solar Energy*

This is going to be a very important investment sector. The twenty-first century is already called "the solar century." And I shall be at the forefront of investing in this quickly expanding energy source.

### 11. *Wind Power*

In Europe, wind-power generation has already taken a great leap, and further wind-power plants are being built from Denmark to Spain. My program can invest in wind-power producers.

### 12. *Water*

I can invest in companies that own important water sources and that sell water throughout the world. As mentioned before, water will become one of the major issues of the twenty-first century. Water will rise in price, and companies that sell water or purify water will do very well.

### 13. *Fuel-Cell Technology*

Gasoline or fossil fuel energy is the biggest polluter on earth. By 2005, several car companies expect to replace their products that run on gasoline with cars that run on pollution-free hydrogen. The technology is based on a reaction between hydrogen and oxygen in fuel cells. The development of fuel-cell-powered components will be one of the major breakthrough technologies of the twenty-first century. And my customers will invest in it. One of the major reasons Chrysler merged with Daimler Benz was to get access to fuel-cell technology.

## NATURAL RESOURCE STOCKS

An investment in stocks of companies that deal in natural resources is a standalone asset class, and it is important to know that the profitability of the investment does not depend primarily on rising prices of the underlying raw material. Stocks of raw materials can also offer very good returns on investments when commodity prices are *not* rising. The profit margins of natural resources stocks are widening because the processing companies modernize and rationalize the production process more and more. They are driven more by volume demand than by commodity price sensitivity. And last but not least, natural resources stocks have performed much better than the underlying commodities. We are in the early stage of a long-term volume-growth story, and simultaneously we will see the start of a cyclical recovery in commodity prices that are hovering around very low levels.

There are around 3,000 exchange-traded stocks in natural resources to choose from. I am engaged in this sector for the following reasons:

• In analyzing investment cycles, natural resources stocks outperform indexes in the second half of an economic cycle, when demand for natural resources exceeds supplies and inventories decrease sharply. This process is underway right now. We are in the eighth year of the current U.S. expansion.

• Following the underperformance of natural resources stocks in the past two years, natural resource companies are valued lower than industrial stocks. Yet the outlook for global resource companies for earnings growth is superior because these companies typically become highly profitable in the late stages of an economic cycle.

• Resource stocks are out of favor (see Figure 13-1) and are underweighted in institutional portfolios. In 1980 resource stocks were 28 percent of an institutional portfolio, and today they are only 8 percent. This is a bullish signal.

The following companies are front-runners in the natural resources sector and look very promising in the coming years. This list is certainly not complete and represents only a small selection of outstanding companies in the resource area. As a fund manager, I can change my opinion at all times and invest or divest accordingly in a large variety of natural resource producing stocks around the globe.

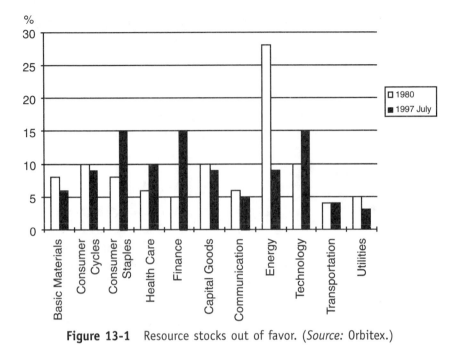

**Figure 13-1**   Resource stocks out of favor. (*Source:* Orbitex.)

## The Oil Majors

If we think of the large oil companies in the world, we automatically think of Exxon, Shell, and so on. But the Russian oil companies are becoming more and more "major," and their stocks offer good investment possibilities.

British Petroleum (BP) is a very well-run oil company. BP also made a huge financial commitment to become one of the major players in solar energy as well. The stock price more than doubled in the past three years (see Figure 13-2), and the sunshine of the solar century will be reflected in the stock price.

The Russian majors are still cheap. Investors who had the guts to invest in these companies three years ago have made truly unnatural profits (see Figure 13-3). Huge profits were made not in the least by Russian tycoons and bank moguls.

The largest gas company in the world is Gazprom, which rose 500 percent in a year and a half (see Figure 13-4).

**Figure 13-2** British Petroleum (May 1995–May 1998). (*Source:* Datastream.)

## Energy Service Industry

The oil exploration business is booming. And the business of "the majors" fuels the business of the oil service industry. Consequently investors have pumped up the stocks in 1997.

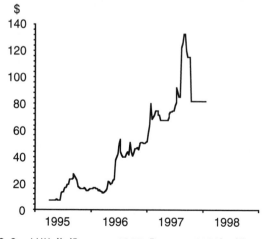

**Figure 13-3** LUKoil (January 1995–January 1998). (*Source:* Datastream.)

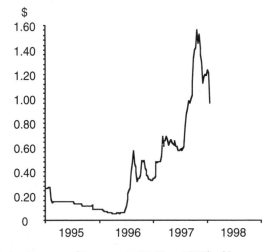

**Figure 13-4**  Gazprom (January 1995–May 1998). (*Source:* Datastream.)

In the energy sector, demand for oil-drilling equipment out-strips supply. In 1979, there were close to 7,000 oil rigs in the world, and today there are only 2,000 rigs (see Figure 13-5). But oil demand is firmly up.

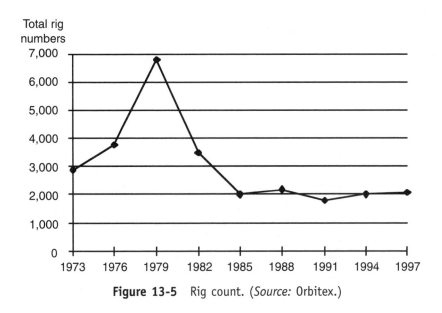

**Figure 13-5**  Rig count. (*Source:* Orbitex.)

**Figure 13-6** Baker Hughes (May 1995–May 1998). (*Source:* Datastream.)

Stocks of oil service companies outperformed the S&P 500 in 1997. Because Asian oil demand has been dampened by the economic crisis, oil prices came down and oil service stocks lost some of their premiums and again represent very attractive buying levels.

If you want to drill for dollars, you might want to take a look at the long-term performance of the following stocks:

• *Baker Hughes* is a drilling-equipment company, and it expects its revenues to double over the next five years (see Figure 13-6).

• *Transocean Offshore* is a leading provider of deepwater and harsh-environment contract drilling services for oil and gas wells. The company currently operates 30 mobile offshore drilling rigs and has contracted with a Spanish shipyard for construction of a new state-of-the-art dynamically positioned drillship. The company provides these drilling rigs, related equipment, and work crews to its customers on either a dayrate or a turnkey basis to drill wells at offshore locations (see Figure 13-7).

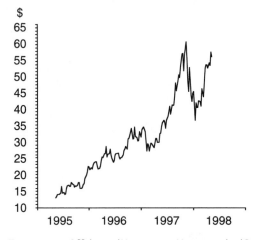

**Figure 13-7**    Transocean Offshore (May 1995–May 1998). (*Source:* Datastream.)

• *Smith International* is a leading worldwide supplier of products and services to the oil and gas drilling and production industries. Smith produces drilling fluids and systems, drill bits, and drilling and completion products (see Figure 13-8).

**Figure 13-8**    Smith International (May 1995–May 1998). (*Source:* Datastream.)

• *Schlumberger* is very well known in Europe. The chance is big that the gas pump at the gas station you use is made by Schlumberger. The share price tripled in three years (see Figure 13-9). Schlumberger also signed a strategic alliance with Russia's largest oil company, Yuksi. Schlumberger will outsource a slice of its $2 billion-a-year oil-field services costs to a new joint venture company. The new company will service a great number of Yuksi's oil fields as well as oil fields of other oil companies.

## Agriculture, Nutrition, and Food Distribution

An important aspect of natural resources investments is the stocks of food companies. Despite trade wars, the food trade between Europe and the United States is expanding at a rapid pace. In the European press, readers get many stories about American and European government agencies bickering about the mad cow disease and genetically altered soybeans. Protectionists and environmentalists try to block imports and exports, but the reality is totally different: today in Europe you can buy American mozzarella and cheddar cheeses and Mahi-Mahi fish from Hawaii. And with prices of French wines going through

**Figure 13-9** Schlumberger (May 1995–May 1998). (*Source:* Datastream.)

the roof, sales of excellent California wines are increasing substantially. In 1996 total agricultural exports from the United States to European Union countries soared by 33 percent to $9.3 billion.

But the European trade to the United States soared as well: it rose 21 percent to a record $6.5 billion in 1996. European products that please the American palate the most are the cheeses, the liquors, and the chocolates. At work are the globalization of food companies and disappearing trade barriers. Import tariffs on dairy products, tobacco, flowers, and spices are being lowered substantially. Also supermarket chains like the British Sainsbury or the Dutch Royal Ahold NV have vast interest in international food-processing plants or in other supermarket chains in countries like the United States or Brazil. Marks & Spencer from the United Kingdom is spending £2 billion ($3.4 billion) to expand their food chain.[1]

• *Unilever* is a very well-managed food conglomerate (see Figure 13-10). It is, among many other things, the biggest frozen-fish supplier in the world. Recently it developed a seal with the International World Wildlife Fund. The seal will be printed

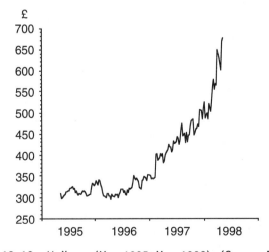

**Figure 13-10**  Unilever (May 1995–May 1998). (*Source:* Datastream.)

on every package of frozen fish, and it will indicate that Unilever fish products come from sustainable fish catch or sustainable fish farming only. I would not be surprised if one day Unilever merged with Nestlé.

- *Sara Lee* is a conglomerate with an excellent food business (see Figure 13-11). It is very big in coffee, and it owns, for instance, Douwe Egberts in Holland.

- Spain's *Telepizza* is one of my favorite companies. Pizzas are as Italian as spaghetti. But the company Telepizza is as Spanish as a paella. In 1988 Leo Pujals, a migrant from Cuba, opened his first pizza shop in Madrid. This was the first home-delivery service of pizzas by motorcycle in Spain. Ten years later he opened store number 440 and expanded the business to Chile, Portugal, Poland, and Mexico. Telepizza has been the darling of the Madrid Bolsa (stock exchange). Telepizza's stock was floated on the Madrid stock exchange in November 1996 at 2.231 pesetas and stood at 22.000 pesetas in April 1998. In less than 18 months, the stock rose 986 percent. Telepizza plans a 1-for-20

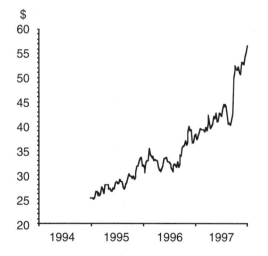

**Figure 13-11** Sara Lee Corp. (December 1994–December 1997). (*Source:* Datastream.)

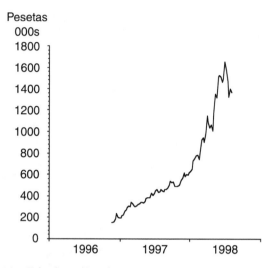

**Figure 13-12**  Telepizza (October 1996–August 1998). (*Source:* Datastream.)

stock split in 1998 (see Figure 13-12). Telepizza has big plans for eastern Europe, and the stock has great potential—an ideal takeover candidate for a big food conglomerate. This is a typical example of an excellent company in Europe started by a motivated man with an entrepreneurial spirit. If you only buy American resource funds, you don't have access to these new ventures outside the United States.

• *ConAgra* is one of the largest and most profitable food companies (see Figure 13-13). This company produces a variety of bulk commodities and food products with—in the United States—strong brand names. Next to fertilizers, flour milling, and speciality grains, ConAgra produces refrigerated products such as Country Pride chickens, Armour hot dogs, and Butterball turkeys. Other grocery products are Peter Pan peanut butter, Hunt's ketchup, and Orville Redenbacher popcorn. ConAgra is a blue-chip corporation of which most Americans have never heard. The stock has a great track record: it has greatly outperformed the S&P 500 in the past 10 years, and it has averaged a 15.6 percent annual increase in earnings

**Figure 13-13**  ConAgra (May 1995–May 1998). (*Source:* Datastream.)

per share since 1980. Therefore it has a leading position in the food industry. The management intends to make Con-Agra the largest and the most profitable food company in the world in the next 10 years. Total sales in the year ending May 25, 1997, reached $24 billion, and the company has 20 products that are selling at more than $100 million.[2] And none of the products bear the name ConAgra. The turnover is comparable to the agribusiness side of the second largest family-owned company of the United States, Cargill Inc. But Con-Agra still has a few competitors with higher annual sales: Philip Morris, the mother company of Kraft Foods; Miller Brewing; Post cereals; and Nestlé of Switzerland, which is the world's largest food company with $45.5 billion in sales in 1996. ConAgra has its foot in the door in every aspect of the food business, from the farm to the dinner plate.

• *Nestlé* is the biggest food company in the world (see Figure 13-14). Nescafé, its instant coffee brand, is the second-largest, best-known global brand after Coca-Cola. And the revenues from water is the company's second-largest source of income. Nestlé has recently rejuvenated its top management. One thing that

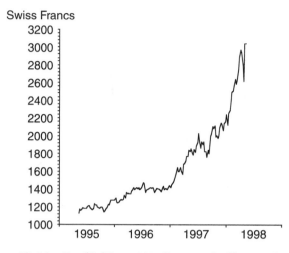

**Figure 13-14** Nestlé (May 1995–May 1998). (*Source:* Datastream.)

fascinates me is how fast Nestlé expands into new markets like central and eastern Europe. In 1995 Nestlé had a very small food business in Poland, an upcoming country with 38 million people, a strong currency, and an area as big as France. Today Nestlé is the leading food company in Poland. Nestlé's headquarters are in Vevey, Switzerland, but only 4 percent of its total production is produced in Switzerland.

• *CPC International* produced foods on the basis of corn and was one of the leading food companies in the world. CPC has been split up in two companies: Bestfoods and Corn Products International. *Bestfoods* has $8.6 billion in revenues. It operates in over 60 countries and sells its products in 110 countries. Among its global brands are Knorr and Hellmann's (a very well-known mayonnaise brand in the United States). The stock symbol on the New York Stock Exchange (NYSE) is BFO. *Corn Products International* generates $1.5 billion in sales. It produces pharmaceutical, soft drink, paper, and corrugated paper products. It is one of the leading producers of cornstarch and dextrose. The NYSE symbol is CPO.

• *Danone*, a French food company, had its stock nearly doubled in 12 months (see Figure 13-15).

• *Seagram* has big plans in China, and its chairman, Edgar Bronfman Sr., takes the long-term view. In 1988 Seagram acquired Tropicana, an orange juice brand with $2.1 billion in global sales in 1997. Seagram now has grand plans to bring Tropicana orange juice to China and let the Chinese drink an American orange juice. In the first phase, Seagram will ship orange juice from Florida to China, but Seagram intends to cultivate land along the Yangtze River in southwest China for growing orange trees. The region has more or less the same climate as Florida, and Seagram started a $55 million joint venture with the Chonqing Three Gorges Construction Group. The company is called Tropicana Beverages Greater China Ltd. Seagram will bring the technology, the seeds, and the fertilizers, and the Chinese will oversee and help 40,000 farm families with financing to plant more than a million orange trees. Both parties will share the cost of constructing a juice-processing factory. Seagram plans that the factory and infrastructure will be opera-

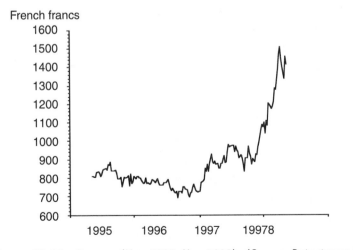

**Figure 13-15**   Danone (May 1995–May 1998). (*Source:* Datastream.)

tional by 2005. I think Seagram will have a great future in China with 1.2 billion consumers right on their doorstep.[3]

## Agricultural Service Industry

In Chapter 10 we offered insight into the oil service industry and oil service funds. We live in a time with buzz words like "lean and mean" production, "first in, first out" inventory management, and "outsource tasks" that other companies can do faster and cheaper. The prime beneficiaries are oil service companies. The same principles, however, count for the companies that offer services and tools for global *agriculture*. This industry sector has cut surplus capacity, modernized production lines, and made components on a just-in-time basis. It is well prepared for great profit figures for the next 10 years. In 1996 the farm-machinery industry had total sales of $43 billion, of which half was tractors and the rest other equipment, including combine harvesters and baling systems. This sector was losing money until the end of 1993, but the general surge in the global economy and the big demand for grain worldwide has intensified the demand for tractors. The combined profit of the big five (Agco, Deere, Case, New Holland, and Claas) was $1.5 billion in 1996.[4] There are some very interesting companies making products to get the grain into the bins. This is a great area for investing with real chances of unnatural profits. The outlook for tractor sales looks especially bright in central and eastern Europe, China, and South America. You can harvest handsome profits by investing in stocks of the big five tractor companies. Sentiment among the producers is excellent because demand for grain worldwide is so high. With firm grain prices, income of farmers rises, and they want the best machinery to achieve the highest yields. Invest in tractor companies that produce farm equipment with high-tech cockpits.

The largest companies in this field are Agco and John Deere. *Agco* is one of the world's five biggest tractor makers. Agco has brands like Massey Furguson, Hesston, and Gleaner. The beauty of Agco is the horizontal structure of the company; 55 percent of all activities are being outsourced to other companies, despite its huge size.

Agco has assembling plants in the United States, in Missouri, Kansas, and Ohio and in the United Kingdom, France, Germany, Brazil, and Argentina. Agco's aim is to assemble products that are totally tailor-made for specific markets. A tractor for Poland is simple in structure and very reliable. An American tractor might have more convenience features. The better the products are tailored for the customers, the higher the sales. Agco practices "lean" manufacturing. They have just-in-time production lines and low stocks, and they rely on outside suppliers to make components. With this strategy, they can accomplish innovations much faster than by being a fully integrated business building a product from A to Z.

Agco seeks to double the company's turnover of $2.1 billion in the next three or four years (see Figure 13-16). In autumn 1997, Agco had $1 billion in cash to go on a shopping spree to achieve these goals. Agco intends to acquire smaller tractor companies to enlarge its market share. "We are not projecting any decline in

**Figure 13-16**   Agco (May 1995–May 1998). (*Source:* Datastream.)

demand [in agricultural machines] for the next three years," says Robert Ratcliff, chairman of Agco.[5]

The *John Deere Company*'s worldwide agricultural-equipment segment manufactures tractors and tillage, soil preparation, seeding, and harvesting machinery. It also produces sprayers and hay and forage equipment—an integrated precision-farming technology. The increasing global demand for agricultural equipment is reflected in John Deere's profits and in John Deere's stock price (see Figure 13-17).

Other big players in the farm machinery area are Case in the United States, Claas in Germany, and New Holland in Italy. The majority shareholder of New Holland is Fiat. For the coming five years the conditions for agriculture are very upbeat, and all these companies intend to increase their tractor sales in central and eastern Europe, in Asia, and in Latin America.

## Life Sciences

Bioengineered crops and food products are bringing about huge changes in agriculture.

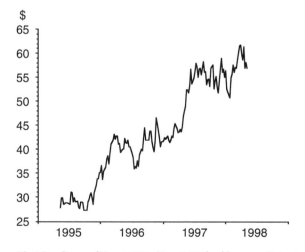

**Figure 13-17**   Deere (May 1995–May 1998). (*Source:* Datastream.)

- *Monsanto* wants to become the Microsoft of bioengineering. Biotechnology was a small side business 10 years ago, but Monsanto has made a huge commitment to make this its core business. Monsanto goes all out to cash in on gene-transfer technology. The company believes that bioengineering will fundamentally change agriculture in the future.[6]

Monsanto has spent $1 billion on in-house research and development, and it has collected a number of smaller companies that specialize in this field, for example, Calgene, a leader in technology in oil seeds and bioengineered tomatoes. It also bought Agracetus, which holds patents in cottonseed engineering.[7]

Now Monsanto wants to blend its bulk-engineered commodities with traditionally grown fare, but this encounters resistance from European consumer groups.

It is also starting to market its first generation of engineered products—insect-resistant potatoes, bollworm resistant cottonseeds, and herbicide-resistant soybeans and rapeseed. But its big success is the range of products under the brand name of "Roundup." There is a Roundup herbicide killing anything looking green. This product has increased the yield per acre in soybeans from 45 bushels per acre to 52 bushels. Suppose that you are a farmer and that you are able to increase the yield of your farmland and thus your income substantially. You can imagine that this product is very popular.

Monsanto is very strong in agricultural biotechnology, and from 1996 on American farmers have started to plant millions of acres with genetically altered corn, soybean, cotton, and potato seeds. The *American* farmer especially has a huge appetite for these designer seeds. According to analysts, the market for transgenic seeds will reach $6.5 billion in 10 years.[8] Many predict that in five years half of the Farm Belt will be planted with crops resistant to worms, fungus, flies, and so on.

But Monsanto has its eyes on China. That is the continent where yields must be increased, and Monsanto salespeople are now learning Chinese.

According to Monsanto, *the future of agriculture lies in herbi-cide-resistant crops with higher yields at lower costs.* Monsanto was an old-line chemical company from St. Louis, but it is turning out to be one of the leaders in agribusiness. This is reflected in Monsanto's stock price, which gained 74 percent in 1995, 71 percent in 1996, and 31 percent in 1997 (see Figure 13-18).

• *Novartis,* Monsanto's biggest competitor, is the Swiss giant that is the net result of the merger between Ciba-Geigy and Sandoz in 1996 (see Figure 13-19). In 1998 Novartis will probably be listed on the New York Stock Exchange.

**My Opinion: If you do not buy natural resources funds but manage your own portfolio actively, you should buy Monsanto stock on the New York Stock Exchange and Novartis stock in Zurich, Switzerland. These companies produce the seeds and are profiting greatly from increased demand for grains. Their seeds will enlarge the world grain crops by 15 percent. The demand is huge, and by buying these shares you participate in the growing earn-**

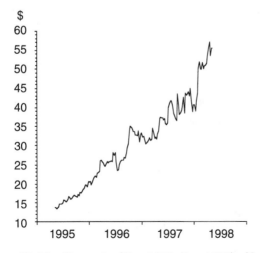

**Figure 13-18**  Monsanto (May 1995–May 1998). (*Source:* Datastream.)

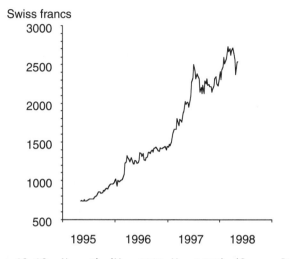

Swiss francs

**Figure 13-19** Novartis (May 1995–May 1998). (*Source:* Datastream.)

**ings these companies generate from seed products that are resistant to diseases, insects, drought, pollution, and herbicides.**

• *Zeneca* is a big player in Great Britain in the "designer genes" business. They predict huge improvements in the coming five years. New seeds of wheat, rice, fruit, and vegetables will be developed that are resistant to infestations by fungus. "Current technologies are like the Model T Ford, compared to what we are coming up with," declares Nigel Poole, Zeneca group manager.[9]

After merger mania in the banking and the information technology worlds, the next takeover wave might take place in the seed business. A prime target in the United States is *Pioneer Hi-Bred International* (PHB), the largest producer of corn seeds and also one of the prime soybean seed producers. PHB's profits have grown nearly 20 percent a year and are rising further as grain demand is rising. So with or without a takeover, this stock has great potential. *Dekalb Genetics* and *Delta & Pine Land Co.* were just gobbled up by Monsanto. Monsanto paid $4.4 billion for them, and it is fast becoming the dominant force in biotech-nology. The company has predict-ed that American farmers will be planting about 49.4 million acres with insect-resistant seeds, versus 19.7 million acres in 1997.

Stocks of food companies that produce health-enhancing prod-ucts are becoming an important investment theme within the food component of natural resources. Pharmaceutical elements are blended with traditional food fare. These new products are therefore called "nutraceuticals" (a combination of nutrition and pharmaceuticals) or "pharma-food." These products are a lot more expensive than conventional products, and profit margins are higher as well. Nestlé and Raisio are two examples of com-panies that are doing well with Pharma-foods.

Nestlé has had great success with its LC1 yogurt products in Switzerland and has captured a fifth of the Swiss yogurt market in the first six months of its existence. LC1 con-tains bacteria that enhance one's digestion and improve one's resistance.

Raisio is a Finnish food and chemical company that produces a cholesterol-cutting margarine called Benecol. Laboratory tests have concluded that cholesterol levels can be reduced by 15 percent when Benecol is consumed on a daily basis. Raisio has had fabulous success with this product in Finland, and it is next to Nokia, the darling of the Finnish stock exchange in Helsinki. Raisio's shares have soared by 1,200 percent in two years. In 1998, Raisio plans to bring to the market a low-fat version of Benecol with only 40 percent the fat content of the original version.

Johnson & Johnson, the U.S. healthcare giant, has signed a contract with Raisio to market Benecol globally and to develop Benecol into a global brand, launching a range of Benecol pharma-food products in the United States.

Pharma-food products are big business in Japan. Already over 80 products are available there that promise to lower cho-lesterol levels or to reduce heart disease and cancer.

## Precious Metals

My investment program can invest in precious metals through a metal account at the Liechtensteinische Landesbank AG in Vaduz, Liechtenstein. In this metal account it is possible to buy and sell metals such as gold, silver, palladium, and platinum. If squeezes in a precious metal occur, customers will participate in a discrete and unleveraged way.

## Electricity

In the long term it is very wise to invest in companies that produce power plants to generate electricity, like the Swiss/Swedish company ABB (Asea Brown Boveri), quoted on the Swiss Stock Exchange (see Figure 13-20).

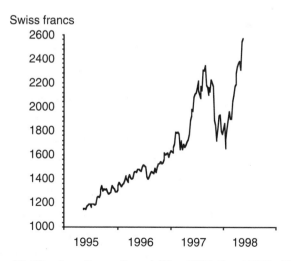

**Figure 13-20**    Asea Brown Boveri (May 1995–May 1998). (*Source:* Datastream).

**My Opinion:  Electricity demand is rising exponentially, just like the global population. You must have stocks in your portfolio of companies that are in the business of building hydropower plants. The Europeans are the big players here, such as the Swiss/Swedish company Asea Brown Boveri, Siemens from Germany, and GEC/Alsthorn from England and France. These companies are engaged in big public projects like building power generators worth $740 million at the Three Gorges Dam in China. In China the Europeans have been eating the American's lunch. And we are not talking about peanuts here.**

The stock price has suffered somewhat from slackening Asian demand, but I think these levels are very attractive to buy long term.

## Fuel-Cell Technology

*Ballard Power Systems* is the Vancouver-based company with a large know-how in the development of advanced-fuel-cell technology. It produces fuel cells that can be used in cars to generate electricity. Cars, as $CO^2$ emitters, are the major source of pollution today, and with the introduction of hydrogen and fuel cells, this can be a phenomenon of the past. Another big advantage will be a substantial noise reduction. It will be like riding a noise-free electrical golf cart. In the near future half of the world's population will live in megacities. The quality of life in a big city is, among other things, greatly influenced by the noise level of the environment. Detroit has made an amazing commitment to environmentalism, and the car industry is running in high gear to develop fuel-cell technology. Hundreds of millions of dollars are being committed to develop "green" cars. Fuel cells provide the fuel to power an electric motor through a chemical reaction between hydrogen and oxygen. Cars can fill up at the same service stations they always used because hydrogen gas can be extracted from liquid fuels. It will take a few more years before fuel-cell cars will be seen on highways. A city or a world without car noises will be a lot closer to Paradise. The car companies are pushing the development of fuel cells at commercially viable volumes.

*Ford Motor Company* will invest $420 million in a partnership between *Daimler Benz* and Ballard Power Systems. This investment will give Ford 15 percent of Ballard shares and also 23 percent of DBB Fuel Cell Engines—a Daimler subsidiary that also develops fuel-cell systems. Thus, Ford joins the leader in fuel-cell technology (Daimler Benz). Daimler Benz's investments in fuel-cell technology total around C$1 billion (Canadian dollars). The goal of this joint venture is to reduce the costs of fuel-cell technology and to make it commercially interesting for practical applications in large series. Fuel-cell products can later also be sold to other car companies.[10]

If you are still not convinced that it is possible to realize

**Figure 13-21** Ballard Power Systems (May 1995–May 1998). (*Source:* Datastream.)

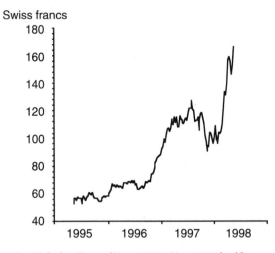

**Figure 13-22** Daimler Benz (May 1995–May 1998). (*Source:* Datastream.)

**Figure 13-23** Ford Motor Company (December 1994–December 1997). (*Source:* Datastream.)

unnatural profits in natural resources of the future, see Figure 13-21 for the stock price development of Ballard Power Systems.

Car companies like Mercedes Benz, Toyota, and Ford are investing heavily in cars with clean energy. Daimler Benz A-class cars will be equipped with fuel cells, and the company hopes to sell 40,000 fuel-cell cars annually by 2006. (See Figure 13-22.) Ford is going green as well and is striving to put its first fuel-cell car on the road by 2004. (See Figure 13-23.) General Motors (GM) has been pursuing its own fuel-cell program, but in 1998 GM also purchased $2.5 million worth of fuel cells from Ballard Power Systems. This added some fuel to the opinion of market observers that GM had run into difficulties in developing its own fuel cells. And I am sure that Daimler fuel-cell technology will be implemented by Chrysler cars, now that Chrysler has merged with Daimler Benz

The big stumbling block to commercializing fuel-cell vehicles is the cost. Ten years ago, a fuel-cell car would have cost $20 million. In 1998 the sticker price would be around $200,000. Ballard Power Systems projects the production of 250,000 fuel cells annually by 2008. A green car by that time will cost no more than a car with a conventional engine.

Despite the general stock market slump in Tokyo, Toyota stock did relatively well (see Figure 13-24). They are very well positioned for the twenty-first century.

## Solar Energy

The oil majors are turning into solar majors. *Royal Dutch/Shell*—the Anglo-Dutch oil giant—is investing HFL 500 million ($220 million) in the development of solar energy. The company Shell Solar will produce in the city of Helmond, Holland, 1 million photovoltaic cells a year. This represents 287,750 square feet of solar panels. In a second phase Shell wants to enlarge the production in 1998 to 1,075,000 square feet of solar panels. This company will be part of a new Shell unit called Shell

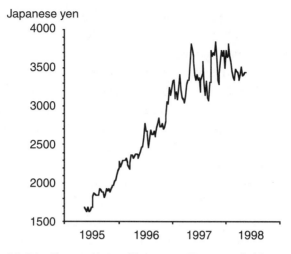

**Figure 13-24** Toyota Motor (May 1995–May 1998.) (*Source:* Datastream.)

International Renewables. Shell wants to become a big player in solar energy and strives to obtain a market share of 10 percent by the year 2010. Shell estimates that by that time global sales in photovoltaics will be HFL 121 billion ($5 billion).[11] Shell is making a serious effort to become a big provider in renewable, clean energy. Shell recognizes that the world market for solar cells is growing at lightning speed and estimates that solar energy needs between 2020 and 2030 will have a market share between 5 percent and 10 percent of total energy. According to Shell, fossil fuel energy will still have a market share of around 50 percent by the year 2050. About half of the solar panels will be exported to emerging markets for solar home systems.

If Shell's forecast proves to be correct, the content of $CO^2$ emissions has a chance to be reduced substantially only in the *second half of the next century.*

*British Petroleum* also has big plans in solar energy. This company has been investing in solar power for the past 15 years. At the end of 1997, BP opened the world's largest and most modern solar-panel-manufacturing plant of its kind, in the San Francisco Bay Area city of Fairfield, California. BP is committed to make the technology competitive in supplying peak electricity demand within the next 10 to 15 years.

Another big player in the future will be the Japanese company *Sanyo*. It is going to mass-produce its HIT Power 21 hybrid solar cells. Sanyo believes that these cells reduce energy loss to an absolute minimum and that they contain the world's highest conversion efficiency.

*Enron* is one of the biggest energy conglomerates in the world (see Figure 13-25). They recently bought Zond, the leading wind-power energy company in the United States, and they have a major stake in Solarex, America's second largest solar cell manufacturer.

*Bechtel Enterprises*, once a leader in nuclear power plants, has formed a joint venture with *Pacific Corp.*, a leader in operating coal-fired generators. Together they formed *EnergyWorks*, to invest in solar power and other "human-scale energy systems." And a big Japanese trading company named *Tomen* is investing $1.2 billion to erect 1,000 wind turbines in Europe during the next five years.

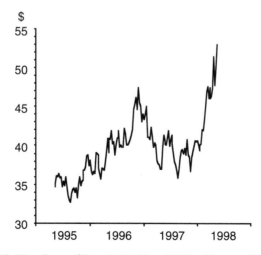

**Figure 13-25**   Enron (May 1995–May 1998). (*Source:* Datastream).

## Water

Great profit opportunities exist in the water purifying industry. French water utility Suez Lyonnaise des Eaux is a good example (see Figure 13-26). The company is the world leader in water-treatment and distribution systems. This area is in tremendous demand in emerging markets. If you want to buy stock of companies that own wells and global water brands, you mustbuy *Nestlé* stock. Nestlé sells water all over the world under brand names like San Pellegrino, Perrier, Vittel, Contrex, Arrowhead, Poland Spring, Buxton, Vera, Calistoga, and so on.

Further excellent water investments in the United States are stocks like Culligan and American Water Works.

## Other Investments

As you can see from the previous chapters, natural resources cover a very wide spectrum. Venture capital projects in natural

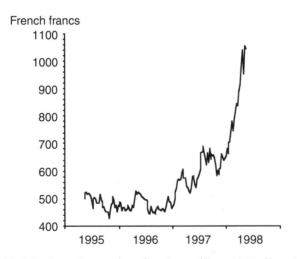

**Figure 13-26** Suez Lyonnaise des Eaux (May 1995–May 1998). (*Source:* Datastream.)

resources can also be very exciting. For instance, the Ukraine has always been the bread basket of Russia and has so-called black soil. This fertile soil offers great investment opportunities, and the Dutch have already started to build acres and acres of new greenhouses. Ninety-five percent of the newly restored flower exports come from the Dutch-built greenhouses. The Dutch also feed cows with Western-style animal feed products, and they have installed robots to milk them. So Ukraine cows are getting healthy again, and nowadays they give as much milk as their counterparts in western Europe or the United States. All in all, there are great agricultural investment opportunities in the Ukraine, and I get requests about them on a regular basis.

I also have promising projects on my desk for purifying water in Malaysia. The big cities there have serious water problems, and industry and hotels alike will be forced to buy water at high prices if they want to stay in business. The area of water-purification systems will be a very profitable one in which to invest. The Malaysian company ETD SDN specializes in modular treatment of toxic and conventional liquid waste. Their Swiss technology is called EMPS (enhanced modular purification system) and it is the new generation of decontamination. The company specializes in water purification, solid waste decontamination, and air detoxification with ozone-enriched water tanks. The company was set up by the Malaysian consul in Switzerland, Jeffery Sandragesan, who introduced both Swiss technology and investors.

## THE LIECHTENSTEINISCHE LANDESBANK AG (LLB)

The oldest bank of Liechtenstein is the Liechtensteinische Landesbank Aktiengesellschaft (LLB). The LLB was founded in 1861, and it was 100 percent state-owned until 1993. The bank is now partly being privatized, but the state will always hold the majority of shares, which gives extra security to its customers. It is the biggest bank in Liechtenstein with a 1997 balance-sheet total of $7.2 billion and a net profit of $58.5 million, with over $17 billion in customer assets. The bank specializes in private banking.

The new headquarters in the capital, Vaduz, were opened in 1996. The ecological awareness of the bank is very big, and solar panels on the roof provide the building with most of its energy needs.

The bank offers a range of in-house and public funds in U.S. stocks and bonds and German and Swiss bond and stock funds. The bank also offers a fund that invests in the big banks of Liechtenstein (LLB Liechtenstein Banken Invest) with an excellent track record. In the first 21 months, the fund rose by 151 percent. Further details of the Liechtensteinische Landesbank and natural resources are published on the Internet Web site www.llb.li.

The author consults and advises large institutions and private clients on investment opportunities in natural resources. Your queries can be directed to:

Roland A. Jansen
Director
LLB Fondsleitung AG
Städtle 17
9490 Vaduz
Principality of Liechtenstein
Phone 41-75-236-81-40
Fax 41-75-236-81-46
E-mail: r.jansen@llb-funds.li

# GLOSSARY

**actively managed funds**  The investment manager of the fund actively executes transactions on behalf of the fund according to his own strategy.

**arbitrage strategies**  Investment strategies that capture price disparities between or within markets. This is the contrary of "buy and hold" strategies: buy a stock and hope and pray the stock goes up. Arbitrage strategies are nondirectional: the success of the strategy only depends on price disparities between markets and not on whether a stock rises in price.

**backwardation**  A market situation in a commodity in which nearby supplies are tight and demand is high. Small supplies and big demand cause cash prices to rise over futures prices and the price difference is called backwardation.

**closed-end funds**  Closed-end funds open their doors to investors during a subscription period. Then the door closes. Investors who still want to buy depend on the sellers of the fund. If the fund is popular, buyers must pay a premium to the net asset value. If the fund at a certain moment is less popular, buyers can buy the fund at a discount of the net asset value. Extreme example: the premium of Soros' Quota Fund was 67 percent over the net asset value in September 1997.

**contango**  A market situation in a commodity where supplies are ample and demand is normal. Cash prices trade below futures prices, and the price difference is called contango. This expression is especially used on the London Metal Exchange (LME).

**CTA**    Stands for "commodity trading advisor," the official title of a registered asset manager in futures in the United States.

**cumulative total return**    Cumulative total return reflects the actual performance over a certain period of time, for instance, the total return over a five-year period.

**custodian bank**    The custodian bank holds the assets of the fund. The custodian bank receives deposits from new investors and pays out redemptions when the investor liquidates his or her fund holdings. In a well-organized fund, the fund manager can only buy and sell securities on behalf of the fund; the manager cannot take the cash out for himself or herself and run away. A good custodian bank is a good protection for the investor, making sure that the investor's money is returned at the net asset value of the fund. In Liechtenstein the custodian bank also has a monitoring function: it must check that all dealings are done in accordance with the prospectus of the fund. For example: If the fund manager of a precious metal fund started to buy stock of a brewery company, the custodian bank would have to remove the position from the fund account.

**disclosure document**    An asset manager in futures in the United States needs to register as a CTA (commodity trading advisor) with the CFTC (Commodity Futures Trading Commission). The manager must publish the trading strategy, performance, fee structure, and company structure in a disclosure statement and update this document on a regular basis. Customers and the CFTC must have access to this document at all times.

**diversification**    Allocating assets among several stocks, bonds, currencies, countries, and so on, to spread risks. If you put all your eggs into one basket, your risk of losing substantial amounts of money rises. When you diversify, you divide your risks among many assets, and you reduce your risks.

**dollar cost averaging**    The goal of dollar cost averaging is to lower the average cost of purchased funds or securities over a certain period of time. The principle is to buy a fixed amount of investments at fixed intervals, irrespective of the investment's price. For example: Take a fund's monthly price during six months: $120, $110, $100, $115, $120, $125. If you invest $6,000 on day one at $120 a share, you have bought 50 shares at $120. After six months your investment is worth 50 x $125, or $6,250. This is a total return on your investment of 4.16 percent. If you apply the dollar cost averaging method, you invest $1,000 in the first month at $120; in the second month you invest

$1,000 at $110, in the third month $1,000 at $100, and so on. The net result after six month looks as follows: you have also invested $6,000 and your average purchase price is $115. The value of your $6,000 investment is $6,556.55, or a total gain of 9.27 percent. This method is excellent for the prudent investor. Advantage: over a long investment horizon, you get the best and lowest average price, and your timing is optimal. Disadvantage: if the fund or stock shoots up in value in the beginning, you miss the boat.

**drawdown**  The biggest temporary loss in a fund. This is a measuring stick of how volatile the fund is. Example: If a fund starts at 100, goes down to 90, and rises subsequently to 120, the drawdown is 10 percent. The smaller the drawdowns, the better the fund is managed.

**expense ratio**  A ratio between the fund's assets and the fund's costs for management, accounting, and custody. Usually the ratio is between 1 percent and 2 percent. When the fund pays performance fees to managers and the fund is profitable, the expense ratio is much higher.

**front load commission**  A sales commission, charged either on top of the fund price or built into the selling or offering price of the fund. Sales commissions vary between 0 percent and 5 percent. The sales agent is paid out of this commission.

**fundamental factors**  The supply-and-demand factors that determine the price of a commodity. This can be, for instance, the weather, consumption, economic up- or downturns, and so on.

**futures market**  On a futures market, investors trade today the price of a commodity, an index, or an interest rate in a certain month in the future. Example: On the oil futures market, investors trade today the value of oil in next December or next March. The future price fluctuates every day, according to supply and demand.

**hedge funds**  Hedge funds have nothing to do with hedging, and the word is a pure euphemism. Hedge funds are allowed to go long and short stocks, currencies, commodities, and so on. Most hedge funds are strongly leveraged and make big bets. It is estimated that 3,500 hedge funds already exist in this world. Most hedge funds are based offshore. The exception is in Switzerland, where hedge funds can be based onshore.

**hedging**  Traders limit their risks with the following simplified hedging examples: when they own physical, unsold positions, they sell their positions forward on a futures exchange. When prices subsequently go up or down, the profit margin of the trader is not at risk. Or when a purchasing manager knows he has to buy a certain commodity, such as airline fuel, on a future date, he can buy the commodity today on a futures market. He has fixed his purchase price and is not worried that oil prices might rise substantially until he buys and pays for the physical commodity.

**high water mark**   The highest previous net asset value of the fund. The fund manager is entitled to a performance fee only if she steers the fund to a new high net asset value. Her performance fee is 10 percent or 20 percent of the new net profits, which are calculated as the difference between the new high net asset value and the previous net asset value. If the fund declines in value, the fund manager must first recoup the losses and push the fund higher above the "high water mark" in order to receive a new performance fee.

**incentive fee**   CTAs and hedge fund managers participate in the new net profits they generate for their customers. The incentive fee varies between 10 percent and 33 percent.

**IRRI**   Stands for International Rice Research Institute.

**leverage**   The investor trades on credit. Example: The investment is $1,000, and total investment exposure is $10,000. The leverage factor here is 10. Generally the volatility of leveraged funds is very high. Leverage should be used only by the full-time, very rich investor who has nerves of steel. Do not use leverage if you are a part-time, not very rich investor and cannot sleep at night because you tinker all the time with the markets. Hedge funds are highly leveraged.

**life science**   This is a euphemism for genetic engineering. A company like Monsanto has sold all its chemical activities and concentrates fully on genetic engineering, or life science, to produce insect-resistant seeds resulting in larger crops.

**LME**   Stands for London Metals Exchange. Here nonferrous metals like tin, lead, copper, zinc, aluminum, and nickel are traded.

**load-adjusted return**   The return includes the fund's sales charge. The sales charge is payable when the fund is purchased, and it lowers the return of the first year.

**long-only fund**   The fund buys stocks, futures, or bonds and expects prices to rise. Subsequently the fund sells the holdings at a profit or loss. All traditional funds are long-only funds. They lose money when prices go down.

**management fee**  The person or company who actually manages the assets of the fund is paid a management fee. This is usually between 1 percent and 2 percent of the fund's assets.

**MBD**  Stands for "million barrels per day." This expression is used to indicate the daily oil consumption.

**net asset value (NAV)**  The administrator of the fund calculates the value per share on a daily or weekly basis. The calculation method is as follows: First, total liabilities of the fund are deducted from the total assets. Then the remaining total net assets are divided by the number of shares outstanding.

**not load-adjusted return**  The return figure is higher because it does not include the fund's sales charge.

**offer price**  Generally it is the lowest price the seller is willing to accept from the buyer. In the fund industry, it depends on whether the fund has a front load commission. When the fund has a front load commission, the offer price is the net asset value (NAV) plus the sales commission. If the fund does not have a front load commission, the offer price is the NAV.

**offshore funds**  Many funds are registered in so-called "offshore" jurisdictions. These are often islands with favorable tax structures and liberal legislation to establish funds within a relatively short time, cheap and fast. Good examples are Cayman Islands, the British Virgin Islands, Bermuda, and the Bahamas. There is one jurisdiction which has one leg offshore and one leg onshore. This is the place where I live: Principality of Liechtenstein. You can remain totally anonymous as a customer when you have fiscal, political, or even family pressure by creating a trust or an "establishment" ("Anstalt"). Liechtenstein is also a member of the European Economic Area and has a new fund law. Therefore equity funds established in Liechtenstein can be promoted publicly in all European member countries. Offshore funds cannot be sold publicly and are not registered with the SEC in the United States. This means advertising campaigns, mass mailing, and so on, are forbidden. They can only be sold privately between four walls. The biggest hedge funds in the world with billions of dollars under management, Soros Funds and Tiger Fund, are offshore funds and cannot be publicly sold within America. Big advantage of offshore funds: they can go long and short the markets.

**onshore funds**  Funds established in jurisdictions with often cumbersome legislation. Funds have many investment restrictions, the registration of the funds takes longer, the fund and the investors generally pay more taxes, but the fund promoters can advertise their product publicly.

**open interest**   Total outstanding futures contracts. If open interest goes down in an upward-trending market, investors lose interest, and this can be an early sell signal.

**open-ended funds**   Open-ended funds can be bought and sold according to the prospectus once a day, a week, a month, or a quarter.

**passively managed funds**   Index funds consist of the shares or bonds of a certain index. The investment manager does not actively buy and sell stocks and bonds according to his opinion, but his task is to buy stocks or bonds so that the fund's asset composition reflects the stocks or bonds of the index. A Standard & Poor's 500 fund will contain the 500 stocks of this index only. The investors know that the fund's performance will reflect the index.

**performance fee**   Some funds where derivatives and leveraged instruments are traded charge a performance fee. The manager receives 10 percent to 25 percent of the new net gain. If the fund declines in value, the fund must first recoup the losses before the manager is entitled again to receive a performance fee. This ceiling is called "high water mark."

**redemption**   An investor who has bought shares in a fund decides to sell her shares and liquidate her holdings. At that moment, she redeems her shares.

**redemption fee**   Some funds charge a redemption fee of usually 0.5 percent. The purpose of a redemption fee is to discourage an investor from redeeming the shares.

**round-turns**   Abbreviation of "round-turn commissions." The number of round-turn commissions is a yardstick showing if a CTA practices high-volume trading or if he follows a long-term slow strategy: 1,000 contracts traded per $1,000,000 assets under management is low; 6,000 trades per $1,000,000 is high.

**sector funds**   Sector funds invest the holdings of the fund exclusively in a certain sector, such as health care, technology, or natural resources. In Great Britain there is even a soccer fund, which very successfully invests the assets in soccer clubs like Manchester United. Because sector funds are confined to one investment sector, they tend to be more volatile than generally diversified funds.

**short selling**   The fund sells stocks or futures as an initial transaction and hopes the asset goes down in value. As a second transaction the fund buys the asset back at (hopefully) a lower price to realize a profit. The fund also can deliver the stock or the future to the buyer. The funds can make money when prices go down.

**subscription period**   When a public fund is launched, there is usually a subscription period during which investors can subscribe to the fund. At the end of the subscription period, the fund is launched, and the investment manager starts to invest the assets of the fund.

**technical factors**   Some investment managers do not take fundamental factors into their buy and sell decisions. They exclusively rely on their proprietary software and look at chart patterns for buy or sell signals. Some managers mix fundamental with technical influences to buy and sell; others let computers make all trading decisions.

**total average annual return**   The total hypothetical rate of return per year during a certain number of years. Example: return year 1: 10 percent; return year 2: 20 percent; return year 3: 25 percent. The total average annual return is 18.33 percent. Year-by-year performances vary, and average annual returns smooth out the variation in performance. The return includes changes in share price, reinvestments of dividends, and capital gains.

**weightings of a fund**   Percentage of assets a fund has invested in certain market sectors or countries or currencies.

# NOTES

## Chapter 2.  The Supply of Natural Resources

1. FAO Food and Agricultural Organization, *World Food Summit Basic Information,* no. 5 (Rome, Italy, February 1996).
2. Data from World Bank, United Nations, World Resources Institute.
3. Lester Brown, in "The Acceleration of History," *State of the World 1996* (New York: W.W. Norton, 1996), 10.
4. USDA/Goldman Sachs & Co., "An Overview of Commodities" (New York, September 1997), 28.
5. Ibid, 27.
6. Ibid, 30.
7. USDA Production, Supply and Demand View. Source: Internet, www.usda.gov, May 4, 1998.
8. USDA/Goldman Sachs & Co., "An Overview of Commodities" (New York, September 1997), 26.
9. Lester Brown, in "Will the World Go Hungry?" by Christopher Hallowel, *Time* (Special Issue, "Our Precious Planet"), November 1997.
10. Gary Gardner, "Preserving Global Cropland," in *State of the World 1997* (New York: W.W. Norton, 1997), 44.
11. Dieter Jäggi and Partner AG, *Gentechnik* (Brochure) (Bern, Switzerland: Gen Suisse, 1994), 28.
12. Rick Weiss, "Engineered Corn Crops Up," *International Herald Tribune,* October 9, 1996.
13. Alison Maitland, "From Petri Dish to Supper Plate," *London Financial Times*, October 15, 1996, 12.

14. Ingo Protykus, "Ich kämpfe gegen den Hunger," in *Schweizerische Illustrierte* (sponsored section by Genforschung Schweiz), November 10, 1996, 25.

15. Rick Weiss, "Gene-Altered Cotton: Warmer, but Still Wrinkles," *International Herald Tribune*, November 13, 1996, 5.

16. Agis Salpukas, "A Growing Insouciant Need for Oil," *International Herald Tribune,* July 25, 1996.

17. United Nations, "World Economic and Social Survey" (New York: United Nations, 1995), 170.

18. Goldman Sachs & Co., "Commodity Watch" (New York, September 1997), 10.

19. Anne Reifenberg in *Wall Street Journal*, August 20, 1996.

20. Geoff Nairn in *London Financial Times*, July 17, 1996, 8.

21. Lester R. Brown, "Zur Lage der Welt" (New York: W. W. Norton, 1996), 32.

22. European Wind Energy Association in *London Financial Times*, July 17, 1996.

23. Hal Kane, "Shifting to Sustainable Industries," in *State of the World 1996* (New York: W.W. Norton, 1996), 155.

24. Christopher Flavin and Nicholas Lenssen, *Power Surge: Guide to the Coming Energy Revolution* (New York: W.W. Norton, 1994).

25. European Wind Energy Association in *London Financial Times*, July 17, 1996, 8.

26. Hal Kane, "Shifting to Sustainable Industries," in *State of the World 1996* (New York: W. W. Norton, 1996), 154.

27. Christopher Flavin, "Clean as a Breeze," in *Time* (Special Issue, "Our Precious Planet"), November 1997.

28. Hal Kane, "Shifting to Sustainable Industries," in *State of the World 1996* (New York: W. W. Norton, 1996), 154.

29. Caspar Henderson, "Solar Power for the Poor," *London Financial Times*, October 1, 1997.

30. "Shell steekt HFL 500 miljoen in opwekking zonne-energie," *De Telegraaf*, October 16, 1997.

31. Simon Holberton, "Energy Demand May Double by 2020," *London Financial Times*, September 16, 1997.

32. Kenneth Gooding, "Zinc Use Ahead of Production Again in 1996," *London Financial Times*, February 4, 1997.

33. Kenneth Gooding, "Report Says Aluminum Prices to Jump," *London Financial Times*, October 24, 1997.

34. Kenneth Gooding, "Warning on Aluminium Growth," *London Financial Times*, November 18, 1997.

35. Kenneth Gooding, "Prices Fell, Not Performance," *London Financial Times*, Copper Supplement, October 6, 1997.

36. All numbers from James Harding, "China Faces Shortage of Iron Ore and Copper," *London Financial Times*, October 7, 1997.

37. Kenneth Gooding, "Electronics Industry Warned of Palladium Shortage," *London Financial Times*, November 19, 1997.

38. Kenneth Gooding, "Platinum in Short Supply," *London Financial Times*, November 19, 1997.

39. Quotes and figures from Michael S. Serrill, "Wells Running Dry," *Time* (Special Issue, "Our Precious Planet"), November 1997.

40. Food and Agricultural Organization, "Irrigated Area," 1990 Production Yearbook (Rome, 1990).

41. Peter Baumgartner, "Wasserholen mit dem Tropfenzähler," *Tagesanzeiger*, November 8, 1996.

42. Henk Donkers, "Amerikaanse boeren verkopen hun irrigatiewater," *Algemeen Handelsblad*, October 4, 1997, 26.

43. Sandra Postel, *Last Oasis: Facing Water Scarcity* (New York: W. W. Norton, 1992), 199, and "Forging a Sustainable Water Strategy," in *State of the World 1996* (New York: W. W. Norton, 1996), 41.

44. Food and Agricultural Organization, *Global Agriculture 2000* (Rome, 1996).

45. J. L. Lorzan, Lenz W. Rachor, E. Watermann, and B. Westerhagen, *Warnsignale aus der Nordsee* (Berlin: Parey, 1990), 85.

46. Jonathan Friedland, "Catch of the Day," *Wall Street Journal*, November 26, 1997, 5.

47. Helene Cooper and Scott Kilman, "Exotic Tastes," *Wall Street Journal*, November 4, 1997, 6.

## Chapter 3.  The Demand for Natural Resources

1. Jacques Diouf, Director-General of the FAO, interview with *International Herald Tribune*, October 16, 1996, 15.

2. World Health Organization, Geneva, video on world population, May 15, 1996.

3. USDA Harvested grain area. Source: Internet, www.usda.gov, May 4, 1998.

4. *Megacity Growth and the Future* (Tokyo: United Nations University Press, 1994), 19.

5. Data from W. Nentwig, *Humanökologie* (Heidelberg: Springer Verlag, 1995), 96.

## Chapter 4.  China, the Swing Factor

1.  Numbers from Lester Brown and Christopher Flavin, *World Watch Magazine* (Washington), September/October 1996.
2.  *The Economist*, in *Manager Magazine*, February 1995, 20.
3.  Sophie Roell, "China Seeks to Quell Fears on Grain Needs," *London Financial Times*, October 26, 1996.
4.  Jikun Huang, in "Grain Imports by China Set to Rise," by Alison Maitland, *London Financial Times*, January 7, 1998.
5.  Kang Xiaoquang, in "Can China Keep Bowls Filled?" by Elaine Kurtenbach, *International Herald Tribune*, November 14, 1996.
6.  Jikun Huang, in "Grain Imports by China Set to Rise," by Alison Maitland, *London Financial Times*, January 7, 1998.
7.  Lester Brown, *Who Will Feed China?* (New York: W. W. Norton, 1995), 30.

## Chapter 5.  The Influence of Our Ecology on Natural Resources

1.  Nancy Dunne, "U.S. Wastes $300 Billion of Energy a Year," *London Financial Times*, December 1, 1997.
2.  Jerry Mahlman, in "Climatologists Agree: World Will Get Hotter," by William Stevens, *International Herald Tribune*, November 4, 1997.
3.  "Ozone Layer Vanishing Fast," *International Herald Tribune*, November 5, 1996.
4.  World Bank, "Earth Faces Water Crisis," press release, Washington, D.C., August 6, 1995.
5.  Gary Mead, "Mixed Fortunes in Asia from El Niño," *London Financial Times*, November 4, 1997.
6.  Dr. Keith Bentley, quoted in *Time*, November 3, 1997.
7.  Data from Climate Diagnostics Center, University of Colorado at Boulder, in "An Ill Wind for Business," by Larry Armstrong and Elizabeth Veomett, *Business Week*, September 29, 1997.
8.  Bushan Bahree, "Slippery Slope," *Wall Street Journal*, July 14, 1997.

## Chapter 6.  Investing in Natural Resources

1.  Neil Behrman, "Silver Surges on Strength in Supply/Demand Status," *Wall Street Journal*, December 5, 1997, 15.

## Chapter 7. Commodity Futures Funds

1. Data from Offering Memorandum, Sabre Fund Management, London, March 1997.
2. Data from Commodity Fund Prospectus and various monthly reports, Northern Light, Stockholm, April 1997.
3. Data from Disclosure Document and various monthly reports, Di Tomasso, Victoria, Canada, April 11, 1997.
4. Data from Commodity Trading Advisor Disclosure Document of Fundamental Futures Inc., Dallas, TX, March 31, 1997.
5. Data from Offering Memorandum and Internet, Finagra Management Inc., www.iasg.com, May 10, 1998.

## Chapter 8. Mining and Metal Funds

1. Data from Offering Memorandum and performance tables, U.S. Global Investors (Guernsey) Ltd., January 15, 1998.
2. Data from Offering Memorandum, Internet, and performance tables, Magnum Global Investments Ltd., Nassau, Bahamas, December 26, 1997.

## Chapter 9. Diversified Natural Resources Equity Funds

1. Data from Internet, Van Eck Global Hard Assets, http://personal32.fidelity.com, May 6, 1998.
2. Data from Internet, State Street Global Resources, www.quicken.com/investments, May 6, 1998.
3. Data from Internet, T. Rowe Price New Era, www.quicken.com/investments, May 6, 1998.

## Chapter 10. Energy Funds

1. Data from Offering Memorandum, Internet, and quarterly reports, Eastern Natural Resources, Geneva, Switzerland, September 30, 1997.
2. Data and quote from "Pumped Up," by Matthew Brzezinski and Bushan Bahree, *Wall Street Journal*, November 18, 1997, 3.
3. Data from Internet, Excelsior Energy & Natural Resources, http://personal81.fidelity.com, May 6, 1998.
4. Data from Internet, Fidelity Funds, http://personal32. fidelity.com, May 6, 1998.

5. Data from Internet, Invesco Strategic Portfolio Energy, http://personal32.fidelity.com, May 6, 1998.
6. Data from Eastgate International brochure, 1997, Fairfield, Iowa, March 1997.
7. Data from Forstmann-Leff documentation and performance updates, Forstmann-Leff, New York, January 14, 1998.
8. Data from Cambridge documentation and performance updates, Cambridge Investments Ltd., 1997, San Francisco, January 15, 1998.
9. Data from Internet, Fidelity Funds, http://personal32. fidelity.com, May 6, 1998.
10. Data from prospectus and performance tables, Wellington Management, April 1997, Boston.
11. Data from prospectus and performance tables, Dawson-Samberg, 1997, Southport, Connecticut.

## Chapter 11.   Nutrition and Food Distribution

1. Data from Internet, Fidelity Funds, http://personal32. fidelity.com, May 6, 1998.

## Chapter 12.   Commodity Certificates

1. Data from prospectus, Di Tomasso, 1997, Victoria, Canada.
2. Data from Goldmann Sachs Internet Web site www.goldman sachs/com.
3. Steve Strongin, "The Strategic Case," Goldman Sachs Commodity Research (New York, 1997), 11.
4. Ibid., 12.
5. Ibid., 13.

## Chapter 13.   The Full Investment Spectrum

1. Numbers from Helene Cooper and Scott Kilman, "Exotic Tastes," *Wall Street Journal*, November 4, 1997, 5.
2. Banaby J. Feder, "ConAgra: Growing in the Shade," *International Herald Tribune*, October 31, 1997.
3. Kathy Chen, "The Big Squeeze," *Wall Street Journal*, January 7, 1998.
4. Peter Marsh, "Tractor Makers Set Sights on Further Growth," *London Financial Times*, October 8, 1997.

5.  Robert Ratcliff, in "Why Mature Industries Should Adopt a Horizontal Strategy," Nikki Tait, *London Financial Times*, October 15, 1997.

6.  Rick Weiss, "Engineered Corn Crops Up," *International Herald Tribune*, October 9, 1996.

7.  Alison Maitland, "From Petri Dish to Supper Plate," *London Financial Times*, October 15, 1996, 12.

8.  Peter Fritsch, Scott Kliman, and Stephen D. Moore, "Seed Money," *Wall Street Journal*, October 26, 1996.

9.  Nigel Poole in "Will the World Go Hungry?," by Christopher Hallowel, *Time* (Special Issue, "Our Precious Planet"), November 1997.

10. Andrew Fisher, "Ford, Daimler in Green Link-Up," *London Financial Times*, December 16, 1997.

11. "Shell steekt HFL 500 miljoen in opwekking zonne-energie," *De Telegraaf*, October 4, 1997.

# INDEX